"SMOKED YANKEES"
AND THE STRUGGLE FOR EMPIRE

"SMOKED YANKEES"

AND THE STRUGGLE FOR EMPIRE

UNIVERSITY OF ILLINOIS PRESS

LETTERS FROM NEGRO SOLDIERS,

:0:0:0:0:0:0:0:0:0:0:0:0:0:0:0:0:0:0:0:0:0:0:0 1898-1902

Willard B. Gatewood, Jr.

Urbana, Chicago, and London

To my Mother and Father

TABLE OF CONTENTS

INTRODUCTION   3

I. OFF TO WAR   19

II. BLACK HEROES: HOPE TO DESPAIR   39

III. AMONG THE BLACK VOLUNTEERS   99

IV. IMPERIAL GUARDS IN CUBA   179

V. FIGHTING IN THE PHILIPPINES   237

INDEX   321

PREFACE

THE PERFORMANCE of Negro soldiers in the Spanish-American War and the Filipino Insurrection inspired black citizens with a sense of pride at a time when the oppressive racial climate in the United States seemed to warrant only despair. "The South is proud of Roosevelt, the North is proud of Hobson," a Negro editor exclaimed in July, 1898, "and we are proud of the colored troops, the heroes of the day." Such pride found expression in a profusion of books, editorials, orations, poems, and pictures celebrating the deeds of black soldiers whose bravery on the field of battle seemed to promise "a new era for the Negro race" in America. Negro soldiers themselves fully appreciated the significance of their participation in America's quest for empire and hoped that by shouldering the white man's burden in Cuba, Puerto Rico, and the Philippines to ease the black man's burden in the United States. They supplied black newspapers with frequent and detailed reports of their activities which rarely received more than passing mention in the white press. Collectively these letters constitute a remarkably complete record of the black man's role in America's struggle for empire at the turn of the century.

The correspondence of black soldiers included in this volume was selected from literally hundreds of letters which appeared in the Negro press. Of the 114 letters in this collection, only five came from sources other than Negro newspapers. An effort has been made to include letters which represent as many Negro military units as possible and which reveal the diverse experiences and attitudes of black soldiers. In an attempt to preserve the flavor of the correspondence, each letter has been reproduced, except for certain deletions, as it appeared in the press. This accounts for occasional inaccuracies in grammar, spelling, and punctuation. The letters are organized into five chapters and appear chronologically, except in Chapter III, which deals with Negro volunteers whose brief term of service was spent entirely within military camps in the United States. It seemed to be more feasible here to arrange the correspondence according to military unit rather than chronologically throughout the chapter.

Many individuals and institutions rendered valuable assistance in the preparation of this volume. Librarians and archivists at the University of Arkansas, University of Georgia, Duke University, Atlanta University, National Archives, and Library of Congress graciously responded to all my requests. My research was also facilitated by a generous grant from the American Philosophical Society. I am particularly indebted to Professor Paul McBride of Ithaca College, Professor Robert Griffith of the University of Georgia, Professor Warren Kimball of Rutgers University, and Professor Edwin Harrell of the University of Alabama for their perceptive counsel. Mrs. Barbara F. Lineberger, who typed the manuscript, was as tolerant as she was diligent. My wife Lu Brown Gatewood maintained a constant interest in the project and is in large measure responsible for its completion.

Let it be said that the Negro soldier did his duty under the flag, whether that flag protects him or not.

EDWARD A. JOHNSON, 1899

▪▫▪▫▪▫▪▫▪▫▪▫▪▫▪▫ INTRODUCTION

THE AFRO-AMERICAN, according to James Baldwin, "is a unique creation; he has no counterpart anywhere, and no predecessors." His uniqueness springs in part from his experience as a slave, for the "peculiar institution" stripped him of his African heritage and bequeathed a legacy that consigned him to an anomalous position in American society. His plight in the United States has been that of an "exile in his own land," of an "unloved stranger" excluded from the American Dream. The "cruel and totally inescapable ambivalence of his status in his country" has forced him to wage a persistent battle for self-identity and self-esteem.[1]

The obstacles encountered by black Americans in their efforts to win acceptance have not only produced what has been termed "the rage of the dis-esteemed," but have also pointed up the irony and incongruities of American life. The frustrations and perplexities experienced by Negroes in striving to "achieve the full height of manhood" reached new dimensions during the Spanish-American War and the Filipino Insurrection. For the first time since acquiring citizenship, black men were called upon to render military service outside the United States. As soldiers, they became spokesmen abroad among "colored people" for a country which made color a badge of inferiority.

If the black Americans' concern over the imperialistic ventures

[1] The quotations from James Baldwin are found in his *The Fire Next Time* (New York: Dial Press, 1963) and *Notes of a Native Son* (New York: Dial Press, 1955).

of the United States at the close of the nineteenth century resembled that of other citizens, their approach to these momentous
events was substantially different. Confronted by a rising tide of
repression at home, Negroes viewed the Spanish-American War
and the acquisition of an overseas empire within the context of
their own deteriorating status. Although such a perspective may
have enabled them to discern the discrepancies between the
rhetoric and realities of American imperialism, it scarcely simpli-
fied their task of formulating a coherent and consistent attitude
toward expansion. Clearly black Americans sympathized with the
oppressed peoples of Cuba, Puerto Rico, and the Philippines, but
as important as the oppressed condition of these peoples was the
fact that many were non-white. That the Spanish colonies included a sizable "colored population" made it easy for Negro
Americans to identify with them and to endorse movements for
their liberation. But because Negroes recognized the degree to
which racism pervaded American society and thought, they could
never become wholly reconciled to the arguments of either the
imperialists or the anti-imperialists. Although they hesitated to
oppose a policy of imperialism when it became identified with
the "party of Lincoln," their traditional allegiance to Republican-
ism did not insure their consistent support for the imperial thrust
of the United States at the turn of the century. In fact, the outbreak of the war with Spain in 1898 evoked widely disparate
reactions within the black community.

At one extreme were the enthusiastic pro-war advocates whose
bellicose rhetoric placed them in the vanguard of the most strident
jingoists. They emphasized the benefits which war would bestow
upon Negroes. Their argument maintained that the black man's
participation in the military effort would win respect from whites
and therefore enhance his status at home. They predicted that
the islands likely to come under American influence would not
only open economic opportunities for Negroes but also would
diminish the color prejudice of white Americans by bringing them

in contact with predominantly "colored" cultures.[2] Opposing such views were the highly vocal, anti-imperialist elements within the Negro community who were also concerned about the impact of the quest for empire upon black Americans. Though sympathetic with the plight of Cuba and especially with Negro Cubans, these black citizens argued that the Spaniards, for all their cruelty, at least had not fastened upon the island a system of racial discrimination comparable to that in the United States. They envisioned a Jim Crow war resulting in a Jim Crow empire, which would leave colored Americans as well as the colored population of the Spanish colonies in a more oppressed condition than ever. At any rate, black anti-imperialists contended that only when the American government guaranteed its own black citizens full constitutional rights at home would it be in a position to undertake a crusade to free Cuba from Spanish tyranny.[3] The polarization of opinion regarding the Spanish-American War represented by the extreme positions of the anti-war and pro-war spokesmen did not, however, characterize the response of Negroes in general. Their attitude was clearly ambivalent. A majority of blacks seemed to consider participation in the military struggle an obligation of citizenship which they would gladly fulfill, if they could do so in a way that would enhance rather than degrade their manhood. Though they hoped that a display of patriotism would help dissipate racial prejudice against them, they were never free of misgivings about a war launched in the name of humanity and waged in behalf of "little brown brothers" by a nation so enamored of Anglo-Saxon supremacy.[4]

As the imperialistic enterprise progressed, and especially after

[2] *The Freeman* (Indianapolis), July 3, 1897; *Iowa State Bystander* (Des Moines), February 18, April 1, 29, 1898; *Wisconsin Weekly Advocate* (Milwaukee), May 14, 21, 1898; *The Colored American* (Washington), April 30, May 28, 1898; *The Colored Citizen* (Topeka), April 21, 28, 1898.

[3] *Richmond Planet*, April 23, 30, May 28, 1898; *The Bee* (Washington), May 21, 28, 1898; *Broad Ax* (Chicago), March 19, 1898.

[4] See *The Gazette* (Cleveland), March 5, 19, 26, 1898, March 4, April 29, 1899.

the United States became involved in thwarting the independence movement among the Filipinos, the misgivings of black Americans re-emerged and by 1900 had hardened into widespread, vocal opposition.[5] A complex of social, psychological, and racial factors was responsible for the increasingly strident note of anti-imperialism in the pronouncements of Negro spokesmen, but clearly the experiences of Negro soldiers at home and in Cuba, Puerto Rico, and the Philippines, especially their encounters with the color line, were important considerations. While the expressions of the soldiers themselves embraced the whole range of attitudes manifested at different times by black civilians, their responses to the quest for empire, like those of other Negroes, revealed a combination of altruism and self-interest. They could never quite reconcile their sympathy with the aspirations of the colored peoples of Cuba and the Philippines with the desire to enhance their own status as American citizens by taking up the White Man's Burden. The black soldier, therefore, often appeared vacillating and uncertain in his observations regarding America's imperialistic ventures. To an extraordinary degree, he became the victim of conflicting emotions and attitudes spawned by his unique position in these ventures.

The first Negro troops mobilized for service in the Spanish–American War were the four black regiments of the regular army, the Twenty-fourth and Twenty-fifth Infantry and the Ninth and Tenth Cavalry, which had been organized shortly after the Civil War. One reason that the black regiments were among the first called for duty in Cuba was the War Department's assumption that Negroes possessed a "natural immunity" to the ravages of the climate and diseases of the tropics. Whatever the motives for mobilizing the black regulars, the soldiers themselves welcomed the assignment as an opportunity to demonstrate their "soldierly

[5] See George P. Marks, "Opposition of Negro Newspapers to American Philippine Policy, 1899–1900," *Midwest Journal,* 4 (Winter, 1951–52): 1–25.

qualities" and to win respect for their race.[6] Commanded by white officers, these Negro regiments had previously achieved distinction for their role in campaigns against the Indians in the West. By 1890 they had become elite units of the army. The black cavalrymen, in particular, who were popularly known as the Buffalo Soldiers, had acquired an enviable reputation.[7] Although the performance of the black troops was a source of racial pride throughout the late nineteenth century, Negro spokesmen persistently protested their assignment to forts west of the Mississippi River and their exclusion from the cadre of commissioned officers. T. Thomas Fortune, editor of the *New York Age,* crusaded for the establishment of a colored artillery unit primarily because such a unit would be located in the East. "We want an artillery unit," Fortune declared, "so that we can come back to civilization and show the whites how to soldier."[8] But such protests and demands proved to be futile. By 1898 there was still no colored artillery unit, nor were there any black commissioned officers except a few chaplains and Lieutenant Charles Young, a Negro graduate of West Point, who was professor of military science at Wilberforce University.[9] And Negro regiments remained in the West. The stationing of a troop of the Ninth Cavalry at Fort Myers, Va., in 1891 as a reward for its part in the successful Pine Ridge campaign against the Indians touched off such opposition among whites in the area that the experiment was

[6] An excellent treatment of the role played by the black regiments in the Cuban campaign is found in Marvin Edward Fletcher, "The Negro Soldier and the United States Army, 1891–1917" (Ph.D. dissertation, University of Wisconsin, 1968), Ch. 8.

[7] For brief surveys of Negroes in military service see Horace Mann Bond, "The Negro in the Armed Forces of the United States prior to World War I," *Journal of Negro Education,* 12 (Summer, 1943): 263–87; L. D. Reddick, "The Negro Policy of the United States Army, 1775–1945," *Journal of Negro History,* 34 (January, 1949): 9–29.

[8] *New York Age,* December 23, 1889.

[9] Abraham Chew, *A Biography of Colonel Charles Young* (Washington: R. L. Pendleton, 1923), p. 13.

abandoned and the troop returned to its western camp.[10] Not until the outbreak of the Spanish-American War were the Negro regiments pulled out of the West and sped to camps in the South in preparation for the invasion of Cuba. For more than a month the black troops remained in the vicinity of Tampa, Fla., where they were forcefully reminded that even their blue uniforms provided little protection from the anti-Negro prejudice of white soldiers and civilians. In the words of a Tampa newspaper, white citizens in the area refused "to make any distinction between the colored troops and the colored civilians" and would tolerate no infractions of racial customs by the colored troops. Because the black soldiers insisted upon being "treated as men," their sojourn in Florida was attended by a series of confrontations with whites. Only the departure of the invasion force for Cuba brought an end to the racial incidents involving Negro troops.[11]

Despite the prejudice which they encountered in Florida, or perhaps because of it, the black troops acquitted themselves with distinction on the battlefield of Cuba, particularly at Las Guasimas, El Caney, and San Juan Hill. Briefly, in the summer of 1898, they enjoyed the status of heroes who received plaudits from whites as well as blacks.[12] Convinced that they had demonstrated their value as combat troops and imbued with a new sense of self-confidence, Negro soldiers expected to be rewarded by means which they considered commensurate with their performance. The failure of the War Department to extend such recognition by recommending Negroes for commissions in the regular army was vigorously protested by the black veterans of the Cuban campaign and especially by black civilians. Their contention was that even if the law establishing the black regiments required white officers, it was the duty of Congress and the War Department to

[10] *New York Age,* March 21, May 9, 1891.

[11] Willard B. Gatewood, Jr., "Negro Troops in Florida, 1898," *Florida Historical Quarterly,* 49 (July, 1970): 1–15.

[12] See Hiram Thweat, *What the Newspapers Say of the Negro Soldier in the Spanish-American War* (Thomasville, Ga.: n.d.).

have the law changed. Neither the promotions of men in the ranks to noncommissioned officers' positions nor the granting of commissions in the volunteer service as rewards for those black regulars who displayed conspicuous gallantry in Cuba dispelled their disappointment and disillusionment.[13]

In the meantime, the martial spirit which engulfed the nation prompted thousands of black Americans to offer their services as volunteers. News of victories in Cuba early in July, 1898, quickened the desire of Negroes in civilian life to emulate the heroism of the black regulars. But as they quickly learned, it was not merely a matter of joining the volunteer army. When President William McKinley issued his first call for volunteers late in April, 1898, the governors of most states, North and South, reacted indifferently to the black man's demand that he be allowed an opportunity to demonstrate his patriotism. The Negroes' difficulties were compounded by the fact that few belonged to the state militias, and the volunteer army was made up primarily of militiamen. Even states which had all-Negro militia units showed little inclination to muster them into federal service. For example, the governor of Georgia refused to mobilize any of the Negro companies of the militia, although they consistently received superior ratings by the state's adjutant general. In Mississippi, where Negroes were busy organizing volunteer companies, the governor announced that no black units would be needed. More disturbing to the Negro community, however, was the refusal of Republican governors in the Midwest and Northeast to accept black volunteers.[14] In spite of a loud protest from Negro citizens in his state, Governor Frank S. Black of New York refused to accept Negro volunteers and explained that the color line had traditionally been enforced in the state militia.[15] As a result of

[13] *Illinois Record* (Springfield), August 13, 20, September 17, 1898; Cleveland *Gazette,* August 13, December 10, 1898; *Richmond Planet,* April 13, 1898.
[14] *Savannah Tribune,* April 30, May 7, June 11, 1898; *Daily Picayune* (New Orleans), June 3, 1898.
[15] *New York Times,* June 23, 1898.

such actions only Alabama, Ohio, and Massachusetts mustered in black militia units in response to the President's first call for volunteers. Company L of the Sixth Massachusetts Regiment, a black company in an otherwise white regiment which took part in the invasion of Puerto Rico, was the only Negro volunteer unit to see action in the Carribbean during the Spanish-American War.[16]

The governors of Illinois, Kansas, Virginia, Indiana, and North Carolina, reacting either to pressure from Negro politicians or to the failure of whites to fill quotas, accepted Negro units under the President's second call for volunteers. But Negroes were not content merely with being allowed to join the volunteer army; they demanded black officers for black military units, a concept which ran counter to that held by the War Department and by white Americans in general. Negroes took up the cry, "No officers, no fight."[17] Such demands gained a few concessions. Ultimately three of the Negro volunteer regiments mustered into federal service—the Eighth Illinois, Twenty-third Kansas, and Third North Carolina—had complete rosters of Negro officers.[18] Always conscious that they constituted an "experiment," these black regiments were impressed with their responsibility to perform in a manner that would reflect credit upon all black Americans. "If we fail," the Negro colonel of the Eighth Illinois Regiment told his men, "the whole race will have to shoulder the burden."[19]

While the states were mobilizing Negro volunteers in the

[16] The role of Company L of the Sixth Massachusetts Regiment is recounted in Frank E. Edwards, *The '98 Campaign of the 6th Massachusetts, U.S.V.* (Boston: Little, Brown, 1899).

[17] *Richmond Planet,* May 7, 14, 21, 28, 1898; Miles V. Lynk, *The Black Troopers, or the Daring Heroism of the Negro Soldiers in the Spanish-American War* (Jackson, Tenn.: Lynk Publishing Co., 1899), p. 92.

[18] See Edward A. Johnson, *History of Negro Soldiers in the Spanish-American War* (Raleigh, N.C.: Capital Publishing Co., 1899), pp. 135–37; Theophilus G. Steward, *The Colored Regulars in the United States Army* (Philadelphia: A.M.E. Book Concern, 1904), pp. 282–98.

[19] Quoted in W. T. Goode, *The "Eighth Illinois"* (Chicago: Blakely Printing Co., 1899), p. 231.

summer of 1898, Congress authorized the War Department to organize ten additional volunteer regiments under its immediate direction. These units were to be made up of men who ostensibly were immune to yellow fever. Four of these so-called immune regiments—the Seventh, Eighth, Ninth, and Tenth Volunteer Infantry—were designated as all-Negro units and were recruited from the black population in the South and the Ohio Valley. In response to the demand for black officers, the War Department commissioned Negroes as lieutenants in the line companies. Although whites occupied all staff positions and all line positions above the rank of lieutenant, the immune regiments at least provided a means of rewarding Negro regulars who had rendered distinguished service in Cuba. Approximately thirty black enlisted men of the regular army received commissions in the immune regiments. The term of service for volunteers, including the black regiments, was of short duration. In most instances it was about a year.[20] During 1898–99 one of the immune regiments, the Ninth Volunteer Infantry, and two state units, the Eighth Illinois and Twenty-third Kansas, performed garrison duty in Cuba. Other Negro volunteers who remained in the United States complained of being shuffled from camp to camp and of being subjected to discriminatory treatment by whites, especially civilians.

The mere presence of armed black troops was sufficient in some areas of the United States to activate anti-Negro prejudices. Black soldiers regularly encountered from whites insults such as "all niggers look alike to me." They were ordered out of "white only" restaurants, saloons, and parks, and forced to abide by Jim Crow practices in trains and trolleys. Negro volunteers, as well as blacks in the regular army, vigorously expressed their resent-

---

[20] For more detailed information on the "immune" regiments see W. Hilary Coston, *The Spanish-American War Volunteer* (Middletown, Pa.: Mount Pleasant Printery, 1899); Steward, *Colored Regulars,* pp. 288, 291; Fletcher, "The Negro Soldier and the United States Army," pp. 231–36.

ment at the various forms of discrimination and prejudice directed at them. On occasion they took action to break the color barrier or to retaliate against some particularly offensive insult. Obviously the Negro soldiers were in a more favorable position than others of their race to insist upon respect and equitable treatment. They not only possessed arms (at least for a while) and whatever legal protection was inherent in their uniforms, but also existed in sufficient numbers to risk forceful action against their detractors.[21] Yet their display of restraint was perhaps more remarkable than their occasional use of force to combat discrimination and to retaliate against insults. At least one factor which helped prevent more frequent and more violent reactions on their part was the feeling of being on trial and the conviction that their actions had consequences for all black Americans. Because of their restraint Negro volunteers were all the more resentful of what they considered the sensational and distorted publicity lavished upon every incident which tended to discredit them. The treatment which black volunteers encountered in various camps in the United States, especially at Camp Haskell near Macon, Ga., coupled with the absence of any opportunity to render service on the battlefield, took its toll on their morale. Disillusioned with military service as a means of improving the condition of their race, most Negro volunteers welcomed the mustering out of their units early in 1899.

About the time these volunteers began returning to civilian life, the United States embarked upon a campaign in the Philippine Islands to crush the independence movement there led by Emilio Aguinaldo.[22] For three years, beginning in 1899, American mili-

[21] See Cleveland *Gazette,* June 25, July 2, September 17, 1898; *Illinois Record,* August 27, 1898; *Richmond Planet,* March 11, April 1, October 7, 1899; Topeka *Colored Citizen,* September 29, November 11, 1898; *Augusta Chronicle* (Augusta, Ga.), August 31, 1898.

[22] See Leon Wolff, *Little Brown Brother: How the United States Purchased and Pacified the Philippine Islands at the Century's Turn* (Garden City, N.Y.: Doubleday, 1961).

tary forces engaged in a bloody guerilla war against the so-called Filipino Insurrectos. From the moment Admiral George Dewey sailed into Manila Bay in 1898, Negroes in the United States displayed considerable sympathy for the independence movement among the Filipinos, whom they identified as "our kinsmen" and "our colored brothers."[23] This sympathy, combined with the disillusionment of Negroes regarding the benefits reaped from their services in Cuba, gave rise to a highly vocal anti-imperialist element in the black community. The indomitable Henry M. Turner, senior bishop of the African Methodist Episcopal Church, characterized the American crusade in the Philippines as "an unholy war of conquest" against "a feeble band of sable patriots."[24] Even the cautious Booker T. Washington declared that Filipinos "should be given an opportunity to govern themselves."[25]

The opposition of Negroes to the policy of imperialism became so loud by 1899 that the War Department questioned whether black soldiers, especially volunteers, should be sent to the Philippines. One official in the department doubted that such troops "if brought face to face with their colored Filipino cousins could be made to fire on them."[26] There was less doubt about the feasibility of using black regulars in the islands than volunteers, presumably because the former were better disciplined and more adequately indoctrinated. In mid-1899 contingents of Negro regulars, who had returned to their stations in the West following the Cuban campaign, embarked for the Philippines. Portions of all four black regiments of the regular army in time saw action in virtually every part of the islands. Negro units participated in many notable battles including those at Iba, Botolan, and O'Donnell, and were constantly in danger of attack by Aguinaldo's forces during their frequent use for sentry, garrison, and rec-

[23] Washington *Colored American,* November 11, 1898.
[24] *Voice of Missions,* 8 (October 1, 1900): 3.
[25] Indianapolis *Freeman,* September 24, 1898.
[26] Washington *Bee,* September 9, 1899.

onnoitering activities. Early in 1900 the black regulars in the Philippines were joined by two regiments of Negro volunteers, the Forty-eighth and Forty-ninth Infantry, recruited by the War Department at the request of the commander in the islands. For a year and a half these volunteers performed creditably against the Filipino rebels.[27]

In the Philippines, as in Cuba, the black soldiers were quick to establish rapport with the natives. General Robert P. Hughes reported from the Philippines: "The darkey troops . . . mixed with the natives at once. Whenever they came together they became great friends. When I withdrew the darkey company from Santa Rita I was told that they shed tears over their going away. I know they begged me to leave them."[28] Although Negro troops proved to be highly effective in subduing the Filipino Insurrection, they were usually solicitous in their treatment of Filipino civilians and often identified with them racially. In letters to acquaintances at home black soldiers frequently extolled the Philippines as a land ripe with opportunities denied black Americans in the United States. Some white officers came to suspect that "the negro soldiers were in closer sympathy with the aims of the native populations than they were with those of their white leaders and the policy of the United States."[29] Indeed, many black American soldiers in the Philippines were painfully conscious of their position as opponents of a movement by a "colored people" to achieve independence and freedom. One Negro soldier wrote: "We black men here [Philippines] are so much between the Devil and the Deep Blue."[30] Although black troops themselves referred to the Filipino

[27] Fletcher, "The Negro Soldier and the United States Army," Ch. 10; Rienzi B. Lemus, "The Enlisted Man in Action, or the Colored American Soldier in the Philippines," *Colored American Magazine,* 5 (May, 1902): 46–54.

[28] *Hearings before the Committee on the Philippines of the United States Senate,* Senate Document No. 333, 57 Congress, 1 Session, Part 1, p. 647.

[29] Stephen Bonsal, "The Negro Soldier in War and Peace," *North American Review,* 186 (June, 1907): 325.

[30] Sergeant Major J. W. Galloway to the Editor, *Richmond Planet,* September 30, 1899.

rebels as "gugus," they understood only too well the implications of the term "nigger" which white soldiers commonly used in referring to all Filipinos.[31] To some Negro soldiers, references to Filipinos as "niggers" and the drawing of the color line which had accompanied Americanization of the islands indicated what was in store for the "little brown brothers" under American rule. Prompted in part by a desire to thwart such a bleak prospect, an unusually large number of black troops deserted during the Philippine campaign. According to Stephen Bonsal, desertions from Negro regiments "were invariably of a different character" than those from white regiments. The white soldier "deserted because he was lazy and idle and found service irksome," while Negroes deserted "for the purpose of joining the insurgents," whose struggle they interpreted as the struggle of all colored people.[32] Lest the black soldier forget the plight of his own people in the United States, the Filipino insurgents regularly distributed posters addressed to "The Colored American Soldier,"[33] which reminded him of the American practice of lynching and encouraged him not to be the instrument of his white master's ambition to oppress another "people of color." Of all Negro soldiers who deserted the most famous was David Fagan of the Twenty-fourth Infantry. He accepted a commission in the insurgent army and for two years wreaked havoc upon the American forces.[34]

In 1902 the last of the Negro troops departed from the Philippines. Notwithstanding complaints about the appearance of American "color prejudice" in the islands, a few Negro soldiers, especially those who had married Filipino women, chose to re-

[31] See Albert E. Robinson, "The Outlook in the Philippines," *The Independent,* 102 (February 8, 1900): 349; *The Times* (Manila), November 17, 1899; *Hearings before the Committee on the Philippines of the United States Senate,* Senate Document No. 331, 57 Congress, 1 Session, Part 2, p. 884.

[32] Bonsal, "The Negro Soldier in War and Peace," pp. 325–26.

[33] *Richmond Planet,* November 11, 1899.

[34] Manila *Times,* December 14, 1901; Frederick Funston, *Memories of Two Wars* (New York: Charles Scribner's, 1914), pp. 376, 380, 431, 434, 435.

main there. Some engaged in business in Manila or received appointments to minor posts in the civil government; others settled in the provinces. By 1903 the Afro-American colony in the Philippines totaled approximately 500 persons. In spite of the agitation in the United States about Negro emigration to the Philippines, the black American population there underwent no spectacular growth.[35]

Throughout their participation in America's imperial ventures from 1898 to 1902, Negro troops provided the black press with an abundance of correspondence. Negro editors not only were generous in opening their columns to the soldiers but also printed their communications in prominent places in their journals. Although white soldiers wrote to newspapers, their letters were either less numerous or white editors were less generous in printing them. At any rate, the more affluent white press, with its staff correspondents and access to wire services, did not have to rely upon white soldiers for news of their activities. In the case of black press the situation was wholly different. Because their newspapers enjoyed limited circulation and possessed scant financial resources, black editors were largely dependent upon soldiers for news about black men in military service. In some instances, soldiers who began writing letters to an editor on an informal basis became, in time, something of regular correspondents. There is no evidence to suggest the soldiers received any fees or salary for their journalistic efforts. On occasion the soldier-correspondents were friends of editors in whose newspapers their letters were printed. For example, C. W. Cordin, a resident of Ohio who was first in the Seventh Immune Regiment and later in the regular army, wrote letters for several years to his friend Harry Smith, editor of the Cleveland *Gazette,* in which he com-

---

[35] Washington *Colored American,* January 12, 1901; Rienzi B. Lemus, "The Negro and the Philippines," *Colored American Magazine,* 6 (February, 1903): 314–16; T. Thomas Fortune, "The Filipino: Some Incidents of a Trip through the Island of Luzon," *Voice of the Negro,* 1 (June, 1901): 239–46; "Race Discrimination in the Philippines," *The Independent,* 56 (February 13, 1902): 416–17.

mented on virtually every aspect of life among black soldiers. Similarly, much of the information regarding the Eighth Illinois Infantry which appeared in the *Illinois Record,* a Negro newspaper in Springfield, appeared in the form of letters from a soldier who had served as a typesetter for the paper before joining the regiment.

But the extent to which the black press relied upon soldiers for military news cannot be explained solely in terms of economics. Negro soldiers who wrote the letters and Negro editors who published them were, generally, convinced that the white press was not doing justice to black troops. The editors were particularly disturbed by what they considered the calculated efforts of the white press to give maximum publicity to every incident of misconduct by black soldiers. Especially objectionable were the extravagant reports of misbehavior by black troops which appeared regularly in newspapers throughout the South. But, as one Negro journalist noted, even when black troops received favorable mention in the white press they were treated as "nameless beings" and identified only as "a negro soldier."[36] Despite the editorial praise bestowed upon the black heroes of the Cuban campaign, Calvin Chase, editor of the Washington *Bee,* voiced a common sentiment among Negroes when he complained that the dispatches of white correspondents from Santiago slighted their exploits and that white editors were more inclined to fill their columns with news of some "racket" or "riot" created by black soldiers in southern camps.[37] Even articles praising the black soldiers which appeared in white newspapers were marred by their patronizing tone. To insure proper coverage of the activities of Negro troops, black editors seriously considered pooling their resources to employ their own war correspondent. But failure to agree upon the

[36] *Richmond Planet,* March 25, 1899; *Savannah Tribune,* December 3, 1898, November 25, 1899; Washington *Bee,* July 23, September 10, 1898, April 22, 1899; *Illinois Record,* August 27, 1898.

[37] Washington *Bee,* September, 24, 1898.

individual for the post meant that the editors continued to rely principally upon the soldiers themselves for military news.[38]

The letters from black soldiers which appeared regularly in black newspapers constituted rich sources of information regarding a wide range of experiences and attitudes related to their participation in America's quest for empire. Some of their letters were primarily descriptions of military activities; others were highly impressionistic accounts of the peoples and cultures found in Cuba, Puerto Rico, and the Philippine Islands; still others interlaced personal opinions with factual reports of various phenomena which they encountered at home and abroad. But regardless of the character of the communication, the racial consciousness of the Negro soldier was evident. Whether they were describing their experiences in the camp at Macon, Ga., or their relations with Cubans and Filipinos, black troops wrote from the perspective of dispossessed Americans striving to share more equitably in the rights and privileges of first-class citizenship. The more perceptive correspondents were acutely aware of the anomalous position of the black soldier who, as a member of an oppressed "colored" minority in the United States, was engaged in suppressing the aspirations of the "colored" Filipinos in an effort to relieve his own oppressed condition at home.

[38] Washington *Colored American,* July 16, 1898.

I

OFF TO WAR

In the eyes of the world the Negro shall grow in the full height of manhood and stand out in the field of battle as a soldier clothed with all the inalienable rights of citizenship.

ILLINOIS RECORD, 1898

THE SINKING of the U.S.S. *Maine* in February, 1898, initiated a lively debate within the black community regarding the appropriate response for Negro Americans to make in the event that the United States went to war with Spain to free Cuba. A vociferous minority agreed with the black Iowan who declared: "I will not go to war. I have no country to fight for. I have not been given my rights."[1] But the majority of black citizens, however much they might understand such sentiments, supported the declaration of war against Spain and displayed their willingness to participate in the military effort. Late in April, 1898, a Negro correspondent in Los Angeles summarized the complex of reasons which prompted black people to support the war: "As in all other cities the Negro is discussing his attitude toward the government in case of war. Shall he go to war and fight for the country's flag? Yes, yes, for every reason of true patriotism, it is a blessing in disguise for the Negro. He will if for no other reason be possessed of arms, which in the South in the face of threatened mob violence he is not allowed to have. He will become trained and disciplined. He will be generously remunerated for his services. He will get much honor. He will have an opportunity of proving to the world his real bravery, worth and manhood."[2] Clearly, both the Negro soldiers already in the regular army and the thousands of black civilians who attempted to join the volunteer army believed the war would help achieve "justice at home as well as abroad."

Among the first troops readied for service in Cuba in 1898 were the four regiments of the regular army (Twenty-fourth and Twenty-fifth Infantry and Ninth and Tenth Cavalry). These black

[1] *Iowa State Bystander* (Des Moines), May 20, 1898.
[2] *The Freeman* (Indianapolis), May 7, 1898.

regiments, all under the command of white officers, began to arrive at Chickamauga Park, Ga., and at Key West, Fla., even before the official declaration of war with Spain. During the first two weeks in May, 1898, all black units of the regular army were ordered to Tampa, the port selected as the one best suited for embarkation to Cuba. During the next month of what was called "the rocking chair period" over 3,000 Negro troops were among the invasion forces concentrated in the area around Tampa. The Twenty-fourth and Twenty-fifth Infantry and the Ninth Cavalry pitched camp on sites near the city. But when the Tenth Cavalry arrived, it could find no suitable camping ground and was ordered to nearby Lakeland along with several white units.[3]

Chaos and confusion prevailed in every quarter, and as Professor Frank Freidel has noted, the "logistics snarl was too complicated" for the commander, General William R. Shafter, to unravel.[4] At Tampa, as at Chickamauga, the Negro units continued to receive an influx of new recruits, because the War Department had ordered regiments to have three battalions of four companies which meant an additional 750 men for each regiment. The arrival of so many raw recruits only compounded the confusion at the embarkation point.

Scarcely had the first companies of black soldiers pitched camp in the Tampa area when white citizens began to complain about their presence. Earlier reports from Key West that Negro infantrymen had forced the release of one of their comrades from a local jail undoubtedly enhanced the existing antipathy toward black troops. While the white press in Tampa treated the rowdiness of white soldiers with tolerance or levity, it viewed similar behavior by Negroes as evidence of their lack of discipline. Almost

[3] Theophilus G. Steward, *The Colored Regulars in the United States Army* (Philadelphia: A.M.E. Book Concern, 1904), pp. 91–97, 100–103; "Record of Events," April-June, 1898, Regimental Records of the 24th and 25th Infantry, Record Group 94, National Archives.

[4] Frank Freidel, *The Splendid Little War* (New York: Dell, 1962), p. 49.

daily, from the time the black regiments arrived until their departure for Cuba, the local press gave front-page coverage to disturbances caused by what it termed "these black ruffians in uniform." Accurate information about racial incidents involving Negro troops was all the more difficult to obtain because of the rigorous censorship exercised by the War Department over all news regarding military activities and personnel. It appears, however, that such clashes usually resulted either from insults by whites or from attempts by black soldiers to break segregation barriers.[5] The animosity toward black soldiers became especially acute whenever they were placed in positions to exercise authority over white troops. White Floridians protested loudly, for example, when Negroes on military patrol duty arrested white soldiers. One white Floridian reportedly told a white soldier, "Son, if any o these yere darkey policemen ever gives yo'all any trouble yo' jest holler an' yo' friends round hyar will come a'runin' an' take keer o' *him*."[6]

Saloons, cafes, and drug stores which insisted upon maintaining the color line became special targets of the black soldiers' ire and several were forced to close "to prevent bloodshed." John Bigalow, Jr., the white captain of a black cavalry unit, claimed that the white Floridians' lack of discretion and subtlety in race relations was the principal cause of friction with the Negro troops. He insisted that if whites treated colored soldiers with civility, "however much they might discriminate against them," there would be little trouble. Local whites showed little inclination to display such civility. As a result racial tension mounted. Black soldiers obviously resented being described as "black brutes" by local newspapers and being told by the owners of various mercantile

[5] *Morning Tribune* (Tampa, Fla.), May 5, 7, 10, 12, 18, 19, 21, 25, June 8, 1898; William J. Schellings, "Key West and the Spanish-American War," *Tequesta*, 20 (1960): 25–26; *Gazette* (Cleveland), May 21, 1898.

[6] Quoted in A. C. M. Azoy, *Charge: The Story of the Battle of San Juan Hill* (New York: McKay, 1961), p. 48; for a similar statement see Charles Johnson Post, *The Little War of Private Post* (Boston: Little, Brown, 1960), p. 56.

establishments that "we don't sell to damned niggers."⁷ Regular encounters with such discrimination and prejudice solidified the determination of black troops to force whites to respect them as soldiers and as men.

Within a few days after their arrival in Lakeland, the Negro cavalrymen demonstrated their unwillingness to abide by the discriminatory racial customs of the area. Angered by the refusal of a drug store proprietor to serve one of their comrades at the soda fountain, a large group of armed black soldiers returned to the scene. After pistol-whipping the owner of the drug store, they moved into the streets where a sizable crowd had assembled. In the confrontation one white civilian, Joab (Abe) Collins, was killed. Although Collins had been hurling insults and urging the crowd to action, his death was apparently caused by a stray bullet. The incident resulted in the arrest of two black cavalrymen and in the disarming of the rest of the regiment.

In the meantime, similar though less serious confrontations occurred in Tampa, where a majority of the Negro troops were stationed. On the eve of the army's embarkation for Cuba, the tension there erupted in the most serious racial clash that occurred in a military encampment during the Spanish-American War. Triggered by drunken white volunteers from an Ohio regiment who used a Negro child as a target to demonstrate their marksmanship, the Tampa riot lasted through the night of June 6, 1898, and was not finally quelled until the following morning. Despite military censorship, dispatches from Tampa claimed that the streets of the city "ran red with negro blood." At least twenty-seven Negro soldiers and three white volunteers were so seriously wounded that they had to be transferred to a military hospital near Atlanta.⁸

⁷ John Bigalow, Jr., *Reminiscences of the Santiago Campaign* (New York: Harper, 1899), pp. 36–37; "Letter from Tampa," *The Ledger* (Baltimore), June 4, 1898.

⁸ For more detailed treatment of the Collins affair and the Tampa riot, see Willard B. Gatewood, Jr., "Negro Troops in Florida, 1898," *Florida Historical Quarterly,* 49 (July, 1970): 1–15.

The following letters indicate the context in which Negro soldiers looked upon participation in a war to liberate Cuba from Spanish tyranny. The treatment of the black regulars at the hands of whites in Florida prompted some to ask whether "America is any better than Spain."

Theophilus G. Steward, Twenty-fifth Infantry, Chickamauga Park, Ga., ca. May 1, 1898; from The Gazette *(Cleveland), May 28, 1898. Chaplain Steward expresses pride in the Negro regiments mobilized for service in Cuba and believes that their performance will improve the condition of "the American colored man of the South."*

[Editor, *Christian Recorder*
Philadelphia, Pa.]
Sir:

Early in the month of April the order reached the headquarters of our regiment to pack up and prepare to start for Key West, St. Augustine and Dry Tortugas. After a few days this order was changed and the regiment was ordered to Chickamauga National Park. On April 10, Easter Sunday morning, we left western Montana for the last named place, and . . . the whole regiment met together for the first time since 1870, in the Union Depot at St. Paul. Here orders were received for the lieutenant colonel and two companies to separate from the regiment and go directly to Key West, the other six companies to proceed to Chickamauga as ordered. These six companies, with the regimental band, were the first troops to arrive in the park. Since then all the remaining colored troops in the army, except the two companies sent to Key West, have arrived, besides a large number of white troops. With the four colored regiments have come three of the colored chaplains. . . . On Sunday, April 24th, the first service was held in the encampment of the 25th [Regiment], and was conducted by myself and Chaplain [George W.] Prioleau of the Ninth Cavalry. . . .

No regiments in the service have a better reputation than the colored regiments and none will do better service, I venture, and yet I hope they may never have to fight. If fight they must, officers and men will do their whole duty, but it is a duty not to be coveted. Our regiment is put in the First Brigade with three white regiments, ours at present being the ranking regiment. It is not known how long we will remain here, but the presumption is that it will require some weeks to get ourselves in readiness for a descent upon Cuba, while no one knows just how long it will take the navy to clear up the way. Our camp is visited by throngs of people and by newspaper men from all over the country. The prejudice toward the colored soldier was very great when we came here, but sentiment appears to be modifying very rapidly. White men of the South are ready to fight side by side with the Negro, so [long as] they do not get too close together. What a sight it is to see artillery, cavalry and infantry, all rushing together for war, and preparing for war as for any other business. The newspaper reports of the plan to be pursued by the Army and Navy in the attack on Cuba ought not to deceive our own people, as they are not likely to deceive Spain. It is not known what either the army or navy will do beyond the attempt at blockade. There may be no invasion of Cuba at all and there may be but little of real war. There is, however, ground to fear a great and prolonged war, and it is not unlikely that the United States will have her hands full before she gets through with the job. Certain it is that it is much cheaper to do the right than the wrong thing. Had our nation walked in the highway of holiness, war would not now come nigh her. I believe this war will very greatly help the American colored man of the South, and result in the further clearing of the national atmosphere.

T. G. Steward
Chaplain, 25th Infantry

George W. Prioleau, Ninth Cavalry, Port Tampa, Fla., May 13, 1898;
from The Gazette (*Cleveland*), *May 13, 1898. The reception of the*
Negro regulars in the South on their way to Cuba prompts Chaplain
Prioleau to ask: "Is America any better than Spain?"

Hon. H. C. Smith
Editor, *Gazette*
Dear Sir:

The Ninth Cavalry left Chickamauga on the 30th of April for
Tampa, Fla. We arrived here (nine miles from Tampa) on
May 3. From this port the army will sail for Cuba. We have in this
camp here and at Tampa between 7,000 and 8,000 soldiers,
artillery, one regiment of cavalry (the famous fighting Ninth)
and the Twenty-fourth and Twenty-fifth infantries. The Ninth
Cavalry's bravery and their skillfulness with weapons of war . . .
is well known by all who have read the history of the last Indian
war. . . .

. . . .

Yesterday, May 12, the Ninth was ordered to be ready to embark
at a moment's notice for Cuba. . . . We are here waiting for
the order to march. Possibly before you shall have been in receipt
of this communication, the Ninth, with the Twenty-fourth and
Twenty-fifth infantries and eight batteries of artillery will be in
Cuba. These men are anxious to go. The country will then hear
and know of the bravery of these sable sons of Ham.

The American Negro is always ready and willing to take up
arms, to fight and to lay down his life in defense of his country's
flag and honor. All the way from northwest Nebraska this
regiment was greeted with cheers and hurrahs. At places where
we stopped the people assembled by the thousands. While the
Ninth Cavalry band would play some national air the people
would raise their hats, men, women and children would wave

their handkerchiefs, and the heavens would resound with their hearty cheers. The white hand shaking the black hand. The hearty "goodbyes," "God bless you," and other expressions aroused the patriotism of our boys. . . . These demonstrations, so enthusiastically given, greeted us all the way until we reached Nashville. At this point we arrived about 12:30 a.m. There were about 6,000 colored people there to greet us (very few white people) but not a man was allowed by the railroad officials to approach the cars. From there until we reached Chattanooga there was not a cheer given us, the people living in gross ignorance, rags and dirt. Both white and colored seemed amazed; they looked at us in wonder. Don't think they have intelligence enough to know that Andrew Jackson is dead. Had we been greeted like this all the way . . . there would have been many desertions before we reached this point.

The prejudice against the Negro soldier and the Negro was great, but it was of heavenly origin to what it is in this part of Florida, and I suppose that what is true here is true in other parts of the state. Here, the Negro is not allowed to purchase over the same counter in some stores that the white man purchases over. The southerners have made their laws and the Negroes know and obey them. They never stop to ask a white man a question. He (Negro) never thinks of disobeying. You talk about freedom, liberty etc. Why sir, the Negro of this country is freeman and yet a slave. Talk about fighting and freeing poor Cuba and of Spain's brutality; of Cuba's murdered thousands, and starving reconcentradoes. Is America any better than Spain? Has she not subjects in her very midst who are murdered daily without a trial of judge or jury? Has she not subjects in her own borders whose children are half-fed and half-clothed, because their father's skin is black. . . . Yet the Negro is loyal to his country's flag. O! he is a noble creature, loyal and true. . . . Forgetting that he is ostracized, his race considered as dumb as driven cattle, yet, as loyal and true men, he answers the call to arms and with blinding tears in his eyes and sobs he goes forth: he sings "My Country 'Tis of Thee, Sweet Land of Liberty," and though the word "liberty" chokes him, he swallows it and finished the stanza "of Thee I sing."

The four Negro regiments are going to help free Cuba, and they will return to their homes, some then mustered out and begin again to fight the battle of American prejudice. Chaplains [Ruter W.] Springer and Prioleau are the only commissioned Chaplains who are so near the seat of war. Chaplain Springer will cross over and engage in the contest, but I will remain here at Port Tampa in charge of thousands of dollars of property of the government. Not a regularly appointed Negro chaplain will be on the field of strife and only one white chaplain. Why, I am unable to state. Perhaps in some instances it was from choice. The colored churches and citizens of Tampa and Port Tampa gave the Twenty-fourth and Twenty-fifth infantries and Ninth Cavalry a grand reception on their arrival. The chaplain of the Ninth was presented with a five dollar pair of shoes and two pairs of silk socks. I trust that my friends will not think because I am on this side while my regiment is fighting that I am a coward. I promised to obey orders. Perhaps this order will be changed by the time Gen. [Nelson A.] Miles gets to Tampa. More anon. I am

Yours truly,
Geo. W. Prioleau
Chaplain, Ninth Cavalry

John E. Lewis, Tenth Cavalry, Lakeland, Fla., June 5, 1898; from Illinois Record (*Springfield*), *June 11, 1898. In spite of the racial prejudice encountered by Negro troops in Florida, Lewis encourages "patriotic young colored men" to enlist in military service and bring "honor to the race."*

Illinois Record

Mr. Editor:

While reading your very interesting paper and noticing the interest you take in the welfare of the colored soldier it might be of interest to you and your readers that I write a few lines, and I hope that you dear sir, will appeal to the young colored men of this country in defense of a common cause. It is the time every patriotic young colored man should come to the front and defend its honor and show that we are true American citizens; that we can protect our homes and government. You, sir, can make an appeal to the young colored man [that] will be an honor to his race. There is many a young man who has had the advantage of an education that has not given our regular army a thought. If some of our best people would encourage their sons to enlist instead of looking down upon a soldier as a debased being, this regular army would be more of an honor to the race. You have young men who are capable of holding a commission in the regular service, but are idle in your cities and will not venture into the service because they would have the scorn of their people. The colored race must venture and seek every avocation of life and it is to the race's interest that they should become skilled in warfare. We have hundreds of young men who have not had the advantage of an education who have risen as high as their ability would permit. To become a commissioned officer in the U.S. service a man must be well educated, more than a public school can afford. Yet there are men capable of leading an army upon a battle-field who have not had that advantage.

. . . .

Mr. Editor, there are many who have the interest of the
colored regiments at heart. This was shown by their public
demonstration when the 10th was on their way from Fort
Assiniboine, Montana, to Chickamauga National Park.

. . . .

Our receptions along the route were more than my pen could
ever tell and we knew no difference until the line of Kentucky was
reached, at Hopkinsville, Ky. It seemed strange that on one
side of the road stood the whites and that on the other colored.
The people of Nashville, Tenn., gave us a rousing reception and
many of the boys longed to return to that city. At Chattanooga
our pleasure was entirely cut off. Several days before the 9th went
in [some Negro soldiers] broke up the Jim Crow car and took
several shots at some whites who insulted them, and the officers
were afraid that serious trouble would arise.

Our camp life at Chickamauga Park was one round of pleasure,
although many white southerners tried to raise enmity between
the white and colored soldiers. One white Southerner talking to
a white soldier [was] running down the colored soldier, and
because the white soldier would not approve of what he said he
commenced to abuse him. It ended in the white southerner being
killed and not one thing was said about it. You would be
surprised, although you live where very little prejudice exists,
[at] the friendly feeling that exists between the colored and
white soldiers and they have resented many an insult that was
cast at the colored troops. Many a resort had to close on account
of refusing them [Negro soldiers] certain privileges. The Jim
Crow car that ran from Lytle, Ga. to Chattanooga was
discontinued. The 25th Infantry broke that up, but yet life was
a pleasure at Chickamauga Park.

But here [Lakeland] we struck the hotbed of the rebels.

Lakeland, Florida, is a very beautiful little town, about 1,500 population and quite thickly settled by farmers or country people; surrounded by beautiful lakes, but, with all its beauty, it is a hell for the colored people who live here, and they live in dread at all times. If one colored man commits any crime, it does not make any particular difference whether they get the right party or not; all they want is a black. The main man, Abe Collins, who was such a dread to the colored people was shot and killed on May 16, 1898 by some [Negro] soldiers. On that date, some of our boys, after striking camp, went to Lakeland, went into a drug store and asked for some soda water. The druggist refused to sell them, stating he didn't want their money, to go where they sold blacks drinks. That did not suit the boys and a few words were passed when Abe Collins (white barber) came into the drug store and said: "You d—— niggers better get out of here and that d—— quick or I will kick you B—— S—— B—— out," and he went into his barbershop which was adjoining the drug store and got his pistols, [and] returned to the drug store. Some of the boys saw him get the guns and when he came out of the shop they never gave him a chance to use them. There were five shots fired and each shot took effect. I suppose that he was of the opinion that all blacks looked alike to him; but that class of men soon found out that they had a different class of colored people to deal with. On the following date the Tampa Tribune had a long article which stated that a colored soldier asked permission of his officer to go to town which the officer refused to grant. Thereupon, the soldier grew abusive, the officer placing him under arrest. The soldier resisted and shot at the officer and hit a comrade, making an ugly wound, which caused his death shortly afterward. The soldier was promptly placed under arrest by the guard; the white soldiers of the first cavalry were so incented at the Negro soldier for shooting at an officer that they threatened to shoot any Negro soldier who was found upon the streets. No wonder there are so many depredations committed against

Negroes of the South when such journalism is allowed to exist.

I will not worry you by writing much more, as this is my first attempt to write a letter to a paper, but if you desire it, I shall try and give you an account of our trip through Cuba.

About the 7th [of June, 1898] eight troops of the 9th [Cavalry] will invade Cuba, A, B, C, D, E, F, and G and I troops. They will be dismounted. The first move will be to establish a supply station. L and M troops were reorganized on the 1st of June. One hundred and seventy-five recruits arrived from Atlanta, Ga. Mr. A. S. Low of the 10th Cavalry band is suffering from fever caused by swimming. I am glad to say that there is very little sickness among the colored troops. All of the boys are in good spirits. My next letter shall be from Cuba. I should like very much to receive your paper that I might know what my people are doing.

> Very respectfully,
> John E. Lewis
> C Troop, 10th Reg.
> of Cavalry

John E. Lewis, Tenth Cavalry, Lakeland, Fla., ca. June 20, 1898; from Illinois Record, June 25, 1898. Lewis comments on the condition of his black cavalry regiment and on the treatment of Negro soldiers by white civilians in Lakeland. He also endorses the movement to place black officers in command of black military units.

Editor:

When I last wrote you I had no idea my next letter would be from this place, but passing events ordained otherwise. The troops mentioned in my last letter are now on Cuban soil, as the vessels left Port Tampa on the 11th inst. and no doubt the boys are now having a hot time. Three troops, H, L, and K were left behind to look after the horses and troop property, but all of them were very anxious to go. On the morning when they were to start, when the first call was sounded, it seemed as if they were going out to a picnic instead of going on such a perilous journey.

The horses will be sent over to the men as soon as a supply station is established. About all of the men who left for Cuba were old soldiers, for an experienced officer knows the value of a man who has seen some service, and from what I have seen and heard I am sure that Uncle Sam will never let his army run down as it has in the last ten years. A soldier cannot be made in a month, as a man must have experience and the class of recruits that we have been receiving of late are not up to the standard; many of whom are mere boys 17 and 18 years of age. They cannot stand the hardship of the soldier's life, yet some of the recruits are an honor. They have only been here a few weeks and their whole heart, purpose and ambition is to be a soldier. These are the boys who have not spent their time idly; they have come from good families and have spent the best time of their life at school. I still maintain that if our best people will encourage their sons to enlist in the army, they will be, when the war is over, an honor to themselves and the race. We must have intelligence as brute force and ignorance are not the requisites upon which our great men won success.

Quite a number of people are of the opinion anyone can enlist in the army. This is a mistake and I was told by a non-commissioned officer who was upon the recruiting service not long ago, that he was surprised at the number of young men who applied to enlist but were refused on account of their inability to read. They have had the opportunity but would not accept.

The 10th Reg. of Cavalry are in need of 300 recruits and you can see by that that the regiment is far from being recruited up to full war strength. We have about 200 recruits who are being

drilled very hard every day, and it is surprising how they stand
up under the warm weather. There are but few cases of sickness
among the men and we have not had one death while the white
troops are having a great deal of sickness and death.

It was a very impressive scene when the regiment formed
into line on their march to the depot, and you could not see one
face that showed sorrow or fear; all were anxious to go and when
the band struck up a march and the command "march" was given,
it seemed as if the troops were on inspection instead of going on
a journey of death and destruction. It was hard to bid the boys
good-bye, for we well know that some of us will never meet again,
and the friendships that have been of years standing made it
hard for the boys to part.

The cry of the boys left behind was "I would rather go than
stay." This is a soldier's life. Hearts must be true and brave.
Sentiment must be discarded and patriotism and bravery must
actuate the man who fights for the love of his country. Many
tried to transfer but their troop commanders would not listen to
them. I, for one, tried to go, but could not, and William Gleaves
of K troop and I were detailed on the commissary department.

In the Commissary or Quartermaster's Department a person
can get some idea of the work and the distribution of goods. No
doubt you have heard much said in regard to the soldier's rations
and how they fare upon the field. The government issues plenty,
but what they issue takes an experienced cook of government
rations to fix up into a good meal. For breakfast we generally
have beef and bacon, light bread and coffee; for dinner beef
stew, tomatoes, beans, hard tack or light bread; for supper,
bacon, bread, and coffee. The bacon is not very good in this
country because of the heat.

Among the troops which were left behind everybody is kept
very busy as they have 840 horses to take care of.

Since the shooting of Abe Collins, the white bully who created
a disturbance some weeks ago because some soldiers wanted to

get a glass of soda water, there has been a marked change in the disposition of the people, and many believe that it was through the providence of God that he was killed. People who were known to refuse to sell colored people what they wished now ask you to their place of business and intimate that they are glad to have you call on every occasion.

The rest of the troops expect to move just as soon as the supply station is established, and I, for one, will be glad to bid adieu to this section of the country, and I hope to never have cause to visit Florida again.

I have noticed by the papers, especially Southern, that they need colored troops with colored officers and that they cannot find any colored man competent. I hope that The *Illinois Record* will keep up its cry for colored troops with colored officers.

This regiment has a few good officers, but it lost its friend when Col. Guy V. Henry was called to a higher command. He was a man who did not care about your color as long as you was a good soldier. Whatever was done under him, if it was worthy, would receive the proper recognition; but I am sorry to say that some look down upon you if you happen to be a dark skin.

Personally, I have been very fortunate in soldiering under good officers; Capt. [Levi P.] Hunt is a very quiet man, and all he wants is for you to do your duty as a soldier, and he will stay with you, and he takes a pride in being with colored troops.

Second Lieutenant Paul Risinger, a Northerner, born in Penn., which speaks for itself, knows no difference [in color] and all the men in his troop would go with him as far as a man could.

I hope to hear of the *Record*'s success, that what colored troops are raised will have colored officers. It will not be long before they are calling heavily upon the colored race, and many colored regiments will be raised to hold what the U.S. has taken in conquest.

We have many non-commissioned officers who are capable of commanding a troop. Sergeant James H. Alexander, James R.

Gillipse, Sgt. Maj. [Edward L.] Baker, Pasco Conly, and others whom I will mention later.

The *Record* is eagerly sought by the soldiers and I hope that you will continue to champion the cause of the Negro soldiers. The friendliness of the white Northern soldier to us is gratifying.

Very truly yours,
John E. Lewis
H Troop, 10th Reg. of Cavalry

BLACK HEROES: HOPE
TO DESPAIR

The Negro played a most important part in the Spanish-American War. He was the first to move from the west; first at Camp Thomas, Chicka- mauga Park, Ga.; first in the jungle of Cuba; among the first killed in battle; first in the block-house at El Caney, and nearest to the enemy when he surrendered.

SERGEANT MAJOR
FRANK W. PULLEN, JR., 1898

Colored men are always forgotten in war when our arms meet with suc- cess, but are speedily remembered when defeat perches above our door.

JOHN MITCHELL, JR., 1898

On June 14, 1898, the American invasion force totaling about 16,000 men finally sailed from Tampa, Fla. It included all four Negro regiments of the regular army. On board the transports bound for Cuba, the Negro troops were segregated into the least desirable quarters. One black soldier described his berth as "under the water line, in the dirtiest, closest, most sickening place imaginable."[1] Disembarking on the southeastern coast of Cuba at Daiquiri, the army prepared for its assault upon the Spanish strongholds in the vicinity of Santiago.

The first battle of the campaign took place on the evening of June 23, 1898, at Las Guasimas, a juncture in the road which ran from the coastal town of Siboney to Santiago and was marked by a clump of guasima trees. The responsibility for precipitating this engagement rested with the plucky ex-Confederate, Joseph Wheeler, a volunteer major general who took advantage of his position as the senior officer in the area to lead the first charge in the Cuban campaign. The Negro troopers of the Tenth Cavalry, who had been held in reserve when the battle began, ultimately moved to the front and attacked the Spaniards at what was considered their most impregnable point. Their conduct at Las Guasimas won for them plaudits from military officers and newspaper correspondents who witnessed the battle, no less than from black citizens throughout the United States. In time, their performance, like that of other units in Cuba, became entwined in a web of folklore. For example, the claim was often made later that the Tenth Cavalry had actually saved the First Volunteer Cavalry (Rough Riders), who were tardy in arriving at Las Guasimas,

---

[1] Theophilus G. Steward, *The Colored Regulars of the United States Army* (Philadelphia: A.M.E. Book Concern, 1904), p. 116.

from utter annihilation in a Spanish ambush. When the Rough Riders came to monopolize the military glory of the Cuban campaign at the expense of other regiments, especially the black soldiers, the story of the Negro cavalrymen's rescue of Colonel Roosevelt's *enfants terribles* at Las Guasimas, replete with embellishments, gained wide circulation and became confused with their later exploits during the Battle of San Juan Hill.[2]

Although most of the Negro troops in Cuba saw action in the vicinity of Santiago, Troop M of the Tenth Cavalry was busy on the southwestern coast of Cuba. Sailing from Florida on June 21, 1898, with several companies of Cuban soldiers who had been concentrated at Tampa, the black troopers landed at Jucaro, where they made contact with the Cuban army under General Maximo Gomez. Isolated from other American forces for about three months while they fought with the Cubans, the fifty black Americans of the Tenth Cavalry took part in several notable battles, including the capture of El Hebro, and won particular distinction for staging a daring rescue operation on June 30, 1898, at Tayabocoa. Four privates who participated in the mission received Congressional Medals of Honor.[3]

Beginning on July 1, 1898, troops of the four Negro regiments were involved in combat which made the encounter at Las Guasimas appear as a minor skirmish. In the twin battles of El Caney and San Juan Hill, which opened the way for the American conquest of Santiago, the black troops won unparalleled praise from almost every quarter. Even the Spaniards fully appreciated the fighting qualities of those whom they called "Smoked Yankees" and "Negretter Soladas." Among the first troops to arrive at the Spanish fort at El Caney were the men of the Twenty-fifth

[2] Ibid., pp. 116–49; E. N. Glass, *History of the Tenth Cavalry* (Tucson: Acme Printing Co., 1921), pp. 32–33.

[3] Glass, *History of the Tenth Cavalry*, p. 32; Marvin Edward Fletcher, "The Negro Soldier and the United States Army, 1891–1917" (Ph.D. dissertation, University of Wisconsin, 1968), pp. 220–21; Irvin H. Lee, *Negro Medal of Honor Men* (New York: Dodd, Mead, 1967), pp. 90–94.

Infantry. While they were demonstrating their prowess as combat soldiers at El Caney, the men of the other three Negro units, the Twenty-fourth Infantry and Ninth and Tenth Cavalry, were participating in the assault upon the Spanish entrenchments atop San Juan Heights. Colonel Roosevelt, finding himself in command of an assortment of cavalrymen including his own Rough Riders and Negro troopers, led the charge up the ridge.[4]

Black soldiers did indeed assist generously in bringing about the most famous military victory won by Americans in a generation. Richard Harding Davis, the famous war correspondent who witnessed the Battle of San Juan Hill, voiced a universal opinion when he remarked that "negro soldiers established themselves as fighting men" in that engagement.[5] Testimony to their heroism was perhaps best indicated by the twenty-six Certificates of Merit bestowed upon black soldiers for their performance in the Santiago campaign. But evidence of their superior qualities as soldiers was by no means limited to their behavior under combat conditions. The promptness with which the Twenty-fourth Infantry accepted the assignment to work in the yellow fever hospitals at Siboney after eight other regiments had refused it tended to confirm the notion that Negro troops belonged to "an excellent breed of Yankee."[6]

The expedition to Puerto Rico following the conquest of Santiago involved few troops and relatively little resistance from the Spaniards. In Puerto Rico the Americans were greeted by a wildly enthusiastic native population. If in any respect the Spanish-American War deserved to be labeled "the splendid little

[4] See Steward, *Colored Regulars,* pp. 150–219; Edward A. Johnson, *History of Negro Soldiers in the Spanish-American War* (Raleigh: Capital Publishing Co., 1899), pp. 39–50; *Annual Reports of the Department of War, 1898,* House Document 2, Part 1, 55 Congress, 3 Session, pp. 323–24, 328–34, 347–49, 434–39, 704–10.

[5] Richard Harding Davis, *The Cuban and Porto Rican Campaigns* (New York: Charles Scribner's, 1904), p. 244.

[6] Steward, *Colored Regulars,* pp. 280–81; Fletcher, "The Negro Soldier and the United States Army," pp. 217–19, 222.

war," it was the campaign, between July 25 and August 14, 1898, that extended American control over Puerto Rico. Although only one Negro unit, Company L of the Sixth Massachusetts Volunteer Infantry, participated in that campaign, individual Negro soldiers attached to other regiments, as well as black sailors and teamsters, took part in it.[7] No less than other Americans, they were impressed by the climate and natural beauty of the island.

For a moment in the summer of 1898, the black soldier was an authentic American hero. Politicians, churchmen, and journalists, as well as their white comrades in arms, extolled the bravery of Negro troops. Even white soldiers from the South were generous in their praise. A white veteran of the Battle of San Juan Hill declared: "I am not a negro lover. My father fought with Mosby's Rangers and I was born in the South, but the negroes saved that fight. . . ."[8] Although Colonel Roosevelt later infuriated black Americans by remarks about the cowardly conduct of certain Negro infantrymen at San Juan, his assessment of the black troops' performance as expressed in speeches during the late summer of 1898 was unequivocally complimentary. And during his campaign for the vice-presidency in 1900 he publicly stated that Negro soldiers had saved his life in Cuba.[9] Shortly after the Battle of San Juan Hill, the well-known correspondent Stephen Bonsal wrote:

I was not the only man who had come to recognize the justice of certain Constitutional amendments, in the light of the gallant behavior of the colored troops throughout the battle, and indeed the campaign. The fortune of war had, of course, something to do with

[7] George W. Braxton, "Company 'L' in the Spanish-American War," *Colored American Magazine*, 1 (May, 1900): 19–25; Frank E. Edwards, *The '98 Campaign of the Sixth Massachusetts, U.S.V.* (Boston: Little, Brown, 1899), pp. 76–280.

[8] Johnson, *History of Negro Soldiers in the Spanish-American War*, p. 85.

[9] Ibid., p. 61; *The Freeman* (Indianapolis), October 13, 1900. Roosevelt's statement about the cowardly conduct of certain black infantrymen at San Juan, which appeared in his article on the Rough Riders in *Scribner's Magazine* (April, 1899), touched off a violent reaction in the Negro press.

it in presenting to the colored troops the opportunities for distinguished service, of which they invariably availed themselves to the fullest extent; but the confidence of the general officers in their superb gallantry, which the event proved to be not displaced, added still more, and it is a fact that the services of no four white regiments can be compared with those rendered by the four colored regiments— the 9th and 10th Cavalry and the 24th and 25th Infantry. They were at the front at Las Guasimas, at Caney and at San Juan, and what was the severest test of all, that came later, in the yellow fever hospitals.[10]

Despite such accolades, few white Americans were willing to grant black troops the one concession which they most desired— black officers. The argument against such a concession was that white officers were necessary for the maintenance of discipline within Negro regiments. The persistence of such ideas after Negro soldiers had acquired greater self-confidence as a result of their feats in Cuba was a source of profound frustration.

Although the commendation of Negro soldiers by the white population was as brief as it was illusory, their role in the Cuban campaign continued to be a source of pride among black Americans. The black warriors of Las Guasimas, El Caney, and San Juan Hill took their places alongside Crispus Attucks, Peter Salem, and others in the echelon of Negro American military heroes. In many Negro homes pictures and plaques depicting the Tenth Cavalry's charge at San Juan occupied places of honor. Hundreds of poems extolled the military exploits of the black troops in Cuba. Of these perhaps the most popular was a lengthy poem entitled "The Charge of the Nigger Ninth."[11] The laurels won by the black regulars may well have provided Negroes with a "much-needed feeling of pride" in an era of repression and discrimination,[12] but those who anticipated that the black man's bravery in

---

[10] Steward, *Colored Regulars*, p. 207.

[11] This poem by George S. Powell is reprinted in Johnson, *History of Negro Soldiers in the Spanish-American War*, pp. 55–58.

[12] Rayford W. Logan, *The Great Betrayal of the Negro from Rutherford B. Hayes to Woodrow Wilson* (New York: Collier Books, 1965), p. 335.

Cuba would improve his plight at home were grossly disappointed. Indeed, Negroes had reason to agree with the black Georgian who insisted that "the Negro's valor has *intensified* prejudice against him."[13]

Letters from black soldiers in Cuba and Puerto Rico revealed their own pride in their accomplishments on the battlefield as the standard-bearers of American liberty and freedom. The soldiers not only provided intimate accounts of military movements in which they participated but also described in detail the conditions under which they fought. Their letters graphically described the gore and destruction of war and suggested that such grim realities had a sobering effect, even upon seasoned veterans. For at least one black soldier, Corporal John R. Conn of the Twenty-fourth Infantry, the death and mutilation caused by the Battle of San Juan Hill constituted sufficient reason to question how civilized men could ever allow themselves to resort to war. Never completely obscured in most of the letters written from the scene of battle was the peculiar context in which Negro soldiers viewed the war and their role in it. Clearly, their perspective was shaped in large part by the deteriorating status of the black man in the United States—a condition which hopefully could be rectified, or at least ameliorated, by a display of loyalty and patriotism on the battle-field. But the letters of John E. Lewis of the Tenth Cavalry which chronicled the return of black heroes from Cuba gave expression to the profound sense of frustration caused by the failure of such hopes.

[13] *Savannah Tribune,* March, 18, 1899.

C. D. Kirby, Ninth Cavalry, Santiago, Cuba, no date; from Illinois
Record (*Springfield*), *August 27, 1898. This black cavalryman explains
how he acquired the nickname "Brave Fighting Kirby" during the Santiago campaign.*

[Mrs. Charles Kirby
West Williams Street
Springfield, Illinois]

[Dear Mother:]

When we got to Cuba, we did not go on land for two days and
remained two miles from shore, believing the harbor to be full
of mines.

The first day Sampson got all his gunboats together and fired
shots all around the landing, tearing everything all around there
all to pieces. The following day we all landed and went about a
mile before we struck camp. That night about 7 o'clock the
Captain asked the 1st Sergeant to send C. D. Kirby to him. I
reported to the Captain, who asked me if I was afraid of the
Spaniards, and I replied that I was not afraid of anything,
whereupon the Captain ordered me to take my gun and belt and
report to him. I soon returned and he said, "Kirby, I want you
to go to the dock and watch the grub, and if anyone comes around
there kill him."

Where I was stationed it was very dark, but about half past
12 o'clock two Spaniards approached. I saw them and kept very
quiet until they were very close to me, and although a little
afraid myself, I commanded them to halt. They did not stop, and
in a loud tone of voice I repeated it twice again, but they kept on
coming, so I stepped behind a rock, took aim and killed one of
them. The other shot at me, but missed, the bullet striking a rock,
glanced and hit me on the shoulder, not doing any damage. I
then shot at him, but did not kill him, although he fell to the
ground. Going to him, I asked him how he was feeling and he

said "pretty bad," whereupon I took the butt end of my gun and knocked him in the head. He groaned and moved.

When morning came, I reported to the Captain and told him what had happened. He asked me if it was I shooting and upon telling him, yes, he said: "Kirby, you are a brave man; you can go to your troop and rest up." I said: "Very well, Captain," and went out. That night about 8 o'clock we broke camp to go to the fighting line, and we walked all night.

Next morning was July 1st when the big fight [Battle of San Juan Hill occurred]. When we got pretty close to our hospital, we met lots of soldiers in wagons with their heads all tied up; some were cut all to pieces; some were shot through the eyes. We all felt badly when we saw them. All the soldiers were hungry, and the Captain went to see about breakfast. After breakfast we all went to the firing line.

We did not do any fighting that day but the next day when the Captain called out, "B troop fall in and count off," I felt pretty badly and said to the soldiers, "Be a sport and die like men." We marched to the pits and got down in them and the Captain said, "Don't a man shoot until General [Nelson A.] Miles fires that bad gun of his." We all loaded our guns and waited for the signal. After a half hour, he fired his big gun and then we all began shooting. That day we fought pretty hard and my gun became so hot I could hardly hold it. The soldiers were falling all around me and I thought every minute would be my time; we fought until dark and our Gatling guns and dynamite guns were knocking everything to pieces.

The Spaniards put up the White flag and then we stopped shooting. When the Spaniards surrendered, our boys yelled and the band played "Star Spangled Banner." We have all we want to eat and never get hungry.

I killed two Spanish spies who were up in trees and saved lots of the soldiers' lives. The Captain and boys were all glad to see me do so, and they picked me up and carried me all around.

The Captain gave me all I wanted to drink and I had a very nice time. They call me "Brave Fighting Kirby."

When the people ask about me, tell them that "The Fighting Kirby" is on top, and that I have thousands of friends in Cuba.

C. D. Kirby
Troop I, Ninth Cavalry

H. B. Bivins, Tenth Cavalry, Santiago, July 8 1898; from Southern Workman, *26 (August, 1898): 166. Sergeant Bivins, who was one of several alumni of Hampton Institute recognized for bravery in the Cuban campaign, expresses pride in the performance of Negro soldiers in the Battle of San Juan Hill.*

Dear Friend,

We had a hard fight. It began at 6:30 a.m. July 1, and lasted until noon, July 3. We drove the enemy within one mile of the city. The city is at our mercy; we can destroy it at any time. Our loss is very heavy, but I don't know how many men we have lost, as our lines are about fifteen miles long. We have the Spaniards bottled up; the only chance they have to escape is to take wings and fly. Sampson did good work. We were within three miles of the naval battle; the very earth trembled.

I was sixty hours under heavy fire; four of our gunners were wounded. I got hit myself while sighting my Hotchkiss gun. I was stunned for five minutes, but soon forgot that I had been hit. I was recommended in the official report for bravery in action. I am well and the boys are cheerful. I need not tell you how my regiment fought. Bravery was displayed by all of the colored regiments. The officers and reporters of other powers said they had heard of the colored man's fighting qualities, but did not think they could do such work as they had witnessed in the sixty hours' battle. Please send me some papers; a paper costs from

ten to twenty-five cents here; the latest paper we have is dated
June 23.

H. B. Bivins

P.S. Sorry to tell you I have killed more than a hundred Spaniards;
some I shot with a carbine. We have taken a number of prisoners.
There are several thousand wounded Spaniards in town.

J. C. Pendergrass, Tenth Cavalry, Santiago, July ?, 1898; from Illinois
Record, *September 3, 1898. In a letter to a former member of the Tenth
Cavalry, Sergeant Pendergrass provides an account of his unit from its
arrival in Cuba through its participation in the victory at San Juan Hill.*

Sgt. R. Anderson, Ret.
Springfield, Illinois

[Dear Sir:]

After the battle of Santiago, I suppose you desire to hear from
us. Well, here it is: We, Troop A, with the regiment, left
Lakeland, Fla., June 7th, dismounted, and embarked on the St.
Leona same date for duty with the first expedition against Spain.
Disembarked June 22, under cover of fire of the navy at
Daiquiri, Cuba, June 23, at 6 p.m. in squadron with B, E, and
I Troops, under the command of Maj. [S. T.] Norvell; pushed
forward as part of the advance guard of the army of invasion.
June 24th struck the Spanish troops strongly entrenched on the
heights of Las Guasima. After a severe engagement of about two
hours, the enemy was driven from his position with great loss.
Men were exhausted from intense heat and unable for further
pursuit. About thirty-five men of our force were killed and about
sixty wounded. No casualties in my troop. Bivouaced on the
field and buried the dead that night.

On the morning of the 27th our brigade proceeded with the

regiment to Servilla, and late in the afternoon of the 30th to El
Paso and took position in front of the defense covering the city
of Santiago. At 4:30 a.m., July 1, batteries of artillery, American
and Spanish, began firing, and we being the support to one
battery were subjected to a galling fire until about 6:30, when
the dismounted cavalry was ordered forward. By this time the heat
from the sun was almost unbearable, and quite a number of
men, both officers and enlisted, fell on the way from its effects,
and all the while the Spanish were throwing volley after volley
into us, and men of every rank fell at each volley. All this time
we were unable to locate the enemy, being in a dense jungle of
about two miles.

About 9:20 we got in about 1000 yards of them when our
small arms fire began, while our advance was rapid and was too
rapid for the Spanish force, who were buried in entrenchments up
to their necks. After our fire got well under way, our shots were
so effective that the enemy was unable to harm us to any great
extent. When a Spanish soldier put up his head to fire, sometimes
as many [as] six of our bullets would strike his head at once, and in
the pit dead everyone fell. This action on our part wholly
destroyed the discipline of the enemy so they would not show any
part of their body, but would simply stick their rifles above their
entrenchments and fire without aim; while our sight was true
almost every time.

By 11:00 o'clock the San Juan hills were ours and the city of
Santiago, and the Spanish troops were annihilated, though the
fire was incessant until 10:00 a.m. the 3rd.

On the evening of the 2nd at about 10 o'clock our troops
opened fire from suspicion in which 350 Spaniards were killed.
In this none of our troops were even injured.

At 12:00 p.m., the 3rd, a flag of truce was sent to the city
saying to the commander demanding that he surrender; of course,
he could not say without the consent of the Queen, so they were
given until 4 p.m., the 10th, under an armistice to conclude. So,

at noon, the 10th, the Queen said to die there, and from 4 p.m. until about 10 the next day the cannons and Gatling guns roared. While the cannons tore away their defenses, the Gatling guns mowed their men. Our dynamite gun, nearly every shot, blew a company of them a hundred feet in the air. After a few hours of this, another flag of truce was sent and they were, at this time, informed if they did not surrender at once the city would be totally destroyed at once, and to which demand they gladly complied with.

In all of this battle our guns were not playing on anything but defensive works. The final surrender, ceremony, etc. took place on the 16th. They turned over 28,000 men, arms, thousands of dollars worth of ammunition, horses, etc. There were 18,000 of us. Of our troops, killed 238 and 1,100 wounded. The Spanish loss is unknown to us, but it is supposed to be upward of 2,000. We are yet finding their skeletons around here in the bushes.

Our men laid on the field were not buried until the third day, at which time some of them were badly eaten by vultures.

.   .   .   .

The half of the suffering on this island is not known to the people of the states. It is appalling. I have not been sick since I left the ship, but on it I had seasickness very bad. It is extremely hot here in the forenoon and rains nearly half of the afternoon by the bucketfulls every day.

For five days during the fight I had no coat; hardly any shirt, it being torn off by wire fences; no blanket; eat before day; not half rations; no coffee; wringing wet from wading streams, sweat and rain. Did not take my shoes off for twenty days. I hope to see no more war.

We have thirty-eight men present in the troop, of which nineteen are down with fever. Poor fellows, they dug about twenty miles of entrenchments here, all at night and guard the next night and bomb proofs all day. They say I am much of a man for not having been sick yet after having worked in the hot sun so hard. Nearly all of the officers have played out and gone.

Our fourth of July is lamentable to think of. We never get any mail, none since June 16 at Lakeland. Now we are almost naked, no medicine, not much to eat, hot water to drink, sleeping on the bare ground, no papers of any kind. I do not know whether you will get this or not, but if you do, please read it to my mother.

It is rumored in our camp this morning that we are to move to Long Island, New York, as soon as the sick are able to travel. When we left the boat, no records or property was unloaded so I have not been able to write till day before yesterday when I received my valise.

Best wishes and kindest regards to all, I am

> Yours sincerely,
> J. C. Pendergrass
> 1st Sergeant, Troop A,
> Tenth Cavalry

W. C. Payne, On Board U.S.S. Dixie, *off San Juan, Puerto Rico, July 24, 1898; from* The Colored American *(Washington), August 13, 1898. Impressed by the economic opportunities of Cuba and Puerto Rico, Payne urges Negro Americans to emigrate to these islands.*

Editor of the *Colored American:*

You, no doubt, chronicle much news of the present war . . . gleaned from a variety of sources. But this news is of a general character, and as I know your aim is to disseminate information pertaining especially to the colored race . . . I take great pleasure in writing you a few facts about Cuba, its people and the opportunities which may be enjoyed by the American Negro, should he choose to take advantage of them.

All well informed people know Cuba is one of the richest . . .

and most fertile spots in the world. To see Cuba is but to realize
the truth of this statement. Lying off the most marvelous harbor
the human eye has beheld, one may look upon hundreds of rich
plantations now going to waste for want of cultivation. Many
little creeks, rivers and brooks can be seen racing oceanward. On
these plantations, sugar cane, tobacco, rice, vegetables and all
kinds of delicious tropical fruit grow in abundance. Cuba is also
a successful stock country. Cattle thrive nicely and there is plenty
of grass. Cuba is divided into five large states or provinces. . . .
I am positive that twenty million souls can live luxuriously in
these provinces. But after the Spaniards have all been transported
to Spain (as they will be), there will be scarcely more than one
million people remaining in Cuba. I am able to tell you that less
than five per cent of the people of Cuba took up arms for their
mother country. The Spanish Army is almost entirely deported,
not a vestige of it will be left to be a future pestilence to the
Cubans. Will Cuba be a Negro republic? Decidedly so, because
the greater portion of the insurgents are Negroes and they are
politically ambitious. I would not recommend Cuba to the greedy
politicians as a rendezvous, because the Cubans are, I am afraid,
going to have political troubles of their own. But in Cuba the
colored man may engage in business and make a great success.
It is evident that America will have the option on Cuban trade.
Can Negroes become shippers and commission merchants?
There isn't the slightest doubt of it, and those of us who have
money should try the experiment. Now as to Porto Rico: Our ship
the United States Steamer "Dixie," with the "Wasp" and
"Annapolis," have just captured a beautiful little city on the
southern coast of that beautiful island. The landing of troops is
now going on. At Ponce our little fleet of three gun boats arrived
yesterday. Captain Davis of my ship is in charge and proceeded
to demand its surrender which immediately followed. This
morning (July 28) we took full possession of the place. At this
writing the harbor is swarming with little boat loads of natives.

They are most all colored people, very enlightened and
tidy-looking. I have been conversing with some of them, as much
English is spoken among them, and they seem particularly
interested in me because I am colored. Some of them asked me
on sight: Are you a Porto Rican?" I answered: "Americano."
They replied, "Viva Los Americano." I answered, "Viva Los
Porto Rico Libre," and they cheered for the United States. They
received us with open arms. Porto Rico is another field for
Negro colonization and they should not fail to grasp this great
opportunity. The weather is fine, the fever scare a fake and the
wild animals are trained to run like Spaniards. The Spanish Army
is fleeing before our troops this minute, and we can exclaim,
"Veni, Vidi, Vici." An opportunity to get this letter off will not
permit me to write more.

> Yours sincerely,
> W. C. Payne

*M. W. Saddler, Twenty-fifth Infantry, Santiago, July 30, 1898; from
The Freeman (Indianapolis), August 27, 1898. Sergeant Saddler extols
the patriotism of the "sons of Ham" in the following letter which describes the role played by his black infantry regiment "in compelling
the surrender of Santiago."*

Dear Sir:

I wish to call attention to the heroic part the Twenty-fifth
United States Infantry played in compelling the surrender of
Santiago. We have no reporter in the division and it appears
that we are coming up unrepresented.

On the morning of July 1, our regiment, having slept part of
the night with stones for pillows and heads resting on hands,
arose at the dawn of day, without a morsel to eat, formed line,
and after a half day of hard marching, succeeded in reaching the

bloody battleground at El Caney. We were in the last brigade of our division. As we were marching up we met regiments of our comrades in white retreating from the Spanish stronghold. As we pressed forward all the reply that came from the retiring soldiers was: "There is no use to advance further. The Spaniards are intrenched and in block houses. You are running to sudden death." But without a falter did our brave men continue to press to the front.

In a few minutes the desired position was reached. The first battalion of the Twenty-fifth Infantry, composed of companies C, D, G and H were ordered to form the firing line, in preference to other regiments, though the commanders were seniors to ours. But no sooner was the command given than the execution began. A thousand yards distance to the north lay the enemy, 2000 strong in intrenchments hewn out of solid stone. On each end of the breastwork were stone block houses. Our regiment numbered 507 men all told. We advanced about 200 yards under cover of jungles and ravines. Then came the trying moments. The clear battlefield was reached. The enemy began showering down on us volleys from their strong fortifications and numberless sharpshooters hid away in palm trees and other places. . . . Our men began to fall, many of them never to rise again, but so steady was the advance and so effective was our fire that the Spaniards became unnerved and began over-shooting us. When they saw we were "colored soldiers" they knew their doom was sealed. They were afraid to put their heads above the brink of their intrenchments for every time a head was raised there was one Spaniard less.

The advance was continued until we were within about 150 yards of the intrenchments; then came the solemn command, "Charge." Every man was up and rushing forward at headlong speed over the barbed wire and into the intrenchments, and the Twenty-fifth carried the much coveted position.

So great was the loss of officers that Company C had to be

commanded by its First Sergeant S. W. Taliaferro, the gallant aspirant for the commission from the ranks. . . . The Company's commander was wounded early in the action by the explosion of a bombshell.

Thus our people can now see that the coolness and bravery that characterized our fathers in the 60's have been handed down to their sons of the 90's. If any one doubts the fitness of a colored soldier for active field service, when the cry of musketry, the booming of cannon and bursting of shells, seem to make the earth tremble, ask the regimentul Commanders of the Twenty-fourth and Twenty-fifth infantries and Ninth and Tenth Cavalry. Ask Generals [Henry W.] Lawton, [Jacob F.] Kent and [Joseph] Wheeler, of whose divisions these regiments formed a part.

The Spaniards call us "Negretter Solados" and say there is no use shooting at us, for steel and powder will not stop us. We only hope our brethren will come over and help us to show to the world that true patriotism is in the minds of the sons of Ham. All we need is leaders of our own race to make war records, so that their names may go down in history as a reward for the price of our precious blood.

M. W. Saddler
First Sergeant, Co. D.
25th Inf.

John E. Lewis, Tenth Cavalry, Lakeland, Fla., ca. August 1, 1898; from Illinois Record, *August 13, 1898. Lewis expresses profound disappointment over the failure of the War Department to recommend the promotion of the black heroes of the Cuban campaign to the ranks of commissioned officers in the regular army. He adds his voice to the growing clamor within the Negro community for black officers.*

Illinois Record
Springfield, Illinois

Mr. Editor:

Sickness has prevented me from writing you, for it is my desire to place before your readers the enlisted men of the regular service, who are fully capable of being commissioned officers. I am very glad to see that you, Mr. Editor, are still fighting with the same spirit for Negro soldiers and Negro officers and that you have taken up our burden upon your shoulders. I assure you that the 10th cavalry will aid you in any way possible. The boys are all anxious for your paper. . . .

Sergt. Pascho Conly is one of the worthiest non-commissioned officers who first entered the service in '79 and who has for eighteen years been a non-commissioned officer. Practical experience in the different departments . . . has added materially to his qualifications and by reason of his superior abilities, some credit should be given. . . . As a leader he is capable of commanding any troop and he retains that self-respect which everyone loves.

Will this war open up a brighter future for the colored soldier? Have not the non-commissioned officers proved that they are fully capable of commanding? Did 1st Sergt. William Givens of D, 10th Cav. fail when the command fell upon him, when their brave officers were shot down? No! It was forward! On to death or victory! About every troop of the 10th lost its officers . . . and non-commissioned officers took their places and led the troops on to a victory that has gained the admiration of the

world. Years of experience have well fitted them to lead our
troops upon the battlefield and it is the hope and prayer of every
Negro soldier to have our capable men receive the recognition
that is so justly theirs.

Mr. Editor, while the different states are organizing colored
troops, there are men in the regular service who should not
be overlooked. I know well that they are not known as the
historian of today has not yet given more than a meagre account
of the valor and patriotism of the American Negro soldier whose
love of his country and valorous deeds have on numerous
occasions been fully demonstrated. We believe that *The Record*
would be proud to champion the cause of good men whose
military records and recommendations from their commanding
officers attest to their capabilities. I know that these soldiers
would be a credit to any organization and that their practical
experience would add greatly to the efficiency of our volunteer
troops.

.   .   .   .

Will this government recognize and reward the brave
non-commissioned officers of the 10th for the gallantry who,
when the white commissioned officers were either killed or
wounded and could go no further, took command. When the
leadership fell upon them, did they cry out in despair, "I want a
white man to lead me?" No! The troops had confidence in their
Negro leaders; they did not become demoralized but marched on
to a glorious victory under the leadership of Negroes whose
names should go down in history. These men showed that they
could be depended upon at a critical moment and why not now?

I have it from men who were upon the field that had it not
been for the boys in black, the recent victory at Las Guasima
would have been a second Custer massacre; yet it is the men of
the Rough Riders and gallant 71st New York who get the glory
and the promotions. The press fails to state how the 1st, 10th

Cav. and 24th Inf. went through the ranks of the Rough Riders urging them on and how, after they had dislodged the Spaniards, the gallant 71st N.Y. came up.

We mourn the loss of many a dear friend and comrade. . . .

There has been a great deal of sickness in the camps, especially in the 1st Ohio Vol. and 1st Regulars. Five deaths have occurred lately in the white regiments, while the 10th Cav. has not lost a man by sickness.

The sanitary condition of the town [Lakeland] is bad and there are many cases of fever. The 1st and 10th Cav. are ordered to Montauk Point, L.I., and we expect to leave here in several days.

Mr. Editor, please keep up the good fight . . . I hope that you will be well paid in the future. Remember that the 10th Cav. will be constant readers of your valuable paper.

I am now glad to state that the people here are treating us better. . . .

Very truly yours,
John E. Lewis
Member of Tenth Cavalry

James Miller, Ponce, Puerto Rico, August 6, 1898; from Savannah Tribune, *September 10, 1898. This Negro soldier, who took part in the invasion of Puerto Rico, relates his impressions of the island which was the first place he had ever been where there was "no distinction in color."*

Dear Sir:

I take the pleasure to write you to tell you I am well at present. I thought I would give you a sketch for your paper. . . . I am now at the above named place. It is the greatest country I was ever in for climate but I find the natives very poor. They are

almost without shelter and without food. They crowd around our
camp all day long.

Children are lying naked about the streets, women and men
are in a starving condition although they are very clean. The city
is under the United States martial laws. They live on fruits,
cocoanuts, mangoes, bananas and saps. They have nothing to
cook on. They value a meat can very highly. Everyone dresses in
white, and the females go bare-headed. They crave for an English
school, and also a minister to hear the Word of God. The church
bell has not rung in four years. Provisions are very dear and
luxuries are cheap. They do not eat beef at all and have no use
for a butcher. They say, "a butcher kills beef, he kills man."

The troops got here in time to save the natives of this place.
The Spaniards had a meeting a couple of days before we arrived
and laid the law down that any man or woman who rebelled
against them would be punished in this manner: Corset jackets
with nails in them for women and children and gloves the same
for men. This was to have been put into effect July 29 but we
arrived July 28, and the executers flew to the mountains in the
inland. Flour is worth $32.00 per bbl., rice 20¢ per lb., condensed
milk 50¢ per can, [and] bacon 30¢ per lb. This is the place for
some merchant to make a fortune selling goods reasonable. A
fifty cents pair of shoes in America is worth $2.00 here.

This is the first place in my life that I have been and found no
distinction in color.

I slept very comfortable last night on the hard ground. Our
corral is in the midst of coffee, cocoanut, date and mango trees.

There are mountains all along the coast, as fine a sight as a
man could dream of. There is room enough between the
mountains and sea coast for large cities. . . . What suits me
best of all, the island is covered with beautiful women and girls
and they fairly worship an American.

Your sincere friend,
James Miller

Unsigned, Member of Tenth Cavalry, Lakeland, ca. August 12, 1898;
from Illinois Record, *August 20, 1898. The writer of this letter, proba-*
bly John E. Lewis *of the Tenth Cavalry, expresses the resentment of*
black soldiers toward the color line drawn against them by the military
and complains bitterly about "the rotten journalism" in the South, which
regularly maligned Negro soldiers.

Mr. Editor:

Yet as time slowly rolls on we have not heard of one
non-commissioned officer of the 10th Cav. recognized for his
bravery, although through the hardest battle, they commanded
troops.

When officers of A, B, C, D, E, and I fell wounded and of G
and P were killed, the command fell on the non-commissioned
officers; they led their troops on to victory, and yet not one has
been recognized.

Is it that the officers of the regiment did not fully recognize
their bravery and that they allow their prejudice which has so
long existed against the Negro soldier to blind them? You can
advance so far and no farther and it seems as if they will allow
this condition of affairs to continue. When Col. [Guy V.] Henry
left the regiment, we all felt his loss, but under existing
circumstances I am afraid that you will not hear of any
non-commissioned officer of the 10th being promoted above a
sergeant, for his bravery as was in other colored regiments, but
we hope that it will be a great change for the better.

Mr. Editor, encourage the best young men of the race to enter
the service as there are plenty of our young men who are well
qualified. Give us these men and there will be no excuse that "He
is a good man but not educated."

Sergeant James H. Alexander should receive recognition for
the long honorable service he has rendered. When the Indians
were on the war path in Arizona, Texas, and New Mexico,
Sergeant Alexander was in the saddle running them down.

L. Troop of the 10th which was recently organized is far ahead
of any young organization in the army. Sgt. Freeman
who is in command looks out well for his troops. The troops
have a very able-bodied set of non-commissioned officers. . . .

.   .   .   .

Four troops of the 9th Reg. of Cavalry passed through
Lakeland, August 9th on their way to Montauk Point, L.I. Before
leaving Tampa they rescued one of their comrades from the Tampa
jail. This trooper was arrested for carrying concealed weapons
and [for] drawing his pistol on a little boy, about ten years old.
He was tried, convicted, and sentenced to six months in the
county jail at Tampa. No member of his regiment would believe
that he drew his pistol upon a little boy, and from responsible
parties we learned that the charge was false. They arrested him
and threw him in jail. He was black, that was enough to convict
him. The *Tampa Tribune* in their morning's issue states, "Negro
soldiers, black brutes, show their lawlessness again by liberating
their comrade from the county jail, sanctioned by their officers,
and they [are] white men. The colored people even knew of it
several days, and did not say anything about it." It seems from
that that they expected the colored people to inform them of
everything that takes place among their people. The paper fails
to state how the colored people have been abused in Miami, Fla.
by the Southern [white] volunteers who shot them down like
dogs and ran them from their homes.

In a crowded store several weeks ago a colored man stepped
on the toes of a white lady and begged her pardon, but regardless
of this, one of the noble sons of this southern country shot this
man down for insulting a white lady. Mr. Editor, I could tell
you of many instances of this kind that makes any man who has
any degree of manhood feel like resenting some of the crimes
which are committed against the colored people and the soldiers
who are soldiering in the South.

On or about the 10th [of August, 1898] a number of soldiers of the 10th Cavalry were at the depot [in Lakeland] waiting to see if any soldiers were going through, when the Sheriff of Bartow took a prisoner on the train, waiting to take his prisoner to the county jail at Bartow. A number of soldiers (white) of the 1st Cavalry took the prisoner away from the sheriff and turned him loose. The whole responsibility fell upon the shoulders of the colored troops. They stated that 25 or 30 [Negro soldiers] with drawn pistols pointed at the sheriff liberated the prisoner. All members of the 10th were assembled to see if the officer could recognize any of the men which he failed to do, but the sheriff did not go to the white camp and request that the men should be assembled that they might be recognized. The colored regiment have not their pistols. They were deprived of them May 16th, 1898. The men who held their pistols on the officer were white, but, no, they would not have it said that white soldiers rescued a colored man from the sheriff, although the white soldiers did save the prisoner.

It is hard to submit to all that is published about us, not one word of which is contradicted; yet our officers know that it is not so. Every colored soldier here would rather be in Cuba than to remain in this section, and I only hope that it will not be long before the government will send us north or to Cuba. It is a shame, and if things do not change soon I will feel sorry for some people. As long as a colored man will permit a white to kick and knock him around, he is a good black, but when he won't permit that he is a "dangerous Nigger, Sah." We are men and demand to have that treatment, and will have it as long as we remain in this section.

The 1st Regular Ohio Volunteers and 10th Cavalry get along well and by their actions you would not know but that they were all one, and they have protected the colored man where he will not protect himself. I don't believe in shielding anyone in crime, and I don't believe in judging a man guilty and sentencing him before he is found guilty. The colored troops did not have trouble with the whites in the north, and all they have fought against here is the insults which were cast upon them. I am sorry to say that some of our [white] officers stated, "If they insult you, walk away from them." That is very well, but if you walk away they will kick and knock you as they did Sergeant D. T. Brown of Atlanta, Ga., but he did not let that go and gave the man who hit him from behind, a severe beating. There is a time when every man should strike back.

What makes everything so bad is the existence of such rotten journalism. Should not our officers [white] resent it when they have published what is not so about their commands? It is just as much upon their shoulders, as it is upon the men. They are in command, and are the responsible party. . . . Will they let it pass and place disgrace upon their command without refuting one word when they know that the members of their command did not have their side arms. . . ?

The troops will leave in several days for Montauk Point, L.I., and every man is glad to leave these parts.

· · · ·

[Unsigned]

John R. Conn, Twenty-fourth Infantry, Siboney, Cuba, August 24, 1898; from The Evening Star *(Washington), September 17, 1898. This articulate and sensitive black infantryman relates the horrors as well as the heroism of the war in Cuba.*

Mrs. J. W. Cromwell
Washington, D.C.

Dear [Sister]:

You request in your letter that I write you an account of my daily life here. There is so much confusion that I do not know

how to commence. We came ashore from transports here at
Siboney June 25, the next day after the Rough Riders had their
famous battle; and here let me tell you the real truth of the case:
Five or six regiments disembarked on the 21st or 22nd—I am
uncertain which date—at a point about twelve miles east of here,
and started west toward Santiago and met with little or no
resistance until they had advanced this far. The morning of
June 24 there were three columns started West—first, the 1st
Volunteer [taking the] bridle path on the very comb of a
mountain, where the underbrush was so thick it was impossible
to walk only in single file; next, the 1st United States Regular
Cavalry, going over a rough and irregular wagon road, running
north or parallel with the route taken by the Rough Riders, the
two roads making a junction about four and one-half miles west
of here, and the third column, the 10th United States Cavalry,
taking a route about a mile or more still further north where
there was no road at all. It was intended that the three commands
should move as nearly abreast as possible, but the difficulties the
10th Cavalry had to contend with in advancing were not taken
into consideration, so they were about twenty to thirty minutes
behind on getting into action.

They all took up the march as above, advancing as blind men
would, through the dense underbrush. . . . The first column,
the Rough Riders, was the first to strike the enemy in ambush
about 500 yards east of the junction of the two roads mentioned,
receiving a volley that would have routed anybody but an
American. The first regulars, hearing the music as they called it,
hurried forward to join in the dance, and awoke a hornet's nest
of Spaniards on the left, north of the party engaging the Rough
Riders, and had more music than they could furnish dancers for.
But, to the credit of the uniform and the flag, there is no account
of either column giving an inch. They advanced sufficiently to
come into line, and holding their ground until the much abused
and poorly appreciated sons of Ham burst through the underbrush,

delivered several volleys and yelling as only colored throats can yell, advanced on a run. Their position being still further to the north and opposite the left flank of the Spaniards, they (the Spaniards) could not stand it any longer, but broke and ran, and did not make a decided stand until they faced us at San Juan July 1. When the battle closed June 24 there were nineteen or twenty killed, but only one of them was colored.

The first thing that greeted us when we came ashore was an exaggerated account of the day before. The killed and wounded, as rumor had it, was something like 200, and in evidence was a column of litters coming down the hill. I counted ten or twelve and they were still coming, and I think I was scared a little. It took us about three hours to disembark, and we marched about a half mile north, going into camp in a beautiful cocoanut grove, where we remained three nights, living almost entirely on cocoanut milk and native fruits. Here is the first place we were issued raw rations, and everybody had to cook for himself. As I can scarcely cook plain water without burning it, I was not benefitted much in the change of cooks.

We camped here three days, while different parts of the army were marching past us taking their places in columns between us and Santiago. At last our turn came—3rd Brigade, 1st Division—to move forward and go in camp on the same ground made sacred by the blood of the Rough Riders, where we also stayed in camp three days. June 30, the army was again put in motion, and all day long there was almost a continual column of soldiers passing our camp until about 4 o'clock in the afternoon, when a general call was sounded in headquarters and we struck tents and took our final position in line. We advanced about four miles further west, but the road was so densely choked with soldiers that it was 10 o'clock before we went in camp, and everybody knew what to expect in the morning.

I slept very soundly that night and was awake very early the next morning. We were issued rations for three days, and I had just started to eat breakfast when the first gun was fired, at 6:30 o'clock. Very soon the Spaniards began replying and the navy began firing, and in a very short time there was a real and terrible duel with modern arms going on. The navy, as it was situated, could render no assistance, and the Spanish guns by using smokeless powder and being posted in well-masked positions, soon forced our artillery to move from one position to another, to their very great disadvantage, but they still could advance and and did advance. I still think the Spaniards had a little the best of it with the artillery the first day.

About 8 o'clock a.m. we started forward, and we were then almost the extreme rear of the army and about four miles from the front, or firing line. Almost immediately our right, I since learned, was hotly engaged, taking a small town called El Caney, on the right of our position. There is where the 25th Infantry distinguished itself. As we advanced we could hear the small arms more and more distinctly. After we had advanced about a mile, we began to meet the wounded coming to the rear, and thought seriously of the situation, and then in a short time the road was almost choked entirely with the wounded and stragglers. Our progress was very slow so when we got into the zone of the small arms firing it was about 11:30 o'clock. It was terrible. There were wounded and dead men lying all along, beside and in the road, and the air seemed alive with bullets and shells of all descriptions and caliber. You could not tell from what direction they were coming; all that we could understand was that we were needed further in front, and we could not shoot, for we could not see anything to shoot at. We advanced until we were assured by our divisional commander that our mettle was about to be tested; that he was depending on his boys of the 24th to make history, and that the fate of his record and possibly of the nation depended on the quality of the mettle mentioned.

We piled up all our extra baggage and our blanket rolls,

nothing but our arms, ammunition, and canteens being needed, and, fully stripped for fighting, we advanced with our regimental chaplain's last words ringing in our ears: "Quit yourselves like men and fight." We were right in it then, in good shape—lots of music and very few drums. From appearance we passed two or three regiments lying in the road, so that we had to stumble over them and pick our way through them to advance. Our colonel took the situation in at a glance and led the regiment down into the bed of the San Juan River until we were in the desired position, and there it was terrible—just one continual roar of small arms, cannon and bursting shells; but our position was comparatively secure on account of the river bank. We were then faced to the right (north), about 900 yards south and right of the now famous San Juan Hill. The order was then: "Third Brigade, (9th, 3rd and 24th Infantry) forward."

The orders from our colonel were: "Twenty fourth Infantry, move forward 150 yards and lie down." With a last look at our arms and ammunition—yes and a little prayer—we started, and such a volley as they sent into us! It was then that Sgt. [D. T.] Brown was shot almost at the river bank. We had to cut and destroy a barbed wire fence. You may form an idea of how strong it was when I tell you it had five to nine wires strung on it, and the posts set from two and a half to four feet apart. How or by what means it was destroyed no one scarcely knows; but destroyed it surely was, and in that angry mob, nearly all their officers having been disabled, there was no organization recognized. Men were crazy. Some one said: "Let us charge" and someone sounded "Let us charge" on a bugle. When that pack of demons swept forward the Spaniards stood as long as mortals could stand, then quit their trenches and retreated to the trenches around Santiago. When we gained the hill they were in full retreat, and our army just occupied their trenches and commenced to get even.

It seems now almost impossible that civilized men could so

recklessly destroy each other. . . . Along the crest of the hill, in
their trenches and along the main road, there were piles of dead
and wounded Spaniards. In the confusion I was separated from
my command and went with a small party to the right of the
block house . . . and there I stayed until I was ordered to the
rear with a man who was shot in the head. It was about 3:30 or
4:00 p.m.; and the firing was terrible and continued from both
sides. . . .

.   .   .   .

We had been on the hill about three hours and my gun was
almost red hot. I had fired about 175 rounds of ammunition,
and being very thirsty, I gladly accepted the detail, as the hill was
ours then and we had been shooting at nothing for about an
hour. What a sight was presented as I recrossed the flat in front
(then rear) of San Juan. The dead and wounded soldiers! It
was indescribable! One would have to see it to know what it was
like, and having once seen it, I truly hope I may never see it
again.

When I returned from the hospital five miles to the rear of our
position, it was dark, and as I passed our pile of rolls returning
I took what rations I could find—a few hard tack and a very
little raw bacon—and kept on to San Juan in search of my
company, which I found busy throwing up entrenchments. We
swapped stories of our experiences and I divided my scanty fare.
We could not make any fire, so we ate and returned to work,
remaining to 2 a.m. July 2, when we lay down in the ditches to
get what sleep we could before daylight, as we knew we would
have to fight to hold our own.

I was awakened at daybreak by the crack of small arms. It
was the Spaniards driving in our pickets. In a short time our
whole line was awake, replying to them, and before sunrise the
battle was raging furiously. It lasted all day with no intermission,
until dark. Everybody being his own cook, and not having

anything to cook, I had a very simple diet that day. Almost all the army had the same—breakfast, canteen half full of water; dinner, full canteen of water; supper, the empty canteen. We were relieved after dark by a part of the 71st [New York Volunteers], and to the rear to get some sleep and rest.

In about one or two hours, at 8 or 9 o'clock, the Spanish made an assault on our position, which was repulsed with terrible losses to them.

The casualties were light on our side, but we learn since that it cost the Spaniards more than 600 men in attempting to drive us from San Juan. They found the Yankee wide-awake and not giving an inch. The attack lasted about forty five minutes, and while it was going on it seemed ten times worse than the battle of the day before. We were finally allowed to return to our position in reserve and go to sleep.

The morning of July 3 we were issued some rations which I will assure you were more than welcome, and our simple fare of boiled bacon, hot strong coffee . . . minus sugar, plus appetite, was more wholesome than any fare I ever tasted in my life. Just as soon as we could swallow some breakfast we were returned to the trenches, and at noon July 3 the first truce was established, and the sword rested while the pen fought for the next seven days.

Corp. John R. Conn
Co. H. 24th Infantry

Unsigned, member of the Tenth Cavalry, Montauk Point, N.Y., August 29, 1898; from Illinois Record, *September 10, 1898. A black cavalryman, probably John E. Lewis, insists that the performances of Negro troops in the Cuban campaign entitle them to commissions in the regular army.*

Illinois Record

Mr. Editor:

The letter you should have received for last week's issue . . . was destroyed by water on the night of the 22nd August. The camp was visited by a terrible thunderstorm which blowed down and flooded the tents. I shall not attempt to give you an account of the trip of the Tenth Cavalry from Lakeland, Florida, here, but will only say that it was a pleasant trip until we arrived here. How anxious the boys were to strike camp and receive their comrades on their return trip from Cuba. We arrived here on the night of the 20th and found the Tenth was in quarantine and had been for two days. How slowly time passed, because we were so anxious to see our comrades . . . but on the 25th the good word spread that the Tenth would be in camp on that date. There was great rejoicing when the boys marched into camp. It was a terrible sight to see men who left Lakeland, Fla. on June 5th for Cuba, looking like the perfect man, and in the best of health, and returning looking like old broken down men from the effects of fever and the hardships in Cuba. It was hard to see some of your dearest friends, pass them by and could not recognize them until they spoke. Their forms were so emaciated no one could realize what suffering these men are undergoing. Stricken by fever, they returned to their mother country once more, but, yet the colored troops . . . were a picture to the whites. Sickness and death were terrible among the white troops . . . and it goes to show beyond a doubt that the colored troops can stand more hardships than the whites under any condition. I have seen the southern whites enlist into the first regular cavalry who were supposed to be immunes and die like sheep, while the Tenth only had one death, and that was in their own country. To now see these troops you would hardly know them; after what the colored troops have done, they are trying to rob them of their laurels. The *New York Journal* of the 23rd states that the colored soldiers are great fighters but they have to have white leaders. Has it not been proven it is false? The troops and companies were without commissioned officers half of the time. Where was the commanding officer of the Tenth[?] Did not Col. [Theodore] Roosevelt take command of the Tenth and lead it into the thickest of the battle? It was hard that a regiment had to go to the front without a leader but it is a fact. If the Tenth had only a few more men like Major [Theodore J.] Wint of the first squadron . . . but [he] was cut down in the first charge at San Juan.

· · · ·

The whole regiment mourned his loss, for he has been their only friend since Col. [Guy V.] Henry left the regiment. He has stood by them not like Lieut. Colonel [T. A.] Baldwin, who was in command of the 10th, stated before we left Florida that the 10th should be mustered out; they were nothing but a set of cowards.

Who showed cowardice, the gallant colonel, or his regiment?

He never led it in a fight. The men never saw him. Where was he at San Juan Hill and before Santiago? No, never to be found, yet after the battle was won, he states, "I knew my men could fight."

Mr. Editor, will the time ever come when the colored soldiers will be treated as men? The white officers who have that hatred against the colored soldiers should sever their connections with the colored regiment. If we have officers let them be men who are not afraid to lead their men into battle.

· · · ·

[Unsigned]

George W. Prioleau, Ninth Cavalry, Montauk Point, N.Y., September ?, 1898; from The Gazette *(Cleveland), October 1, 1898. Chaplain Prioleau calls attention to the cruelties and ironies spawned by racial prejudice in the following account of his trip through the South as a recruiting officer for the Ninth Cavalry.*

[Editor, Christian Recorder]

Tuskegee, Alabama, normal and industrial institute furnishes the town with electricity. Think of it! The slaves of Alabama furnishing material and intellectual light for their former masters. Yet when an officer of the United States Army, a Negro chaplain, goes in their midst to enlist men for the service of the government, to protect the honor of the flag of his and their country, and this chaplain goes on Sunday to the M.E. Church (White) to worship God, he is given three propositions to consider, take the extreme back seat, go up in the gallery or go out. But as we were not a back seat or gallery Christian, we preferred going out. We did not fail to inform them on the next day that the act was heinous, uncivilized, un-christian, [and] un-American. We were informed that niggers have been lynched in Alabama for saying less than that. We replied that only cowards and assassins would overpower a man at midnight and take him from his bed and lynch him, but the night you dirty cowards come to my quarters for that purpose there will be a hot time in Tuskegee that hour; that we were only three who would die but not alone. We stayed there ten days, enlisted 34 men, left a sum of $110 of Uncle Sam's money for services rendered. We took the train for Montgomery. There our stay was more pleasant. St. Matthews and Orangeburg, S.C. were our next places. Having spent a number of years around these places, we met with favor and appreciation. It was about the first time that a recruiting officer for the regular army for colored men ever opened office in this state. Charleston is the same old hotbed of rebellion and prejudice, and the prejudice of the city is not so much with the

better element of the whites, but among the backwoodsmen
who make up the [Benjamin R.] Tillman element in South
Carolina. The prejudice is not so much against the ignorant
Negro, the riff-raffs, as it is against the intelligent, educated,
tax-paying Negro; the Negro who is trying to be a man, and in
Charleston and other cities in the south you will find many. On
the public highway, street and railroad cars I received insults
daily for 30 days in my own city. My recruiting party was most
brutally treated, and there was no redress.

. . . .

Having business at the station with the chief of police, I asked
him why it is that the Negro of the South is so badly treated;
are they not the builders of your cities? Were they not the
protectors of your families from '61 to '65 while you were fighting
to keep them in bondage? He said: "The Negroes of the South
are perfectly happy, satisfied with their treatment and if you
Northern Negroes would stay away from them, and your
Northern papers would attend to their own section, we would
have no trouble with our Negroes." I replied that I was not a
Northern Negro; that I was born on Tradd Street, Charleston,
S.C., and was owned by the grandparents' of [his] sergeant who
sits there at that desk; that his father was reared on my mother's
milk; that his father, a month younger than I, owed his life to my
mother, his father's slave; that I, as a slave boy, gave him many
good thrashings and sent him to his mother, and my mistress,
howling. When he found that I was a Charlestonian and had not
disgraced my city and state, but gave it more prestige, that rebel
said that he must welcome me back to my native home. Out of
105 men, we enlisted 85, yet they say that the Negro is diseased
and weak and is dying out. If you want to see young Afro-
Americans, go to Charleston.

We are now in camp at Montauk Point, Long Island. The
men who returned from Cuba are doing well; they have done

well; they were the heroes before Santiago, if there were any heroes there. The historian must recount the four colored regiments in that fearful and bloody conflict or history will be a lie. We are here; we want to get home, [and] we do not want to return to Cuba, but if it is the decree of the Secretary of War, bravely and unmurmuringly we will go and do our commander's bidding—we will lay our lives again as a sacrifice upon the altar of our country.

George W. Prioleau
Ninth Cavalry

Member of the Tenth Cavalry, Montauk Point, N.Y., no date; from Illinois Record, *October 1, 1898. The following letter, which in all probability was written by John E. Lewis, maintains that the part played by Negro soldiers—"smoked Yankees"—in Cuba has been slighted in order to heap praise upon white officers "laying in the rear under cover" during the heat of combat.*

Mr. Editor:

I am very sorry that duty at times interferes with me writing you a letter every week, but you are well aware that time is not my own. The regiments are fast leaving the island, and to look where only a few days ago all was full of life and the tented field, called the "White city" was alive with soldiers and citizens now reminds one of the "Deserted Village."

The Rough Riders were mustered out on the 12th and 13th, and when Colonel Roosevelt bade the regiment good-bye he paid a glowing tribute to the 9th and 10th Cavalry, especially in saving them from ambush.

Mr. Editor, if your readers could have heard the Rough Riders yell when the 10th Cav. was mentioned as the "Smoked Yankees"

and that they were of a good breed, they would have been
doubly proud of the members of their race who rendered such
signal service on the battle field. . . .

When a troop of the 10th made their famous charge of 3,000
yards under the command of Capt. [William J.] Beck, the
non-commissioned officers, all colored, distinguished themselves
in a manner that will redound to the glory of the race. Among
those who distinguished themselves are Carter Smith, acting 1st
Sergeant, Sgts. Geo. Taylor, James F. Cole, James H. Williams,
Smith Johnson and Corpl. Joseph G. Mitchell who was wounded
at San Juan.

All are soldiers whose names should go down in history.
They never faltered in the thickest of the battle; they encouraged
on in a rain of shot and shell and showed by their actions that
they were the leaders. They did not hesitate to take the lead, and
when that charge was made it was "save your cartridges, don't
waste a shot."

The half will never be told of their deeds upon the battlefield.
All deserve praise from the private up, but the praise has been
given those who should have been in the lead instead of laying
in the rear under cover. And yet they say that the black is not fit
to lead.

If our war reports would only give credit where credit is due
there would be no need writing these poorly composed lines that
your readers might know of the deeds and hardships their dear
ones have passed through.

You will read that colored troops, or companies did so and so,
but the white papers never mention a name and the world only
knows one who has done an act of bravery as a Negro soldier,
nameless and friendless. It was never mentioned how, at that
famous charge of the 10th Cav. and the rescue of the Rough
Riders at San Juan Hill, the yell was started by a single trooper
of C Troop, 10th Cav. and was carried down the line.

Brave 1st Sgt. Adam Huston at the head of his troop
commanded "forward" which seemed into almost certain death.
In him the troop found an able leader; Lieut. [E.D.] Anderson
who was in command and fell to the rear and when the command,
"Forward March," was given, the brave Major [Theodore J.]
Wint only smiled, for he admired bravery and did not change
the command although he knew that the troop was in a desperate
position. The troops were carried safely through. . . .

Will it ever be known how Sgt. Thomas Griffith of Troop C
cut the wire fence along the line so the 10th Cav. and Rough
Riders could go through?

Never once did these brave men give thought to danger and to
Sgt. [George] Berry of G Troop, the color bearer who marched
on with colors in each hand, unstinted praise should be given.
He has seen over thirty years of service and when the war broke
out could have retired, and regardless of the advice of friends,
he went with the boys. . . . It was "forward boys, follow me,
they can't hit us; come on." Such was the courage characteristic
of our Negro troops: Yet we hear nothing and not even a name
is mentioned. Sgt. Berry, called "Blood" by all the boys,
returned in good health.

·   ·   ·   ·

The Spaniards would have sent our army home in disgrace
had it not been for the daring and almost reckless charge of the
Negro regiments. God was with them in that charge and no man
who has ever seen the place will say that it was possible to make
the charge without being slaughtered.

There has been much said in regard to the health of the
colored regiment of whom about one-fifth are sick; of the whites
two-thirds have been sick, [and] on account of this there has
been some talk of sending the colored troops back to Cuba, but
for my part I don't care to go. We have fought one battle and

have passed through many hardships, and the 10th Cav. should
be honored that much to have a long needed and well deserved
rest. But yet we would all willingly go if ordered to do so.

.   .   .   .

[Unsigned]

Member of the Tenth Cavalry, Montauk Point, N.Y., no date; from
Illinois Record, *October 8, 1898. In his regular letter to the* Record,
*this Negro cavalryman returns to a favorite theme by insisting that the
bravery of black soldiers under fire in Cuba stood in sharp contrast to
the cowardly conduct of certain white officers. He pleads for a military
system which will allow qualified men, regardless of color, to become
commissioned officers.*

Mr. Editor:

Our camp is about deserted. . . . Everyone is on the wonder
because orders have been issued several times that we would go
to the post and in several days we would again hear that it would
be Huntsville, Ala. and finally Cuba. On every side you will hear
Cuba in preference to the South, as the boys all dread that section
of Uncle Sam's domains; yet they will have to treat us right if
we go there.

It is not the desire of any man to have trouble with the
Southerner but the conditions will be the same as when we went
South last April, an insult and a blow.

It is to be regretted that a southern point is our destination,
and I only hope that it will not be long before we are either sent
to our post or to Cuba, should the regiments who have served in
Cuba, be returned.

The health of our men is not what it should be as they are

still suffering from the effects of the fever and it is a question whether half of the regiment would return, although the army will return to Cuba under different conditions.

Very few men who have returned from Cuba care to go there again, as they suffered greatly from the fever, and dread the climate and, again, what laurels are they to win? The battle at Santiago de Cuba was an individual fight: it was a fight with a very few officers, and the soldiers, whether non-commissioned officers or privates, who were capable of leading the boys on to victory then, are surely worthy of leading them now.

If the Negro soldier is not so well educated, let the government educate him that he then may be qualified to hold any position in which the government may desire to place him. Has it not been shown that, with all the expense the government has been put to for the purpose of maintaining such schools as West Point and Annapolis, that in times of peace they might drill the soldiers and prepare them for battle and to lead as officers in time of danger, the result has been very unsatisfactory. How many of these trained officers failed to be leaders on July 1st and 2nd. The 10th Cavalry would have been in disgrace in regards to officers had it not been for Captains Beck, Ayers and Watson.

. . . .

If you want good soldiers, you must have good leaders, men who are not afraid to go to the front of battle.

It is hard for an enlisted man to see those who are over them to lead and advise, seek the shelter of some, convenient bank during the battle and just as soon as the firing ceases, take command of them. Give us leaders who are not afraid, men like sergeant [H. B.] Bivins of G Troop, Sgts. [James] Elliot, [?] Winburn, and [?] Hamilton, of D Troop, Pvt. [Luschious] Smith but recently appointed Corporal of D Troop for the brave part he played, also young Charles White who, although yet not out of his teens, fought bravely and deserves recognition.

M Troop of the 10th, under command of Lieut. [Carter P.] Johnson, is the last detachment of our regiment to return from Cuba. They arrived here on the 19th. . . . The detachment was with General [Maximo] Gomez of the Cuban army. The men have a bitter complaint to make against the lieutenant for the way they were treated. The whole company came near getting massacred on account of his getting drunk. After the Cubans and his command had taken a fort and block house, he got a barrel of rum, got drunk, pulled down the Spanish flag and ran up his blouse as the American flag. He was given just one-half hour to leave the fort. He ordered his men to fire upon the Cubans, which they refused to do, as they would have been massacred had one shot been fired.

The men who returned to us tell an awful tale of suffering. . . . Out of seventy-five men who were the pick of the 10th Cav. only a corporal's guard returned in good health. Lieutenant Johnson won his record and advance from the ranks and now brings disgrace upon himself and the command.

.   .   .   .   .

The 9th Cav. left on the 26th for Arizona and how lonesome it made the boys feel to see them go. . . . Only six regiments remain in camp. . . .

[Unsigned]

George W. Prioleau, Ninth Cavalry, Fort Grant, Arizona Territory, October ?, 1898; from The Gazette *(Cleveland), October 22, 1898. In chronicling the return of black veterans of the Cuban campaign from Montauk Point, N.Y., to a fort in the West, Prioleau points up the difference in the reception given white soldiers and those of his own unit. The black chaplain is keenly aware that the war with Spain has failed to dissipate Negrophobia as some Negroes had predicted it would. In his view, "hatred of the Negro" is no longer confined to the South: it has become a national rather than a sectional phenomenon.*

[Sir:]

On October 4th the Ninth Cavalry broke camp and by orders of the Adjutant General, U.S.A., we left Camp Wikoff, Montauk, New York, for Fort Grant, Ariz. For the first time in the history of this country three Afro-American chaplains were blessed in being together to give their experiences of army life. It was strikingly noticeable that on September 24, Chaplains T. G. Steward, W. T. Anderson, Dr. Arthur Brown, formerly of Cleveland, ranking as First Lieutenant, and the writer were seen dressed in fatigue uniforms with the insignia of their rank, riding through Camp Wikoff.

On Sunday night, September 25, the Ninth and Tenth Cavalry, and the Twenty-fifth Infantry had a union service under Y.M.C.A. tent no. 2. Chaplain Steward preached the sermon while Anderson and myself with the Tenth Cavalry Band conducted the music. Chaplain Steward preached a very interesting sermon. We made a few remarks afterward and the men joined in singing that stirring gospel song, "Throw Out the Life Line," etc. It was a very interesting meeting which will be long remembered. It was a remarkable sight to see colored and white soldiers hold up their hands for prayer and at the close of the meeting come up and shake hands, saying: "Chaplains, pray for us." One man of the Ninth came up to me on Tuesday morning saying: "Chaplain, bless the Lord, I have found the Christ."

On our arrival at Long Island City, the Red Cross Society gave
to the entire regiment a splendid supper. While crossing the
Hudson on ferry-boats to Brooklyn, we were greeted by cheers
from laborers, and saluted by tugs and steamers as we passed by.
One of the grandest sights that we ever beheld were five war
vessels of our navy. . . . Our reception all along the line on the
B. & O. [Railroad] . . . was all that could make the hearts of
soldiers glad, and to inspire them with courage and renewed vigor
to lay their lives as sacrifices upon the altar of their country. We
were on our way to far distant Arizona to guard the settlers of
this territory from the uncivilized red man, far away from
railroads, electric lights, paved walks, cable cars, crowded cities
. . . lecture halls, operas, and the association of friends and
relatives.

While the cheers and the "God bless you" were still ringing in
our ears, and before the warm handshakes had become cold, we
arrived in Kansas City, Mo., the gateway to America's hell, and
were unkindly and sneeringly received. The First Cavalry,
U.S.A., arrived a few minutes before we did. The two regiments,
regulars of the U.S.A., were there together. Both were in Cuba.
The Ninth faced the enemy amid shot and shell up San Juan hill.
Its members fought, they bled, some died to vindicate the rights of
our country and to revenge the loss of the Maine and 250 brave
men. They were victorious, and returned home with victory
perched upon their country's banner. The First [Cavalry], well,
let history tell it. However, both were under the same flag, both
wore the blue, and yet these black boys, heroes of our country,
were not allowed to stand at the counters of restaurants and eat a
sandwich and drink a cup of coffee, while the white soldiers were
welcomed and invited to sit down at the tables and eat free of cost.
You call this American "prejudice." I call it American "hatred"
conceived only in hellish minds.

There are but few places in this country, if any, where this
hatred of the Negro is not. You will find it in every department

and walk of our country. Some say that it is not in the army. No, not so long as the Negro has no aspiration to command. But whether it's here or not, and he is fortunate enough to wear the insignia of his rank upon his shoulder instead of his arm, let him behave himself and no man can take his place. His pay goes right on as long as he behaves himself. Walking on Euclid Avenue, sitting at your desk in Case Library building, reading a few items concerning the treatment of the Negro is not sufficient. It is theoretical and hearsay knowledge. Go down in the South and get practical knowledge. Why, sir, this thing is getting worse every day. An expression of Senator [Benjamin R.] Tillman's June speech is: "Down with the niggers, but if we must tolerate them, give us those of mixed blood." And yet if a Negro man marries, or even looks at a white woman of South Carolina, he is swung to the limb of a tree and his body riddled with bullets. It seems as if there is no redress in earth or Heaven. It seems as if God has forgotten us. Let us pray for faith and endurance to "Stand still and see the Salvation of God."

After an eight days' journey we arrived at Wilcox, Ariz. on Tuesday. . . . We rested on our arms, and on Wednesday mounted our chargers and for 28 miles over a sandy and dreary [and] hot desert marched, with not a stream or well in sight. We arrived at Fort Grant hungry and thirsty. . . .

Fort Grant is a beautiful post at the base of Mt. Eaton. The climate is excellent, the water is fine and pure. Our houses are built of unpolished stone right from the mountains.

Geo. W. Prioleau
Ninth Cavalry

Member of the Tenth Cavalry, Montauk Point, N.Y., no date; From Illinois Record, *October 15, 1898. The* Record's *regular correspondent in the Tenth Cavalry, who is probably John E. Lewis, laments the assignment of his unit to a camp in Alabama and indicates that the black soldiers are in no mood to tolerate insults from white southerners.*

Mr. Editor:

This leaves on the eve of the departure of the 10th Cav. for Huntsville, Alabama, and it is with a feeling of regret that we all start again for the south. Not a man in the regiment cares to soldier again in the South because the soldiers have very little protection. Too many believe that if you are insulted that it is the proper thing to turn and go away because a white man insulted you, and that you must remember that you are *black*. This don't go in the 10th, and I am glad that we have men who have enough manhood to resent any insult cast upon them. The officers, I have noticed, who were the greatest to try to dog the men, were the greatest cowards and were just as meek as kittens in Cuba. I have noticed in the last few days that they have been great to treat the men like dogs instead of as human beings, but it is mostly toward recruits and is an unfair advantage. . . .

[Unsigned]

Member of the Tenth Cavalry, Huntsville, Ala., no date; from Illinois Record, *November 5, 1898. In the following letter the writer (probably John E. Lewis) condemns the discrimination practiced against the Negro soldiers stationed in a camp near Huntsville.*

Editor, *The Record:*

Since the trouble some weeks ago everything has been very quiet and but a very few words have been passed. The case is being fully investigated and it is sure to turn out bad for the men who fired on our hospital men. It was another case where we were virtually disarmed, our side arms having been turned in at Lakeland, Fla. May 16, after the trouble and killing of Abe Collins.

On all sides the whites were making threats against us and being disarmed they would have been very brave to have made the attempt.

We are all soldiers of the U.S. and should enjoy the same privileges. If the black regiment is to be disarmed of their side arms, then let the white regiment be treated likewise.

Take the record of the different regiments and you will know that the whites have caused more trouble and killed more men in disgraceful and uncalled for fights than the members of the 10th. It is true that we do have a few men in the regiment who like to play bad, but the whole regiment should not be held responsible for the doings of a few men and be disarmed . . . and be at the mercy of any set of thugs.

The trouble on the 11th of October would never have happened had the men been allowed to have their side arms.

Those white soldiers found that our men did not have their arms with them, otherwise they would not have fired a shot. I don't believe in giving every recruit who comes out the full use of his arms until he has been with the troop or company for a year.

. . . .

[Unsigned]

Member of the Tenth Cavalry, Huntsville, Ala., no date; from Illinois Record, *November 12, 1898. Depressed by the treatment of black veterans of the Spanish-American War, the* Record's *regular correspondent in the Tenth Cavalry again lashes out at the practice of restricting black soldiers to the ranks of noncommissioned officers.*

Mr. Editor:

.   .   .   .

And yet our non-commissioned officers and privates have not been recognized as they should be. It is true that a few have received appointments in volunteer regiments, but would it not be more of an honor if they had the appointment in their own regiment. Is this prejudice to be continued? If they are worthy to step to the front and take command and lead through the greatest danger and yet are not worthy to hold a commission in their own regiments? I know the cry will be that they are brave soldiers but are not educated well enough to hold that position and have not had that military experience, and, as I have read in different articles before the war, "that they were good soldiers but would have to be led by white officers." Mr. Editor, it has been proven beyond a doubt that they were wrong. Where were our white officers on July 1st and 2nd; about one half were left behind in safety and made their appearance after the battle. . . .

.   .   .   .

Mr. Editor, I hope the time will soon come when our colored troops and companies will be fully recognized. The 25th Infantry deserves the greatest credit and that regiment is now enjoying the rest the 10th should also be enjoying.

[Unsigned]

Member of the Tenth Cavalry, Huntsville, Ala., no date; from Illinois Record, *December 3, 1898. The writer of the following letter relates the circumstances surrounding the murder of two black cavalrymen, which in his opinion helps explain why the men of the Tenth preferred Cuba to "any part of the South."*

Mr. Editor:

It is with regret that I state certain facts which exist here at present. Did I not state [earlier] . . . that the members of the 10th Cav. being disarmed were at the mercy of any set of thugs. Two of our best and most respected soldiers, Private John R. Brooks, Troop Clerk of H Troop and Corporal Daniel Garrett [were killed].

These soldiers were returning to their camp about 9 or 9:30 p.m. after visiting friends. They were waylaid and shot down, Private Brooks being killed instantly. Corp. Garrett died on the 13th inst . . . "Horse" Douglas, colored, was captured as he was running past a policeman with a pistol in his hand. . . . It seemed very strange at first that Douglas who has borne a good reputation should commit such a deed, but many did it, Mr. Editor. Some low [white] scoundrel put out a reward for every black 10th Cavalrymen that was killed. . . . A black man tried to commit the crime. Just think of it. When this man attempted to draw his pistol, his cylinder became loose, several cartridges falling upon the ground and when he stooped to pick them up a soldier placed a pin knife at the throat of the would-be murderer and made him give his pistol up, which he turned over to his Captain. . . . This man called the next day for his pistol, but the Captain refused to give it up, but otherwise he took no action in the matter. This is the kind of protection men in the 10th Cav. receive. This man even made a statement that there was a reward on the head of every 10th Cavalryman. Are we to stand by and see our comrades foully murdered?

There were no two men more respected than Garrett and

Brooks. They faithfully performed their duties as soldiers . . . and for such men as these, in particular, to meet their death at the hands of paid Negro assassins is a condition of affairs not easily understood by those of us who have never lived in the South.

Mr. Editor, I do not blame the whites of the South for killing off so many blacks in this and other sections of the South. They will never be respected as a race until they work for the interest of their own race. Think of it, men of our own race accepting money to murder those who have aided largely to bring the race up to its present standard [and] who fought so bravely in Cuba. It is truly a sad commentary, Mr. Editor, but shows the brutish ignorance of those of our people who belong to the class usually lynched by the whites of this country. Cuba was a paradise. There we expected and looked for trouble. Our enemies were there, but here it is among our supposed friends and own people that we face a more deadly enemy, an assassin who lays and waits for you at night.

. . . .

I only hope the time will come when we can leave this place [Huntsville], as it has not been the desire of one man to remain in this section. There is not one soldier in the camp who would not rather go to Cuba than remain in any part of the South. The war department knows of what hatred there is against the colored troops in the South and what troubles they have. Why don't they send us to Cuba, or to the north, anywhere, or give us our side arms so that we might protect ourselves. I hope when the new Colonel takes command they will be issued to us again. If the white regiments were disarmed, it would be alright. We are soldiers of the U.S. and let all soldiers be treated alike, whether white or black. Don't disarm one branch so that they might slaughter the others like dogs.

[Unsigned]

Member of the Tenth Cavalry, Fort Sam Houston, Tex., March 17, 1899; from Illinois Record, *March, 25, 1899. This letter, which was probably written by John E. Lewis, is largely devoted to an incident at Texarkana, Ark., involving the Tenth Cavalry during its journey from Huntsville, Ala., to a fort in Texas.*

Illinois Record
Springfield, Illinois

Mr. Editor:

My time has been so taken up of late that it has been almost impossible for me to take time to write you, although there are several things the public should know. At this time I would not attempt to make a statement, but our good southern papers still harp upon the action of the Negro soldiers.

Mr. Editor, must the Negro soldier submit to all the indignities that are cast upon them without one word of resentment? The citizens of Texarkana found a different class of Negroes to deal with. They could run a thousand there, take them out, burn and hang them at their pleasure. You will find enclosed a clipping of the Texarkana affair.[1] It is such rotten journalism that causes so much trouble in this section of the country.

You will also find a clipping marked where the district attorney refuted the stories and false report of the newspapers.

Mr. Editor, on Jan. 31st when the regiment passed through Texarkana [en route from Huntsville to Fort Sam Houston] several of the men went up into the city and into a house where they were directed by some citizens. Upon entering they found it to be white and, of course, they were ordered to leave at once. A big black bully was sent for and attempted to use force, but they

[1] The Texarkana affair described in this letter was the subject of much newspaper publicity, especially in the South. Southern dailies claimed that the black cavalrymen "terrorized" Texarkana and described how a mob of whites threatened to blow up the troop train with dynamite because the soldiers had "kicked in the door to a resort and taken it over." The "resort" was apparently a bawdy house.

quieted him. One of the women ran out upon the street calling for the police, telling them that the nigger soldiers had taken charge of her place.

The soldiers were returning to the cars and reached the platform when the city officers came running down to the train, attempting to arrest someone, anyone, just so they got a Negro soldier. Our sentry was walking up and down the platform with his carbine over his shoulder when one of the officers [policemen] tried to relieve him of his gun, thinking that he was one of the parties at the house. He would have escaped with the gun if it had not been for some of the soldiers taking the carbine from the officer. No sooner was this done than word was sent down the line, "Get your carbine," which was most promptly obeyed, and there would have been serious trouble if the officer had continued to be aggressive as they started in. To me it was a great wonder that the man who attempted to take the gun did not get shot, for it is very serious to attempt to take a sentry's gun.

It went hard for the "bullies" of Texarkana to bow to a black face, for they had always been used to using a black just as they pleased. One would run a thousand, but I am glad to say that they did not run any of the 10th and as for them destroying us by dynamite, we were not the least bit afraid, for the cars were well guarded and it would have been almost impossible for them to have placed it to have destroyed us.

Mr. Editor, I am sorry to state that this will be about my last letter from here, for all who enlisted under the Hull Act will get their discharge. . . .

. . . .

Mr. Editor, I have partly enjoyed my stay in the army, although it has been short. I will soon be in my eastern home so I bid you good bye.

Respectfully,
[Unsigned]

*Presley Holliday, Tenth Cavalry, Fort Ringgold, Tex., April 22, 1899;
from* New York Age, *May 11, 1899. A veteran of the Cuban campaign,
Holliday refutes the charge made by Colonel Theodore Roosevelt in a
magazine article regarding the cowardly conduct of certain Negro troops
during the assault on San Juan Hill.*

To the Editor of the New York Age:

Having read in The Age of April 13 an editorial entitled "Our
Troops in Cuba," which brings to my notice for the first time a
statement made by Colonel [Theodore] Roosevelt,[1] which,
though in some parts true, if read by those who do not know the
exact facts and circumstances surrounding the case, will certainly
give rise to the wrong impression of colored men as soldiers,
and hurt them for many a day to come, and as I was an eye-witness
to the most important incidents mentioned in that statement, I
deem it a duty I owe, not only to the fathers, mothers, sisters and
brothers of those soldiers, and to the soldiers themselves, but to
their posterity and the race in general, to be always ready to make
an unprejudiced refutation of such charges, and to do all in my
power to place the colored soldier where he properly belongs—
among the bravest and most trustworthy of this land.

In the beginning, I wish to say that from what I saw of
Colonel Roosevelt in Cuba, and the impression his frank

[1] This letter is typical of many which appeared in the Negro press in response to
an article by Theodore Roosevelt which appeared in *Scribner's Magazine* early
in 1899. In describing the Battle of San Juan Hill in this article, Roosevelt wrote
that he had stopped a group of black infantrymen from retreating to the rear by
drawing his pistol on them. Like other white Americans, he also demonstrated
that he believed Negroes made good soldiers only if commanded by white officers.
The article set off a violent reaction among Negroes, and its accuracy was challenged by both black and white soldiers. Despite complimentary remarks about
the bravery of black soldiers in the Cuban campaign which Roosevelt made during
the campaign of 1900, Negroes never forgot his article. In 1906, when he dismissed
three companies of black soldiers for their alleged involvement in the Brownsville
affair, it was offered as evidence of his long-standing prejudice against Negro
troops. For Roosevelt's controversial article see "The Rough Riders," *Scribner's
Magazine*, 25 (April, 1899).

countenance made upon me, I cannot believe that he made that statement maliciously. I believe the Colonel thought he spoke the exact truth. But did he know, that of the four officers connected with two certain troops of the Tenth Cavalry one was killed and three were so seriously wounded as to cause them to be carried from the field, and the command of these two troops fell to the first sergeants, who led them triumphantly to the front? Does he know that both at Las Guasima and San Juan Hill the greater part of troop B, of the Tenth Cavalry, was separated from its commanding officer by accidents of battle and was led to the front by its first sergeant?

When we reached the enemy's works on San Juan Hill our organizations were very badly mixed, few company commanders having their whole companies or none of somebody else's company. As it was, Capt. [James W.] Watson, my troop commander, reached the crest of the hill with about eight or ten men of his troop, all the rest having been accidentally separated from him by the thick underbrush during the advance, and being at that time, as was subsequently shown to be the firing line under some one else, pushing to the front. We kept up the forward movement, and finally halted on the heights overlooking Santiago, where Colonel Roosevelt, with a very thin line had preceded us, and was holding the hill. Here Captain Watson told us to remain while he went to another part of the line to look for the rest of his troop. He did not come to that part of the field again.

The Colonel made a slight error when he said his mixed command contained some colored infantry. All the colored troops in that command were cavalrymen. His command consisted mostly of Rough Riders, with an aggregate of about one troop of the Tenth Cavalry, a few of the Ninth and a few of the First Regular Cavalry, with a half dozen officers. Every few minutes brought men from the rear, everybody seeming to be anxious to get to the firing line. For a while we kept up a desultory fire, but as we could not locate the enemy (he all the time keeping up a

hot fire on our position), we became disgusted, and lay down
and kept silent. Private [Lewis] Marshall was here seriously
wounded while standing in plain view of the enemy, trying to point
them out to his comrades.

There were frequent calls for men to carry the wounded to the
rear, to go for ammunition, and as night came on, to go for
rations and entrenching tools. A few colored soldiers volunteered,
as did some from the Rough Riders. It then happened that two
men of the Tenth were ordered to the rear by Lieutenant [R. J.]
Fleming, Tenth Cavalry, who was then present with part of his
troop, for the purpose of bringing either rations or entrenching
tools, and Colonel [Theodore] Roosevelt seeing so many men
going to the rear, shouted to them to come back, jumped up and
drew his revolver, and told the men of the Tenth that he would
shoot the first man who attempted to shirk duty by going to the
rear, that he had orders to hold that line and he would do so if he
had to shoot every man there to do it. His own men immediately
informed him that "you won't have to shoot those men, Colonel.
We know those boys." He was also assured by Lieutenant
Fleming, of the Tenth, that he would have no trouble keeping
them there, and some of our men shouted, in which I joined, that
"we will stay with you, Colonel." Everyone who saw the incident
knew the Colonel was mistaken about our men trying to shirk
duty, but well knew that he could not admit of any heavy detail
from his command, so no one thought ill of the matter. In as much
as the Colonel came to the line of the Tenth the next day and told
the men of his threat to shoot some of their members and, as he
expressed it, he had seen his mistake and found them to be far
different men from what he supposed, I thought he was
sufficiently conscious of his error not to make a so ungrateful
statement about us at a time when the Nation is about to forget
our past service.

Had the Colonel desired to note the fact, he would have seen

that when orders came the next day to relieve the detachment of
the Tenth from that part of the field, he commanded just as many
colored men at that time as he commanded at any other time
during the twenty-four hours we were under his command,
although colored as well as white soldiers were going and coming
all day, and they knew perfectly well where the Tenth Cavalry
was posted, and that it was on a line about four hundred yards
further from the enemy than Colonel Roosevelt's line. Still when
they obtained permission to go to the rear, they almost invariably
came back to the same position. Two men of my troop were
wounded while at the rear for water and taken to the hospital and,
of course, could not come back.

Our men always made it a rule to join the nearest command
when separated from our own, and those who had been so
unfortunate as to lose their way altogether were, both colored and
white, straggling up from the time the line was established until
far into the night, showing their determination to reach the front.

In explaining the desire of our men in going back to look for
their comrades, it should be stated that, from the contour of the
ground, the Rough Riders were so much in advance of the Tenth
Cavalry that, to reach the latter regiment from the former, one
had really to go straight to the rear and then turn sharply to the
right; and further, it is a well known fact, that in this country most
persons of color feel out of place when they are by force
compelled to mingle with white persons, especially strangers, and
although we knew we were doing our duty, and would be treated
well—as long as we stood to the front and fought, unfortunately
some of our men (and these were all recruits with less than six
months' service) felt so much out of place that when the firing
lulled, often showed their desire to be with their commands. None of
our older men did this. We knew perfectly well that we could give
as much assistance there as anywhere else, and that it was our
duty to remain until relieved. And we did. White soldiers do not,

as a rule, share this feeling with colored soldiers. The fact that a white man knows how well he can make a place for himself among colored people need not be discussed here.

I remember an incident of a recruit of my troop, with less than two months' service, who had come up to our position during the evening of the 1st, having been separated from the troop during the attack on San Juan Hill. The next morning, before the firing began, having seen an officer of the Tenth, who had been sent to Colonel Roosevelt with a message, returning to the regiment, he signified his intention of going back with him, saying he could thus find the regiment. I remonstrated with him without avail and was only able to keep him from going by informing him of the Colonel's threat of the day before. There was no desire on the part of this soldier to shirk duty. He simply didn't know that he should not leave any part of the firing line without orders. Later, while lying in reserve behind the firing line, I had to use as much persuasion to keep him from firing over the heads of his enemies as I had to keep him with us. He remained with us until he was shot in the shoulder and had to be sent to the rear.

I could give many other incidents of our men's devotion to duty, of their determination to stay until the death, but what's the use? Colonel Roosevelt has said they shirked, and the reading public will take the Colonel at his word and go on thinking they shirked. His statement was uncalled for and uncharitable, and considering the moral and physical effect the advance of the Tenth Cavalry had in weakening the forces opposed to the Colonel's regiment, both at Las Guasima and San Juan Hill, altogether ungrateful, and has done us an immeasurable lot of harm.

And further, as to lack of qualifications for command, I will say that when our soldiers, who can and will write history, sever their connections with the Regular Army, and thus release themselves from their voluntary status of military lockjaw, and tell what they saw, those who now preach that the Negro is not fit to exercise command over troops, and will go no further than he is led by white officers, will see in print held up for public gaze, much to their chagrin, tales of those Cuban battles that have never been told outside the tent and barrack room—tales that it will not be agreeable for some of them to hear. The public will then learn that not every troop or company of colored soldiers who took part in the assaults on San Juan Hill or El Caney was led or urged forward by its white officer.

It is unfortunate that we had no colored officers in that campaign, and this thing of white officers for colored troops is exasperating, and I join with The Age in saying our motto for the future must be: "No officers. No soldiers."

Presley Holliday
Troop B, 10th Cavalry

AMONG THE BLACK VOLUNTEERS

We don't need white officers for our leaders, we can lead ourselves.
W. T. GOODE, 1898

Separate colored brigades mean separate colored officers. . . . No officers; no fight.
JOHN MITCHELL, JR., 1898

WHEN THE RECRUITMENT of volunteers first began in 1898, the intention apparently was to follow the policy regarding Negroes which then prevailed in the regular army. The basic assumption of the War Department and of white Americans in general was that Negroes made good soldiers if organized into separate units under the command of white officers.[1] For a variety of reasons this policy failed to be uniformly enforced in creating the volunteer army. The agitation of Negroes for black officers, coupled with the need for blacks in filling state quotas and the exigencies of politics, resulted in considerable deviation from the traditional practice. In fact, a few Negroes even belonged to predominantly white volunteer outfits. These so-called "mixed" units usually contained no more than two or three Negro members. Most Negroes, however, belonged to separate, all-black volunteer companies, battalions, or regiments.[2]

Three states, Ohio, Alabama, and Massachusetts, responded to President William McKinley's first call for volunteers by mustering in Negro units. In Ohio, Senator Mark Hanna endeared himself to Negro voters by expediting the acceptance of the Ninth Battalion (Colored) into volunteer service. But because the Negro commander of the battalion had alienated Governor Asa Bushnell, he was replaced by Charles Young, a Negro graduate of West Point whose anomalous position as a black commissioned officer in the regular army had been solved by assigning him to

[1] *Richmond Planet,* April 30, May 7, June 11, 1898; *The Bee* (Washington), May 21, 28, 1898; *New York Times,* July 13, 1898; Captain R. L. Bullard, "The Negro Volunteer: Some Characteristics," *Journal of the Military Service Institution,* 29 (July, 1901): 29–39.

[2] It is difficult to ascertain how many states allowed "mixed" volunteer units, but Negroes belonged to predominantly white regiments from Maine and Iowa.

Wilberforce University as military science instructor.[3] In order to fill Alabama's quota for volunteers the governor of that state mobilized a battalion of Negro troops under the command of white officers. One of the black companies demonstrated its discontent with white officers by refusing to obey their commands. Although the incident created a sensation, it did not result in the appointment of any black officers. The Negro battalion from Alabama was increased, under the second call for volunteers, to a full regiment, known as the Third Alabama Infantry.[4] Company L of the Sixth Massachusetts Infantry, also mobilized under the first call, was a black militia company with a long and distinguished record dating from the Revolution. The only black volunteer unit sent into combat in the Spanish-American War, it took part in the invasion of Puerto Rico. The resignation of the regiment's white officers during the Puerto Rican campaign was prompted at least in part by the discriminatory treatment accorded the black company.[5] The Ninth Ohio Battalion spent its time in camps located in Virginia, Pennsylvania, and South Carolina, and the Third Alabama Regiment, despite rumors of being sent to Cuba as a part of the occupation force, never left its native state.[6]

Under the President's second call for volunteers, four other

[3] *The Gazette* (Cleveland), May 28, 1898, January 20, 1900; *Colored American* (Washington), May 7, 28, 1898; Wendell P. Dabney, *Cincinnati's Colored Citizens: Historical, Sociological and Biographical* (Cincinnati: Dabney Publishing Co., 1926), pp. 125–27; E. O. Randall and D. J. Rayan, *History of Ohio: The Rise and Progress of an American State*, 5 vols. (New York: Century Historical Publishing Co., 1912), 4: 424–25.

[4] *Biennial Report of the Adjutant General of Alabama, 1896–1898* (Montgomery: Rover Printing Co., 1898), pp. 3, 12–15; *Biennial Report of the Adjutant General of Alabama, 1900–1902*, pp. 4–6; *Daily Picayune* (New Orleans), May 30, 1898.

[5] *New York Times*, May 17, 1898; Frank E. Edwards, *The '98 Campaign of the Sixth Massachusetts, U.S.V.* (Boston: Little, Brown, 1899), pp. 43–44, 115, 124.

[6] For a detailed account of the Ninth Ohio Battalion, see Lieutenant Wilson Ballard, "Outline History of the Ninth (Separate) Battalion, Ohio Volunteer Infantry," in Theophilus G. Steward, *The Colored Regulars in the United States Army* (Philadelphia: A.M.E. Book Concern, 1904), pp. 295–98.

states responded to the demand by Negroes that they be allowed opportunities for military service. Governor James A. Mount of Indiana, after considerable hesitation, mustered in two black companies of infantry which occupied the status of "separate colored companies" and divided their time between camps in Indiana and Chickamauga Park.[7] In North Carolina, Republican Governor Daniel L. Russell, whose election in 1896 owed much to the Negro vote, paid a political debt by organizing and mustering into federal service a black regiment with black officers. This unit, the Third North Carolina Infantry, was under the command of Colonel James Young, a prominent Negro politician and a strong supporter of Governor Russell.[8] In a similar vein, political considerations figured in the decisions of Republican Governor John R. Tanner of Illinois and Populist Governor John W. Leedy of Kansas to organize and muster in Negro regiments with complete rosters of Negro officers.[9]

Undoubtedly the black regiment which received most attention, especially in the white press, was the Sixth Virginia Infantry. Negroes in Virginia, led by *Richmond Planet* editor John Mitchell, who coined the phrase "no officers, no fight," waged a persistent and vigorous campaign for a black regiment with black officers. They argued that the record of the black companies of the Virginia militia entitled them to special recognition. Democratic governor J. Hoge Tyler finally decided to accept a black volunteer regiment with all black officers except the commander, R. C. Croxton, a white Virginian and former officer in the regular army.

[7] Indianapolis *Freeman*, April 9, June 25, July 2, 1898; see also "Reminiscences of Camp Life," *The Recorder* (Indianapolis), February 11, 1899, which presents a sketch of Indiana's two Negro companies.

[8] Helen G. Edmonds, *The Negro and Fusion Politics in North Carolina* (Chapel Hill: University of North Carolina Press, 1951), pp. 97–99; *Colored American* (Washington), June 11, July 16, 1898; *The News and Observer* (Raleigh), April 29, May 1, 2, 6, 26, June 24, July 7, 1898.

[9] For the Eighth Illinois, see W. T. Goode, *The "Eighth Illinois"* (Chicago: Blakely Printing Co., 1899), and for the Twenty-third Kansas see *The State Ledger* (Topeka), June 25, July 23, 30, August 20, 27, 1898.

From the beginning the appointment of Croxton was a source of discontent within the regiment. In the fall of 1898 a group of the black officers resigned rather than submit to an examination which they described as a maneuver by Croxton to discredit them. The resignation of the Negro officers and their replacement by whites prompted a "mutiny" by several companies of the Sixth Virginia then in camp near Knoxville, Tenn. Although the difficulty was resolved, the regiment continued to be referred to as the "mutinous Sixth," especially by whites who objected to the use of black men as volunteers.[10]

By late 1898 the volunteer army included over 6,000 Negro troops mustered into federal service by eight states and another 4,000 who belonged to the four "immune" regiments—the Seventh, Eighth, Ninth, and Tenth Infantry—organized without regard for state boundaries by the War Department. The largest concentration of black volunteers in any one camp was at Camp Haskell near Macon, Ga., where the Sixth Virginia, Third North Carolina, and the Seventh and Tenth Immunes were stationed for several months in 1898–99.[11] The 4,000 black volunteers at Camp Haskell were no more inclined to abide by Jim Crow customs or to tolerate insults than the Negro regulars in Florida had been. The presence of so many armed black soldiers bent upon receiving equitable treatment inspired both fear and resentment among white civilians accustomed to a submissive black population. Racial incidents involving Negro troops and white civilians occurred regularly in the vicinity of Macon. By the time the Negro soldiers left Camp Haskell early in 1899, white Georgians were claiming that their presence had sorely disturbed "the peaceful race relations"

[10] *Richmond Planet*, April 30, May 7, June 4, 18, 1898; "Virginia's Colored Volunteers," *Southern Workman*, 27 (July, 1898): 132; *Report of the Adjutant General of the State of Virginia, 1898–1899*, pp. 6, 47–50; Edward A. Johnson, *History of Negro Soldiers in the Spanish-American War* (Raleigh: Capital Publishing Co., 1899), pp. 140–52.

[11] *Congressional Record*, 56 Congress, 1 Session, Appendix, pp. 440–41; *The Macon Telegraph*, January 6, March 9, 1899.

of the state. Governor Allen D. Candler even placed the responsibility for the outbreak of lynching in Georgia in 1899 upon the
"baneful influence" exercised by the Negro troops.[12]

The following letters from black volunteers stationed in various
camps in the continental United States are arranged in five groups.
The first includes two letters from soldiers of the Third North
Carolina Infantry. The second consists of communications from
troops of the Ninth Ohio Battalion under the command of
Colonel Charles Young, which provide commentaries on the
morale and daily routine of this black unit. The third group is
made up largely of correspondence from two soldiers of the Sixth
Virginia Infantry who signed themselves "Ham" and "Black
Man." Their letters chronicle the events which befell this Negro
regiment and explain in detail the incident which gained for it the
label "mutinous Sixth." The letters in the fourth group describe
life among black volunteers at Camp Haskell, Ga. The principal
correspondent is C. W. Cordin, a native of Ohio and a corporal
in the Seventh Immunes. The final selection is a single letter from
a soldier in the Third Alabama Infantry just prior to the muster-
out of the regiment.

[12] See *Atlanta Journal,* November 16, 21, 1898; *Atlanta Constitution,* November 30, December 5, 21, 23, 29, 1898; *Macon Telegraph,* January 6, 8, 9, 15,
1899; Washington *Bee,* March 25, 1899; *Savannah Tribune,* April 1, 1899.

THIRD NORTH CAROLINA INFANTRY, U.S.V.

*N. C. Bruce, North Carolina Battalion, Raleigh, N.C., May ?, 1898;
from* The News and Observer *(Raleigh), May 22, 1898. Bruce, a young
instructor at Shaw University in Raleigh, who volunteered for service in
a unit that was later expanded into the Third North Carolina Volunteer
Infantry, pleads for recognition of Negro patriotism.*

To the Editor:

Much is being said about Negro soldiers in the present war
that is unmanly, unwise and uncharitable, and yet there is one
cheering, refreshing thought among heaps of trashy talk: It is
that nobody seriously suggests any want of patriotism, courage,
intelligence or boldness on the part of the black soldier boys.

It seems to be a settled truth that these can fight and fight well
and long and hard. It is freely admitted that, for instance, an
implicit obedience to orders, for imitativeness and aptness to time
and tune, and for holding together in the midst of danger, the
Negro is a superior man for making the true soldier. And, further,
he has an enviable record already for tent cleanliness, fearlessness
under fire and capacity for enduring privation and hardship.

Just a few fools or worse of the race are taking the view,
either ignorantly, or, from meanness, that the colored man has
nothing to fight for in this country, where he is subject to more
humiliation, maltreatment, lynching and other contumely than
the "unspeakable Turk," the treacherous, barbarous Spaniard
or the alien anarchist, nihilist or socialist.

But now the country dearer to us than life is in peril, and
everybody who thinks knows that negroes have in every past
crisis forgotten their little hardships, forgotten their chains even
. . . and have unhesitatingly come to their country's call. They
know that this is our country, that Negroes helped to make it
what it is in war and in peace. They know further, that all they

think, and breathe, and enjoy is theirs through the power of a
country whose honor is maintained and whose voice is heard
and heeded both on land and on sea. As for lynching and other
inhuman treatment we are no apologist, but we regard these as
sentiments existing chiefly among the baser classes, and that the
larger majority of this nation is against unfairness to anybody.

It is not believed that this war is for spoils of any sort, either
as affording an opportunity to some to blot past disgraces by
some present great achievement; nor is it waged to bring North
and South together and leave out ten millions of patient, kind,
peacable, hard-working negro citizens; nor is it waged to give
rising young white men a chance to become famous. The war was
begun for Justice to Humanity—Justice at home as well as
abroad, and if this is true, it will not end until any and every
color of American man will be gladly welcomed into the trenches
alongside of the other boys to fight for Christ's peace and justice
on earth.

Moreover, some are trying to make excuses for those who are
prejudiced and who are unwilling to fight side by side with
negro soldiers, by hatching up an idea of "immunes" to fever, hot
weather, foul air, bad stenches, and hard work. They forget to
speak of the hundreds of thousands of "poor whites" who also
live in the hot and sultry and miasmatic swamps of the Sunny
South. Where are these? They can hold captured islands and
endure the hot sun and hard work, not better, but equally as well
as their black fellow laborers. At least they have stood it as well
all these years with even a smaller death rate than the negro who
lives in the same swamp and does the same work. This plea
is false and undignified—only made to deceive and to get negroes
into service respected by the other soldiers to begin with as a
person respects mules and oxen—only for heat and heavy
hauling. Negroes want to fight, are anxious to fight, but only on
the same footing as the rest—they want an equal chance from
start to finish to rise even to the highest possible place by merit.

Negroes are willing to wait until such time as the state Governors and the officials at Washington are ready to give them an equal call to furnish men and officers according to their ability and fighting population. They want no men to apologize and invent damaging and base excuses for calling them into service to die. It is wicked to misrepresent the negroes by saying that their heads are too thick for the sun's strokes, their bodies are too filthy to do otherwise than to grow fat upon Spanish filth. . . . Let negroes wait until such a time that the South as well as the North will only be too glad to stop a Spanish bullet with a black Yankee's hard pate or healthy, undying body.

The stars and stripes, the eternal emblem of Liberty, equality, fraternity, justice to everybody, must not, shall not, touch the dust, if the black arms of ten million negro Americans are given a full and fair chance to help hold it aloft. God save the nation of Washington, Attucks, Douglass, Lincoln and McKinley, by making it do right by all her children, black and white alike.

N. C. Bruce
Accepted for Service
in the North Carolina
Battalion

Members of All Companies, Third North Carolina Infantry, U.S.V., Camp Poland, Tenn., September 23, 1898; from The Journal and Tribune *(Knoxville), October 5, 1898. The following letter, which claims to express the views of the men of North Carolina's black regiment, indicates that these volunteers have no desire to remain in service since they will have no opportunity to take part in combat.*

Secretary of War
Washington, D.C.

Dear Sir:

We the undersigned many soldiers, heard that you had been instructed that we wanted to stay in service, as garrison duty, but, my dear sir, we are now pleading with mercy and deny any such report as there has been reported, and we feel that our superior officers has treated us wrong to hold us in service without we knowing anything about it.

We the undersigned did not join the service for garrison duty. We only sacrificed our lives and left our homes simply for the honor of our flag . . . as the War was going on at that time, but now the war is over and we do feel that we might be mustered out of service because we are getting letters from our families every day or two stating their suffering condition, and oh my-God, the way we are treated. We have to drill harder than any other regiment on the grounds and after drilling so hard we have to work so hard. We have to cut ditches, sink holes and fill up gullies, put in water pipes. We, the 3rd N.C. regiment soldiers, have not had but one pair of pants, one coat, two undershirts, one top shirt. We are in a bad fix. Our food is not fit to eat, and oh, my dear sir, we are bound up in a little place about 400 feet long, 3 feet wide. Just think of the confinement we are under because we volunteered freely to fight for our country.

We, the undersigned many soldiers, did not volunteer for garrison duty and we do not think that our honorable gov't will take advantage of willing and faithful men who came to the rescue of the flag, stars and stripes. We have a great deal more to tell you but we cannot express ourselves like it ought to be done.

Down at Fort Macon[1] we was misled. The question was asked who wanted to stay in the service and go to the front if necessary [and] called upon them to raise hands, but the question never was asked if we wanted to do garrison duty. If they had of asked that question we never would of been in Knoxville today. Why, don't you know as a good thinking man that we don't want to have to leave our wives and families to go on garrison duty. Why, if so you would have had more applications in the white house than the mail box would have helt.

You know that these officers is getting a very good salary and they would go in three miles of hell after that dollar, but we who are brave men did not come for the sake of that $15.60, but we gloried in the flag and come to hold it up. . . . So as we did not get a chance to do so we hope that you will consider the matter. Look it over, give us the judgment of justice and if you do we will go home to our families who are in a suffering condition, so we will not write any more.

We the undersigned await your earliest reply. . . .

Members of all Companies,
Third N.C. Regiment

[1] The Third North Carolina Infantry was mustered into federal service at Fort Macon, N.C., and remained there until mid-September, 1898, when it was transferred to Camp Poland, near Knoxville.

NINTH OHIO BATTALION, U.S.V.

J. Madison Pierce, Ninth Ohio Battalion, Camp Alger, Va., June 27, 1898; from The Gazette *(Cleveland), July 2, 1898. Pierce, a young Negro lawyer who volunteered for service in Ohio's black battalion, reports from Virginia shortly after the arrival of his unit at Camp Alger.*

[Sir:]

Everything is in status quo at camp at present. The weather is intensely hot. Until last Saturday the yellow Virginia dust was ankle-deep, so when a strong wind arose preceding Saturday's rain, battalion drill had to be given up. But rain does not do this sterile soil much good; dust can be seen flying two hours after any amount of rain. The boys of the Ninth [Ohio Battalion] were favored with visits from distinguished persons last week. Major Charles Douglass[1] and his wife and Hon. Judson W. Lyons,[2] Register of the Treasury, were among the visitors. Gen. O. O. Howard[3] addressed the soldiers in general at the Pennsylvania Y.M.C.A tent last Tuesday night. . . .

To-day is wash day in camp. It is an amusing sight to see some of our boys, who have never washed a handkerchief, bent double over tubs. Some of them, more industrious than others, "take in" washing. Very desirable husbands they will make when they return to civil life, won't they?

We have been changed for the third time from the second to the first brigade. We are no longer brigaded with any Ohio troops. In order to test our celerity in preparation Maj.

[1] Charles Douglass was the son of the famous Negro leader Frederick Douglass.

[2] Judson W. Lyons of Augusta was a prominent Negro lawyer and politician who was a member of the Republican National Committee. He was appointed Register of the Treasury by President William McKinley.

[3] General O. O. Howard had formerly served as head of the Freedman's Bureau.

[Charles] Young, or "Dynamite" as he is called by the boys, ordered us to prepare to move at once, last Monday. We were ready in fifteen minutes. We have no sick in our battalion at present, though some of our boys would like to be so, especially in the mornings, when we take the one mile sprints. Pies and spiritous liquors are not permitted on the grounds. This is the first locality I have visited in which live chickens are an unknown quantity. We can't hear a rooster's crow within three miles of any of the camps. We do not expect to move soon. My candid belief is that we shall not go to the front at all. I have never heard of anything less than a regiment being called into active engagement.

More next week.

J. Madison Pierce

J. Madison Pierce, Ninth Ohio Battalion, Camp Alger, Va., July 26, 1898; from The Gazette (*Cleveland*), *July 30, 1898. Pierce notes with regret that his battalion may never see combat duty.*

Editor, *Gazette*

We have been changed again, this time we are detached from all brigades and divisions. I believe that this is the third time we have been detached, each time from a brigade or division which was to move to the front. Major [Charles] Young informed us that we shall now do provost duty during the remainder of the summer and then participate in the siege of Havana, which will occur next fall. Of course, if peace is declared after the fall of Porto Rico and Manila, Havana will not be besieged, and like Othello, our occupation will be gone. . . .

J. Madison Pierce

J. Madison Pierce, Ninth Ohio Battalion, Camp Alger, Va., August 2,
1898; from The Gazette (*Cleveland*), *August 6, 1898. Pierce's letter*
describes an encounter between a black sentry and a white Virginian.

Editor, *Gazette*

All is quiet in camp at this writing. Last week we performed
our duty around general headquarters to the entire satisfaction
of those in authority. A few days ago, one of our boys, in
pursuance of Gen. [W. M.] Graham's orders, halted a
distinguished Virginian who was driving through the guard lines
at a very rapid pace. Of course it went against his grain to be
stopped . . . by an Afro-American soldier. Not undaunted,
however, the irate Southerner drove to Falls Church, and shortly
afterward returned with a warrant a half a yard long in length
charging the soldier with assault with intent to do bodily
injury. He was not allowed to arrest the soldier then, but was
promised by our commanding officer that the soldier would be
in Falls Church the next morning. That was before the matter
reached Gen. Graham. It is reported that when he heard of
the incident he declared: "None of my boys will be taken to
Falls Church or anywhere else to be tried for executing my
orders. If anybody is to be arrested, let them arrest me." That
ended the matter.

. . . .

In all probability the whole Second Army Corps will be
reviewed within a few days. Before this time next week our
boys will experience a change from abject poverty to
comparative opulency. The most popular man in the army—the
paymaster—will have visited the camp by that time.

[J. Madison Pierce]

J. Madison Pierce, Ninth Ohio Battalion, Camp Meade, Pa., August 23, 1898; from The Gazette *(Cleveland), August 27, 1898. Pierce not only describes life in the battalion's new camp but also notes the change in the attitude of the black volunteers "now that the hope of participating in battle is gone."*

Editor, *Gazette*

Our new camp is much better than the one we left. We are camped on a hill to the rear of Gen. [W. M.] Graham's headquarters. This section abounds in hills and beautiful scenery. We are within two miles of Middletown and seven miles from Harrisburg. As we are near the Susquehanna our boys go to that river daily for bathing. Upon our arrival here we found that our reputation had preceded us. People from Harrisburg and neighboring places streamed along the road last Sunday inquiring all the way: "Where is the Ninth Battalion?" I venture to assert without the slightest degree of vanity that we have larger crowds than any other command on the grounds.

Now that the hope of participating in battle is gone, our boys, in common with all volunteers, are eager to don the habiliments of civilians. There is a good deal of apathy among us since the peace negotiations began. Previous to that time there was no complaint or fault finding. Now the sentiments of the boys are expressed in the following characteristic strain which some of our musical soldiers have improvised: "Po' ole soljer aint nothin' but a slave." We are still Gen. Graham's guard. He is exceedingly fond of the Afro-American soldier and is unstinting in his praise of us. Last Saturday night about 12 p.m. we were aroused from our slumber by an order that a special detail of ten men from every company was needed immediately. We hurried over to the guard house at headquarters and found thirty drunken and hilarious soldiers from the First Delaware and Third Missouri regiments. They had been brought in by the provost guards because they tried to turn the little town of

Highspire upside down. They made all sorts of threats after
learning that they would be guarded by Afro-Americans, but
soon quieted down and slept till morning.

Dr. [William G.] Wren,[1] formerly of Springfield, is now
our surgeon. He arrived last week. "All's well."

J. Madison Pierce

*Taliaferro Miles Dewey, Ninth Ohio Battalion, Camp Meade, Pa., ca.
September 20, 1898; from* The Gazette *(Cleveland), October 8, 1898.
Dewey conveys the impression that the men of the battalion are becom-
ing increasingly disillusioned with military life and implies that Major
Charles Young is less interested in their welfare than in his own pro-
motion to a captaincy in the regular army.*

Editor, *Gazette:*

Yours of a few days ago was read by me with a good deal of
interest. I have this to say: If there is anything for which
"dynamite" (Maj. Charles Young) should be commended it is
his vigilance over the food that is given his men. When a man
fails to get enough to eat all he has to do is to report the fact to the
major and he will see that the soldier gets enough. In the face
of this I cannot see how it is possible for anybody in the Ninth
to starve. Of course, the fact that we get enough to eat is no
criterion that we have not any reason for complaint from
other sources. For the benefit of those who believe that we have
all play and no work I will give the following as our daily
routine. Reveille at 5:30 a.m., then roll call. Immediately after
roll call we have exercises, usually ending up by a foot race or

---

[1] Wren replaced Dr. John H. Dickerson of Columbus as battalion surgeon.
Dickerson resigned when he and Lieutenant William H. Brooks were accused of
raping a "young white woman, who kept a stand on the grounds" at Camp Alger,
Va.

jumping match; mess at 6:00 a.m., guard mount at 8:30; company drill from 9:00 to 10:00; non-commissioned officers' school from 10:30 to 11:30; mess from 12:00 to 1:00 p.m.; battalion drill from 3:00 until we are called in; mess at 5:00 p.m.; parade from 5:45 p. m. until dusk. Our parade is different from that of the white soldiers. They pass in review before their commanding officer then march in. We are frequently compelled to go through bayonet exercises, hand, foot and body exercises for the edification of the crowds of white people who come for the purpose of seeing the show. We are applauded and praised but that does not make us feel any less tired. Now, about the Porto Rico affair, Capt. [John C.] Fulton and every other officer on these grounds knows the majority of the men want to go home. Those who desire to go to Porto Rico are the men who never had homes; men to whom this army is a boon. Major Young . . . is the only officer who is indifferent in the matter [of going to Puerto Rico], and he says he has a "sure thing" on getting a captaincy of a troop of cavalry, as many of the officers of the Ninth and Tenth Cavalry were killed, that he also knows the longer he remains in the battalion the less will be his chances when this battalion is disbanded. The other officers know that they would be compelled to hustle during the next winter should we be mustered out. You cannot imagine how much conceit some of these officers have acquired since they have been drawing good salaries for the first time in their lives. The men who earned five or six dollars a week at home are the most pompous and most unbearable.

Taliaferro Miles Dewey

Winslow Hobson, Ninth Ohio Battalion, Camp Meade, Pa., ca. October 15, 1898; from The Gazette (*Cleveland*), *October 15, 1898. Hobson suggests that the black volunteers from Ohio are thoroughly demoralized largely as a result of the treatment accorded them by their own officers. He also objected to the practice of using black soldiers as servants for General W. M. Graham and his staff. For him, it was no honor to be one of "Gen. Graham's 'Nigs'."*

Editor, *Gazette:*

I have always read The Gazette with much pride and interest, but when I read your "Taliaferro Miles Dewey" article last week it made me feel that I had a right to write to your paper, even if I did have to sneak it out of camp and to some other post office so that it might reach you. Our mail (I mean the privates' mail) is inspected by our superior officers, just to be sure that we do not receive or send out any word that might express the true feeling of the battalion. Every word in the letter of your last issue is true and when men have the nerve to set up as a reason that we should be satisfied because we are getting enough to eat, the heads of such men should be examined. Why should we not have enough such as it is? I believe the government allows each man about 27 cents each day for food. Buying it as Uncle Sam can in large quantities, I defy the largest eater in our company to eat what is allowed him. But I assure you that it is not a matter of eating that is causing so much discontent in this battalion—it is the treatment we are receiving. Just think of it. The United States military law requires that every petition asking for a furlough be forwarded, approved or disapproved by the officers of a battalion or regiment. Do they do that here? No! It is simply handed back to you by your officer with some sarcastic or insulting remark, and you must drop your head and walk slowly away or you will soon feel and know just what such officers, as we are under, can and will do to you. We have now nearly as many men away from camp

without leave—possibly deserters—as you would find leaving
the Ohio penitentiary if the walls were torn down suddenly. All
say they will take any kind of chance to get away rather than
continue to receive the kind of treatment they now receive.
Yes, every man with a bit of pride and love for family is more
than anxious to get out of this hell. The war is over now and
[Theodore] Roosevelt, [Nelson A.] Miles and others (white
of course) have all there is to be gotten out of it. Now, shame
on our officers! They are willing to be called at the last moment
to play the lackey and watch-dog for the remaining white men
who want to remain in the service—not for glory but for the
money in it. We have, as you have heard, the honor (?) of
being Gen. [W. M.] Graham's guard. Well! I have been for
some time trying to find where the honor lies. It costs every
man in the battalion not less than one dollar per month of his
money for white gloves, and we are compelled to draw clothes
against our will, so that we (Gen. Graham's "Nigs") may look
better than anyone else. Some members of the battalion now
owe the government nearly a whole month's pay for clothing
over-drawn, and I assure you it is not because they want it so.
Guard duty is not all we do. Every servant, such as orderly,
hostlers and table waiters are all drawn from our battalion, so
you can see we are kept very busy watching and caring for the
general and his staff. This is the kind of honor we are
receiving. Just to show you how much they care for us after
the good work we do for them; between 12,000 and 15,000
soldiers have been asked to attend the Jubilee at Philadelphia.
Not one word was said about the Ninth Battalion. Unless we go
as Gen. Graham's bodyguard, we will not be there. Still, when
other regiments are willing to relieve us of our duties. . . .
Major [Charles] Young says, No, let us continue to be the
monks for the general. I have several times asked of what
service we could be in Cuba or elsewhere, being only 400 of us,
and the only answer I can hear is Major [Young]. Well, I am

satisfied that every officer is willing to go and resort to any means
to continue in service. But nine-tenths of the battalion would cry
with joy if at one of our dress parades, the order should be
posted to leave for Columbus [Ohio] on 30 days' furlough;
then to be mustered out. Just think of how the officers guard
themselves. Not a man that can either tell or explain how
things are managed in the battalion can get as much as five days'
furlough, but all officers and men who are satisfied with their
lot or worship the king (Major Young) get 10 days'
furlough and with no trouble. We are sick of this and want to
come home. We have worked hard since being in service and
we need a well-earned rest, but will never get it as long as there
are any white people to see us drill. I say white people
because the major does not try as hard to please his colored
visitors as he does the whites. We hope our friends will help us
out of this.

Winslow Hobson
Ninth Ohio Battalion

T. Miles Dewey, Ninth Ohio Battalion, Camp Meade, Pa., no date; from
The Gazette *(Cleveland), October 22, 1898. Dewey confirms rumors
regarding the demoralization of the Ohio Battalion and suggests that
Major Charles Young was more interested in satisfying the curiosity of
white spectators at drill exercises than he was in the welfare of his troops.*

Sir:

I read the Gazette's two articles on the conditions here in the
Ninth Battalion, O.V.I., with a great deal of interest. I don't
know who furnished you the information but it is nevertheless
true in every respect. Unless something is done pretty soon I
believe that most of our boys will desert, though for the sake of
our race I sincerely hope it [is] not so.

Camp life is very disagreeable at present. We have had a strong cool wind during the last few days. We build fires in our company "streets" to keep us warm. We shall remain here until the latter part of November, at least that is the intention of Gen. [W. M.] Graham.

The following is the manner in which we are treated by our surgeon. Whenever a sick man goes to the hospital our physician gives him a sarcastic smile and says, "Why, you are all right" or "there is nothing the matter with you." Sometimes a man is given a pill or some liquid solution. Of course, it makes no difference what the complaint is. A man suffering with diarrhoea, or indigestion gets a pill from the same bottle as the man with a sprained ankle or weak back. The medical department is the biggest farce in the army.

Maj. [Charles] Young left a week ago . . . for Ohio. He returned the first of the week. It is true that he takes pains to gratify the curiosity of white people to the neglect of our race. Whenever there is a large crowd of white people on the grounds, we can be expected to "be drilled to death" as the boys say.

The only men in the Ninth Battalion who are satisfied with their condition are those who never had homes. I am very thankful to you for fighting the cause in our behalf. It makes the officers sore, but they can't help themselves. Our captain hinted to a friend of mine . . . that some enlisted men ought to refute the statements the Gazette is printing about them. But as they are the truth we will back up the Gazette, our friend indeed. Our officers would be the saddest and most disappointed men in the country if we are mustered out before Christmas.

T. Miles Dewey

[Unsigned], Ninth Ohio Battalion, Camp Marion, S.C., November 12, 1898; from The Gazette *(Cleveland), November 19, 1898. This unsigned letter from a member of Ohio's black battalion focuses on the racial climate in the "southern backwoods."*

Sir:

There is but one company (A) of the Ninth Battalion, O.V.I., here as yet. We were sent ahead to clean up the camp for the others. This is the worst place we have struck as yet. Summerville [S.C.] is a piney woods crossroads village about 22 miles from Charleston, S.C. The water supply is very poor. We have been felling trees and clearing off underbrush since our arrival last Sunday. Camp Alger was bad enough but it was a paradise in comparison to this place.

The Afro-American is largely in the majority here, but his condition is most deplorable. The Southern "cracker" is seen at his best here. I don't know whether Williams, of Co. D, (L'Ouverture Rifles of Cleveland) was shot or not. We expect them about Monday or Tuesday.

I have not received a copy of The Gazette for the last two weeks being so far in the southern backwoods. Please send me an exact account of the election returns, as the Charleston papers say almost nothing of the elections in the north. The editorial and front pages are filled with articles on "white supremacy," "Negro domination," "shot-gun campaign" and the like.

The Ninth is brigaded with the Fourteenth Pennsylvania and Third Connecticut regiments. Brigadier Gen. [Adelbert] Ames is in Command. I shall write every week hereafter.

[Unsigned]

SIXTH VIRGINIA INFANTRY, U.S.V.

"Ham," Sixth Virginia Infantry, U.S.V., Camp Corbin, Va., July 18, 1898; from Richmond Planet, *July 23, 1898. "Ham," the* nom de plume *of a member of Virginia's regiment of black volunteers whose letters appeared regularly in the* Planet, *reports on life among the Negro soldiers at Camp Corbin shortly after they were mustered into federal service.*

[Editor:]

Co. C [Sixth Virginia Infantry, U.S.V.] under the command of Capt. B. A. Graves reached camp Friday evening, were met at the station and escorted to camp by Co. B under command of Lieut. [Lee J.] Wyche.

The men are getting use to camp life. They arise at 5 o'clock, roll call at 5:30, breakfast at 6, surgeon's call at 6:30, guard mount at 9, drill from 9:30 until 11, dinner at 12, drill again in the afternoon, dress parade at 5, supper at 6, taps are sounded at 9:30 when all lights are required to be extinguished in the camp.

The weather has been extremely hot but the men have experienced few serious inconveniences, and there are very few cases in the hospital, and only one serious trouble has occurred.

The men as a rule are well-behaved. On Saturday one man attempted to pass a sentinel, and received a bayonet thrust through the thigh. He is confined to his tent under arrest, but is doing as well as can be expected. Capt. [William A.] Hankins, being the ranking captain, is in command of the camp.

Sunday was a gala day in camp, and was marred only by a severe lightning and rain storm.

·　·　·　·

The men seemed to be perfectly contented and spend their leisure moments in playing cards, baseball and writing letters home.

Company C is building their own kitchen and mess hall, and in a few days will be doing their own cooking.

The roads are miserably dusty and it is next to impossible to keep clean. The men are required to bathe twice a week.

Starting today, the quartermaster's department is issuing supplies of clothing, shoes and underclothes, which some of the men are sorely in need of.

A few Planets were brought down to the camp Sunday and were warmly welcomed. The editorials were freely commented upon and the Planet will always be a welcome visitor.

Considerable excitement was caused in camp by one of the pickets on an outpost a few nights ago. He was attacked by a gang of tramps and was quite badly hurt. The alarm was sounded and the entire camp called out. Two shots were fired, but it was impossible to catch the gang, who escaped into the woods.

Ham

"Ham," Sixth Virginia Infantry, U.S.V., Camp Corbin, Va., no date; from Richmond Planet, *September 3, 1898. The following letter is largely devoted to a racial incident at Camp Corbin.*

[Sir:]

The weather for the past few days has been intensely hot; but the men have been able to go through their regular drills without any serious inconvenience. Muster of the entire camp was held on Wednesday, also Inspection, and the men presented a very creditable appearance. The pay rolls having been signed the men look forward to the visit of the paymaster with eager expectancy. This has been a very busy week with the officers. . . .

The Hospital Department is doing a remarkable good work in caring for the sick and emergency cases. Only three patients are now confined under treatment. The men as a rule are under good discipline and very few are confined in the guard tent.

The recruits, under regular and steady training, have shown a remarkable tendency to learn, and now they move together like clock work. It is not our purpose to criticize the actions of visitors to our camp, but an incident which happened on the occasion of the picnic of the "Nineteenth Century Club" has called forth the indignant protest of the officers as well as the men of this camp. The officers and men stationed here are in the U.S. service—they are soldiers, but they are gentlemen. The soldiers appreciate the visit of all picnic parties who visit them, but they will not stand for any unjust slurs cast upon them by anybody.

One of the committee of this club made the remark that they did not care to come in contact the "D——d black nigger soldiers anyhow." That may be very well, but they forget that these men have given up their homes to serve their country, aside from the fact that it was through the courtesy of the officers that the grounds and pavillion were secured. One of their number, Mr. Harvey Wilder, after being stopped from creating a nuisance around the springs which are used for drinking and cooking purposes, used abusive language to the sentinel on duty and was locked up in the guard tent for the rest of the day. This is carrying matters a little too far, and with all respects to the members of this club, the officers of this camp publicly request all visitors to behave themselves while on this government reservation. They desire it be understood that all

persons or visitors to the camp under the Articles of War come
under the Rules and Regulations of the camp which are strictly
enforced.

. . . .

Ham

"Ham," Sixth Virginia Infantry, U.S.V., Camp Poland, Tenn., September 19, 1898; from Richmond Planet, *September 24, 1898. "Ham" provides an assortment of news about Virginia's black regiment from its new camp near Knoxville.*

[Sir:]

On Thursday, the 15th instance, our command was ordered
to join the review which had been ordered for Maj. Gen.
[J. C.] Breckinridge. The troops left Camp Poland at 6:30 in the
morning, marched about three miles . . . reaching the parade
grounds about 8:00 o'clock. It was a grand and imposing sight
to see over 10,000 men marching. . . .

. . . .

Another Review has been ordered for Wednesday, the 21st
instance, when Secretary of War [Russell] Alger will visit the
camp for inspection and review.

The 3rd North Carolina [Regiment] with all colored
officers has reached camp under command of Major [James]
Young. They are encamped in the valley just below our camp,
on the grounds occupied [previously] by the Pennsylvania troops.

We had quite a little battle in the vicinity of our camp last
Saturday night. Some of the 3rd North Carolina's and 1st
Georgia's [white regiment], the terrors of the camp, came into

collision and blazed away at each other for nearly an hour. None of our men were concerned in it. The Georgians started the row, and as a consequence, their whole camp is now under arrest and will be kept so until they are sent home to be mustered out.[1]

. . . .

Ham

"Ham," Sixth Virginia Infantry, U.S.V., Camp Poland, Tenn., October 12, 1898; from Richmond Planet, *October 15, 1898. "Ham" reports on the uncertainty within the ranks of the Sixth Virginia caused by the resignation of nine black officers of the second battalion.*

[Sir:]

Quite a sensation was caused in camp last Wednesday by the resignation of nine of our officers. The order for the examination of the officers, as to their fitness, qualification and conduct, was issued Monday evening. By Tuesday afternoon every single officer affected by the order had tendered his resignation. When the [review] board met Wednesday morning, they found nothing to do and retired. The resignations have been forwarded to the President and much speculation is

[1] The clash between the Negro volunteers from North Carolina and the white regiment from Georgia took place on September 18, 1898, the day after the arrival of the North Carolinians. When Colonel James Young first appeared on the drill field with his Negro troops, men of the First Georgia fired upon them from a nearby forest. Young's men returned the fire. To protect the black troops from further attacks of this kind, the brigade commander stationed a detail of men from the Second Ohio in the woods alongside the drill field. Such precautions were thought to be necessary in view of the open boast by men of the First Georgia that they intended to "get" the Negro soldiers from North Carolina. See Colonel James H. Young to Adjutant General, September 18, 1898, Regimental Records, Third North Carolina Colored Infantry, U.S.V., Record Group 94, National Archives.

indulged in as to what the result will be. According to rules and regulations, if the resignations are accepted, the appointments will be made from the ranks on the recommendations of the regimental commander, the Governor of the State, and the President.

There is so much red tape concerning military affairs there is no possible way of telling or forecasting the result.

. . . .

Our camp is very popular with the people of Knoxville, and they flock out to camp every afternoon. The boys are reviving interest in the Literary Association, and on Tuesday night gave a concert at the Little Zion Baptist Church, which was crowded to the doors. The entertainment was for the benefit of the church.

The Invincible Quartette of H Company, and the orchestra of Company C made the hit of the evening. The orchestra is composed of William Page, John Richardson, Albert Jenkins, Eddie Jefferson of Company C and Corporal Joe Robinson of Company B.

An examination of all the books and accounts of this command were had a few days ago, and were found to be in satisfactory condition.

The paymaster has arrived and will pay our men off in a day or two. We have been attached to the First Brigade and will leave in a very short while for Macon, Georgia, where we will be quartered for some time. We see from the Richmond papers that a strong effort is being made to have the 6th [Virginia Regiment] mustered out of the service, but from the indications here, we don't think there is much possibility of its being done.

. . . .

Ham

J. B. Johnson et al., Sixth Virginia Infantry, U.S.V., Camp Poland, Tenn., October 27, 1898; from Edward A. Johnson, History of Negro Soldiers in the Spanish-American War (Raleigh, N.C.: Capital Publishing Company, 1899), pp. 149–50. In the following petition to the Adjutant General, Major J. B. Johnson, and sixteen other black officers of the Sixth Virginia urge the appointment of Negroes to fill the vacancies in the Second Battalion created by the resignation of nine black officers. In their view, the appointment of white officers would violate the pledge made to black volunteers at the time of enlistment and would cause "continual friction" within the regiment.

To the Adjutant General, U.S. Army
Washington, D.C.

Sir:

We, the undersigned officers of the Sixth Virginia Volunteer Infantry, stationed at Camp Poland, Knoxville, Tennessee, have the honor to respectfully submit to you the following:

Nine officers of this command who have served the state militia for a period ranging from five to twenty years were ordered examined. They resigned for reasons best known to themselves. We, the remaining officers, were sanguine that Negro officers would be appointed to fill these vacancies, and believe they can be had from the rank and file, as the men in the various companies enlisted with the distinct understanding that they would be commanded by Negro officers. We now understand through various sources that white officers have been, or are to be, appointed to fill these vacancies, to which we seriously and respectfully protest, because our men are dissatisfied. The men feel that the policy inaugurated as to this command should remain, and we fear if there is a change it will result disastrously to one of the best disciplined commands in the volunteer service. They are unwilling to be commanded by white officers and object to do what they did not agree to at first. That is to be commanded by any other than officers of the same color. We furthermore believe that should the appointments be confirmed there will be continual friction between the officers and men of the two races as has been foretold by our present commanding officer. We express the unanimous and sincere desire of seven hundred and ninety-one men in the command to be mustered out rather than submit to the change.

We therefore pray that the existing vacancies be filled from the rank and file of the command and by men of color. To all of which we most humbly pray.

> J. B. Johnson, Major 6th Va. Vol. Inf.
> Pleasant Webb, Capt. 6th Va. Vol. Inf.
> Benj. A. Graves, Capt. 6th Va. Vol. Inf.
> Jas. C. Smith, 1st Lt. 6th Va. Vol. Inf.
> L. J. Wyche, 1st. Lt. 6th Va. Vol. Inf.
> Charles H. Robinson, 1st. Lt. 6th Va. Vol. Inf.
> John H. Hill, 1st Lt. 6th Va. Vol. Inf.
> Jno. K. Rice, 1st Lt. 6th Va. Vol. Inf.
> Edwin T. Walker, 1st Lt. 6th Va. Vol. Inf.
> C. R. Alexander, 1st. Lt. 6th Va. Vol. Inf.
> John Parham, 2nd Lt. 6th Va. Vol. Inf.
> James St. Gilpin, 2nd Lt. 6th Va. Vol. Inf.
> W. H. Anderson, 2nd Lt. 6th Va. Vol. Inf.
> George W. Foreman, 2nd Lt. 6th Va. Vol. Inf.
> Frederick E. Mangrum, 2nd Lt. 6th Va. Vol. Inf.
> Richard Hill, 2nd Lt. 6th Va. Vol. Inf.
> James M. Collin, 2nd Lt. 6th Va. Vol. Inf.

"Ham," Sixth Virginia Infantry, U.S.V., Camp Poland, Tenn., November 2, 1898; from Richmond Planet, *November 5, 1898. The following letter from "Ham" indicates the dissatisfaction among Virginia's black volunteers created by the appointment of white officers to replace the Negro officers who had resigned.*

[Sir:]

The greatest indignation has manifested itself in our command, over the appointment of white officers to fill vacancies occasioned by the recent resignations. A petition has been formulated and forwarded to the War Department signed by 797 of the enlisted men asking that they be allowed their own officers or be mustered out of the service. No examination or suggestion of one has ever been held here to determine the competency or fitness of any of the non-commissioned officers who are in the direct line of promotion. Had this been done and had they been given an opportunity or test of their fitness many would have been found who were capable of holding any position in the Government Service. The boys are still loyal to the Stars and Stripes, but they feel that their days of usefulness are at end and to a man want to give up the business and return home to their families and friends. . . .

They feel that there is nothing for them to work for or hope for, and that all they do goes to the credit of others. They have not manifested any insubordination, but they feel they have been unjustly treated, and while the enlisted men understand that they are not allowed to criticize the actions of their superior officers, they have entered their solemn protest against the appointment of officers not of color, as it was distinctly stated and understood by all, before they left home, that they should select their own officers and would be allowed to do so in accordance with Va. Regulations. This has not been done and the only intimation of the Governor commissioning white officers was seen in the Richmond papers.

The boys learn with deep appreciation of the efforts that are being made by their friends, the press, and the pulpit at home to have the Governor rescind his action or have the War Department muster this command out of service.

One of the newly appointed [white] officers is here. . . . Others are expected to arrive during the week. In fact, some of them are in the city now but have not made their appearance at camp.

We have not yet received orders to move South, but they are daily expected, and the boys want to see the vexatious question settled here before the movement commences, as each step carries us farther from home and friends.

The weather here continues very cold. The men have improvised stoves of all kinds . . . in their tents. . . . The health of the men, however, continues good, only four being in the hospital and thirty six in quarters with minor diseases.

.   .   .   .

Ham

"Ham," Sixth Virginia Infantry, U.S.V., Camp Poland, Tenn., November 2, 1898; from Richmond Planet, *November 5, 1898. In this brief letter, "Ham" informs the editor of the* Planet *of the "mutiny" staged by the men of Sixth Virginia (Second Battalion) in protest of the newly appointed white officers.*

[Sir:]

Things are getting very interesting here now. Several of the new [white] officers have arrived, and this morning when they took charge, not a man would move. The boys have hooted and hissed them ever since their arrival, and have refused to drill. It is getting warmer and warmer, and they expect to be put under arrest—the whole camp. The men have even refused to go on fatigue duty.

Capt. [George A.] Bentley and Lieut. [John W.] Healy, two of the white officers, say they don't care to be where they are not wanted.

Ham

"Ham," Sixth Virginia Infantry, U.S.V., Camp Poland, Tenn., November 9, 1898; from Richmond Planet, *November 12, 1898. Contrary to rumors, "Ham" insists that those soldiers of the Sixth Virginia who took part in the "mutiny" had not begged forgiveness and still preferred "being mustered out rather than serve under white officers."*

[Sir:]

Considering the seriousness of the situation last Wednesday morning, everything has quieted down in a remarkably short time. The men have decided to accept the situation and obey all orders that are given them until their grievances have been acted upon, but they are far from being satisfied.

Yesterday a committee from the non-commissioned officers waited upon Colonel [Croxton] in regard to a letter which appeared in Sunday's *Richmond Dispatch,* and requested him to see all non-commissioned officers. In a few moments all of the non-coms in the command were gathered around the colonel's tent. The article in the *Dispatch* was a letter purported to have been written by Capt. R. Le Masurier, one of our new Captains, and saying, in effect, that the non-commissioned officers were the cause of the uprising Wednesday, Nov. 2nd, and that they had become sorry for what they had done and had been to Col. Croxton and begged for forgiveness, and that they had started the trouble because they had been disappointed in not securing promotions, and that most of the men were dissatisfied and wanted to be mustered out anyhow.

Captain Masurier was sent for and stated that the letter in

question was taken from a private one that he had written his mother who was fearful for his safety, that it was not exactly as he had written, and that it was not intended for publication anyhow. No satisfaction was obtained, however, and the non-commissioned officers considered it a reflection upon them, and they don't want the impression to go out that they influenced the men to disobey orders, simply because they were not promoted to any of the vacancies. Naturally they are indignant that every chance for them has been cut off, but they have used every effort to keep the men within the hands of the law.

As for being mustered out, there was not a dozen in the whole command who actually desire to be mustered out, but we would to a man prefer being mustered out rather than serve under white officers. As to begging for forgiveness, that has never been done and never will be. We are of the same opinion as before this unfortunate affair occurred, that is, that we have been unjustly treated. The men did not go before the Colonel, and state that they regretted that they had taken the wrong steps to secure redress for their grievances, and that they had no intention of mutiny against the supreme law of the land, but that they wanted their wrongs righted, and their rights as citizens and soldiers respected.

No official orders for removal from Knoxville have been received by our command, but it is rumored that the movement will begin next week, at the rate of a regiment a day. This will take from 12 to 15 days to remove all of the troops, and all of the government property from here. Much of the lumber, including the stables and tent flooring will not be transportable and will be disposed of here to the highest bidder.

The command has received a beautiful Regimental stand of colors. They are of the purest silk, and includes the National Flag and the state flag of Virginia, both have 6th Virginia Infantry, U.S. Volunteers painted in gold, on the front side of the flags and are embroidered with gold tassels.

.   .   .   .

In the afternoon we witnessed a novel sight. Regimental parade was held and when the command was given, "Officers, front and center!" They (white and colored, side by side) marched up and reported to the commanding officer, with Captain Benjamin A. Graves as the ranking officer — very amusing indeed.

.   .   .   .

The weather continues very cold, heavy frosts every night and ice in the mornings. The government has allowed a 50 percent increase in the fuel allowance, while we are quartered in this cool climate, but even with this the men have a hard time keeping warm and many are suffering from colds and sore throats.

.   .   .   .

Ham

William H. Johnson et al., Sixth Virginia Infantry, U.S.V., Camp Poland, Tenn., November ?, 1898; from Richmond Planet, *November 19, 1898. Major Johnson and six other black officers of the Sixth Virginia who resigned their commissions explain in the following letter why they chose to resign rather than submit to an examination by a board of review.*

Editor John Mitchell
Richmond Planet

Dear Sir:

As the daily papers have given their supposed version of the resignations of the nine officers of the Sixth Virginia Volunteers, and it has all been unfavorable to the officers in question, it may be well to let our friends hear our side.

To begin with, by an act of Congress, the commanding officer of a regiment is allowed at any time he sees fit, to ask for a Board

to examine into the qualifications, efficiency, conduct and
capability of the officers under him.

This, of course, gives a commanding officer an opportunity to
get rid of any officers who may be objectionable to him, whether
on account of color or anything else. A West Pointer can have
room made for his fellow school mates to the detriment of the
volunteer officers, and the colored officers can be gotten rid of for
the volunteer officers of [his] choice.

It is stated that we were incompetent. If West Point is to be
taken as the standard of efficiency, we admit that we were
incompetent, so is everyone else not a West Point graduate.

Again, if we were incompetent, what is to be said of any who
are inferior to some of us resigned, in mental capacity? When we
reason along this line, we can see that the object was not to find
out our efficiency, etc., but to throw us out.

Had the Board met at the time appointed, we would have been
summoned to appear before the Board, not knowing what was
wanted of us. The order called for a meeting of the Board on
Monday, Oct. 3rd, at 10 a.m. We received the order from the
Adjutant's office, Monday, Oct. 3rd, 9 p.m. Snap judgment.

We were not aware of anything of the kind to take place till we
read the order. Tuesday, 7 a.m., some of our resignations were in
the Adjutant's office. At 9 a.m. the President of the Board arrived
in camp. We were sent for. While some of us were standing in
front of the commanding officer's tent waiting for the others to
appear, we heard the question coming from the tent, "Are there
any officers or men fit for promotion?" The reply was "No". In a
few minutes the President of the Board came out, and said to us,
"The Board will convene Wednesday, 5th, at 9 a.m." "If any of
you wish to resign you had better do it before the Board meets. If
your resignations are not in before we meet we'll have to report on
you." Those words were significant. Why should he have said that?

The intention to get rid of colored officers was evident. We did
not fear a fair examination as some of us had been examined more

than once, and one of us three times, being always successful, but we were satisfied that it was a case of trot them out and knock them down.

We consider that the officers composing the military board of the State of Virginia, Colonel Jo Lane Sterp, General Charles J. Anderson and other prominent gentlemen who examined us, or some of us at least, and pronounced us qualified for our positions, knew their business as well as the commanding officer of the Sixth Virginia Regiment, and their signatures to our papers are enough for us. The signatures of all the examining boards that could be established would not have added any more honor to, or attested to our qualification any more so than the names of these two officers above referred to. The Commonwealth of Virginia felt satisfied at their action, hence our entry into the service.

We can say without fear of successful contradiction that from the 9th of August, possibly from the establishment of the camp beyond Richmond not one regimental drill has been had by the Sixth Virginia Volunteers up until the 22nd of October, saving a few maneuvers executed preparatory to a review by General [J. C.] Breckinridge . . . neither had there been one officer's school of instruction other than those held in which the two Majors were the instructors up to the 12th of October.

We did our duty. The regiment was complimented time and again upon its efficiency, yet after any drill or at any time any shortcoming was noticed on [the] part of enlisted men on the field or sentinels on post, the officers were liable to be summoned to listen to a tirade of execration and oaths. Oaths were always on hand. They were often and very loud.

Our friends have stood up boldly for us, and if our pretended friends could have witnessed the work done by the officers, and the assistance given us, and then seen what we had to contend against, instead of criticizing and condemning our action, they would have commended us. Charity would have dictated that they say nothing until they had heard more, but unfortunately for some of our people, the less they know about a subject the more they discuss it, and the discussion is ridiculous, without sense or reason. We were there and know.

These critics were at home and tried to know more than we and what they do not know about military regulations and usages would fill forty encyclopaedias. We did just what the white officers of a Massachusetts Regiment did under the same circumstances barring color. We do not wish money at the expense of right treatment. One thing has been demonstrated, yes two, that the commanding officer of the 6th Virginia Regiment has no respect for a man of color, refined or vicious.

All look alike to him. Second, that in the eyes of a certain class of army officers, an enlisted man, or an officer if he be a colored officer, is no more than a yellow dog.

We do not wish it understood that we were utterly friendless. We were certain that we had one, and probably two officers, on the board who would have given us justice, but one of the other officers was from a regiment closely allied to the Georgia Regiment [white] which gave us more trouble than all Camp Poland combined, while the other two, one of whom was the president, was from a regiment, the 4th Tennessee, who hated us intensely as evidenced by their action on learning that we were to be temporarily assigned to the same brigade with them. We had nothing to hope for —only swift judgment.

Signed

Wm. H. Johnson

J. A. C. Stevens

David Worrell

James E. Hill

Edward W. Gould

C. B. Nicholas

S. B. Randolph

"Ham," Sixth Virginia Infantry, U.S.V., Camp Haskell, Ga., November 28, 1898; from Richmond Planet, *December 3, 1898. In the following letter, "Ham" explains the incident that led to the arrest of the Sixth Virginia Regiment shortly after its arrival at a new camp near Macon.*

[Sir:]

After a very interesting trip over the Southern Road from Knoxville, Tenn. our command reached Macon, Ga., Saturday the 19th inst. Camp was broken and the first section left Knoxville at 2:30 p.m., Friday the 18th. We stopped at Cleveland, Tennessee, at 7:30 p.m. for coffee. . . . At Dalton, Ga., about 100 miles from Atlanta our train was delayed nearly three hours by running into an open switch. Everybody was considerably shaken up, but nobody was hurt.

Atlanta was passed about 3:30 a.m. and a stop of a half hour made there. The scenery along the route was superb. After the Georgia line was crossed miles and miles of magnificent cotton farms spread out as the train sped onward to its destination. On every hand could be seen massive cotton gins and cotton oil factories in full blast. Here cotton is king. Macon was reached at 10 o'clock and coffee was served to the men, who were nearly exhausted, having been in the train for 20 hours. It was nearly two hours later before the train was hauled out to camp about 1½ miles from the city.

Our camp is located on what is known as the "Huff" place. It is named Camp Haskell, in honor of Lieutenant Colonel [James T.] Haskell of Ohio who was mortally wounded at El Caney and who died shortly afterwards. It is a beautiful camp site, and reminds one very much of Camp Corbin in Virginia. The soil is sandy and flat, but when it rains, does not get very muddy. The drainage is as near perfect as can be.

·   ·   ·   ·

Among the regiments stationed here are the 7th and 10th Regiments of Immunes and the 3rd North Carolina with whom we

were encamped at Knoxville. The other Regiments here are the
2nd Ohio and the 3rd Engineers, both white. Among the Immune
regiments we have met several boys from Richmond, and they
gave us a hearty greeting. . . . They have been encamped since
August, and for a time were at Augusta, Ga., and then at
Lexington, Kentucky, having reached Camp Haskell, only a few
days ahead of us.

The press reports concerning our trouble and arrest, since
coming here, have been greatly exaggerated, and have never
assumed the proportions some of the Virginia papers try to make
it appear.

Soon after arriving here, someone pointed out to the boys a tree
on which a colored man named Singleton was lynched several
years ago. It was a large persimmon tree, and some of them got
axes and cut it down. The owner was not troubled at all. The
trouble about the park amounted to this. A few of them went into
a park about a half mile from the camp, that had little signs tacked
on the trees, "No Niggers and Dogs Allowed in Here." They got
into a row with the park keeper, and tore the signs down. A few of
the men went to town with their guns, but none of them had
cartridges and they were arrested by the Provost Guard, and
brought back to camp. Our camp was placed under arrest and the
guns of the men taken away.

Sunday morning, the 20th inst., since which time, no one has
been allowed to go out or from the camp . . . but now
everything is working smoothly and we have mail twice daily.

. . . .

The boys are all well and take things philosophically, believing
that all their troubles will be peaceably settled. Out of the whole
command not more than sixty were concerned in the rumpus
anyhow.

Through all of our troubles the Y.M.C.A. tent stands as a
ministering angel, and Mr. T. F. Binn, the secretary in charge, is
kept busy all the time. . . . All kinds of religious and pictorial

literature, daily papers, paper and stamps are to be found there, and the tent is crowded all the time between drills and mess calls.

.   .   .   .

Ham

"A Black Man," Sixth Virginia Infantry, U.S.V., Camp Haskell, Georgia, December 1, 1898; from Richmond Planet, *December 10, 1898. The following letter from a soldier in Virginia's black regiment expresses the resentment of his comrades toward what they consider unfair and unjust treatment.*

Sir:

At this writing the Sixth Virginia is still under arrest, and for what? The regiment has been in this city thirteen days and not one enlisted man has been allowed beyond the camp limits on pass. There are many among the men who are inclined to the belief that this wholesale arrest of the entire regiment is not for the reason that some thirty or forty enlisted men, without the knowledge of their company commanders, took their rifles out of camp on the Saturday night of their arrival into the city; and for which they have been tried by a summary court and fined but it is the first opportunity some blindly prejudiced officer has had presented him to punish the men for their point blank refusal to drill under white officers, that memorable day at Camp Poland, until they were given positive assurance that the objectionable officers would resign or the regiment would be mustered out.

To disarm the men, a subterfuge had to be resorted to: The men, before stacking their arms were told that they were to be given the Kraq-Jorgensen magazine rifles. After they had willingly stacked their arms and the arms removed into the city, then they were placed under arrest. Any old pretext was to be made as the cause for disarming and placing under arrest the entire regiment so "mutiny" is given as the charge. Why not have an investigation? One is courted.

While the incarceration is only quasi, the men being allowed full liberty to anywhere within the camp limits and to the Y.M.C.A. tent, yet this is felt keenly by the men, many of whom gave up decent jobs, left comfortable homes and families, and sacrificed personal liberty in response to their country's call in her hour of sore distress and need.

Notwithstanding the injustice of this arrest and the indignity and humiliation to which the men have been subjected, the more discreet among them keep up a cheerful air, and try to encourage the more despondent, so during the long evenings after the day's duties are done . . . tales are told, songs sung and for the time being all are oblivious to trouble.

Last Saturday, the colored officers were summoned to appear before Gen. [William J.] McKee, brigade commander. Capt. Benj[amin] Graves acted as spokesman for the officers. In his remarks which were forcible, he expressed the sentiment of every Negro in the regiment. He gave a brief history of the colored volunteers of Virginia, taking occasion to inform Gen. McKee that in the entire history of the organization, not one white officer ever volunteered his service, nor had the prejudiced white press ever aided or encouraged the Negro militia; on the contrary whenever the men paraded they were made the subject of jest and ridicule. Even in speaking of an officer quotation marks were used when his title was given.

The good or efficiency of the service was never thought of in those days, for then there was no pay attached to it; but now everything was changed, dollars and cents cut a big figure in the eyes of some who wish to see the efficiency of the service improved.

Continuing, he said that the Sixth Virginia was made up of men who moved in the higher walks of life — skilled laborers, mechanics, artists, expert accountants, successful merchants, lawyers, doctors, journalists, teachers and preachers, and not of the riff-raff element of which the Immunes, our erst while guards were. These men had left comfortable homes and devoted families to fight, if need be for National honor and the cause of suffering humanity. After Capt. Graves' remarks which must have made a favorable impression, the other officers addressed the General.

Each and every one was careful to give him to understand that the men were not insubordinate, that there was no desire on the part of the men to be mustered out, nor was a mutinous spirit stalking through the regiment, that refused to be downed, but that the men had come into the service with the distinct understanding that they would be officered by colored men and until the terms upon which the men enlisted were complied with, there would be trouble. As to what the result of this conference will be remains to be seen.

It is hard to see why self-respecting white men should try to force themselves upon Negroes who do not wish them, unless they are men whose penury and lack of ability to secure decent employment forces them to this. Surely, this could not have been the condition of affairs of the white men who have, and who are, anxious to accept commissions in the Sixth Virginia.

But the want of money makes even the best people cast to the winds all thoughts of social equality, amalgamation, miscegenation, mixed schools, mixed companies, mixed regiments, in short, black and tan of any kind just so they "put money in their purses." The men of the Sixth were well-drilled and excellently disciplined before the advent of the white officers in their midst. The high order of discipline still exists in the 1st Battalion of which the soldierly Major J. B. Johnson is in charge and where all the officers are colored, but not so with the Second Battalion. Here all of the officers are white with but two exceptions, and the battalion, once well drilled, is no longer so, and the officers do not, nay cannot, command the respect of the men. The men of the 1st Battalion are in sympahty with the men of the Second Battalion.

The officers of the 1st Battalion were in no wise responsible for the acts of the men who went out of the camp two Saturday nights ago, as the men found out and arrested belonged to the Second Battalion, whose white officers are afraid to poke their heads from [their] tents after dark, and they know why. The report sent out by the press that some of the men were bucked and gagged was false . . . nor has a man been placed in the guard house.

It is rumored that the Governor will appoint Negro officers in all probability to the place of the whites whose resignations have been handed Col. [R. C.] Croxton, to be forwarded to him, but that these appointments will not be made by promotion from the ranks as there are no men in the ranks who are capable of filling the positions. To deny that there are no men in the ranks capable would be a waste of time and paper. . . .

. . . .

The men of the Sixth are anxious that the regiment shall, in discipline and efficiency of drill, measure up to the standard of any of the volunteer regiments, and if the press of the state [of Virginia] has any state pride, in view of the fact that the Third [Virginia Regiment] disgraced itself at Camp Alger,[1] and the Fourth [Virginia Regiment] made itself ugly in refusing, no not refusing, but in kicking against being paid by Major [John R.] Lynch,[2] it would not be so quick to sit in judgment upon the Sixth. The Sixth wishes it understood now and for all time that they do not intend to allow an agreement, though unwritten, made between them and the state that when they volunteered (and they

[1] The Third Virginia Infantry, U.S.V., attracted much publicity while at Camp Alger, Va., for attempting to lynch a Negro who had been involved in a fracas with a white hospital steward. General M. C. Butler set off a lengthy controversy when he ordered the discharge of all soldiers of the Third Virginia who had paricipated in the affair. See *The Dispatch* (Richmond), August 10, 11, 12, 13, 14, 16, 17, 18, 19, 20, 1898.

[2] John R. Lynch, a Negro long prominent in Republican politics in Mississippi, was appointed paymaster wth the rank of Major. Another Negro paymaster with comparable rank was R. R. Wright of Georgia.

were the first in the state to volunteer to defend the flag at home or abroad) that they were to have colored officers be broken and trampled upon as every agreement made between the whites and Indians have been.

It is not so much a question of race or color for which they now contend, but one of principle and they do not intend to have it violated so long as Negro men of capacity, integrity and character can be found among the men of the regiment or in the state's broad domain. To be fair is all they ask.

A Black Man

"Ham," Sixth Virginia Infantry, U.S.V., Camp Haskell, Ga., December 6, 1898; from Richmond Planet, *December 10, 1898. In his regular letter to the* Planet, *"Ham" describes the manner in which the men spend their time while under arrest and notes the prevalence of homesickness with the approach of Christmas.*

[Sir:]

For the past few days the weather has been intensely cold, the wood allowance ran short, and the men have had an extremely hard time in keeping warm. Added to this it has rained three days. Saturday night a severe wind storm struck the camp. The velocity of the wind at times reached nearly 60 miles an hour. Several tent poles were actually twisted apart. Tents were blown away and for a time it looked as if the entire camp would be completely destroyed.

It was a miserable night for the lonely sentinels on post, with the thermometer at the freezing point and water up to their knees. When the storm was at its height, the sentinels discharged their pieces to awaken our men, and this of course occasioned considerable alarm as nobody knew what the firing was about. The 10th Regiment of Immunes was on guard throughout the night, and they say it was a night not soon to be forgotten. Everything continues quiet in the camp; we are still under arrest and don't know how long it will last.

It is rumored that the time will expire in about 20 days and our pay for this month withheld for that length of time. . . . The boys continue to work as if nothing had happened, and at night they gather around their camp fires in the company streets and each amuses himself according to his own inclination.

It is a noticeable fact that while under arrest, the boys are cheerful and in good spirits. They have several good quartettes and their ringing voices can be heard from mess call to taps. . . . Every preparation is being made for an early departure for Cuba.

An inspection of the camp has been held and an inventory has been taken of everything. . . . Everything needed for foreign service will be supplied at once. There does not seem from preparations going on here [any prospect] of muster out. Orders have been issued for physical examination of all commissioned officers in this brigade to determine their condition for service in the tropics.

The health of the boys continues remarkably good. A few have colds and sore throats, but the general condition of men speaks well for the medical department of our command.

. . . .

A unique and interesting secret organization has been formed in camp and takes the place of the Wednesday Club. It is known as the Grand United Council of Uglies. Ugliness is a prerequisite for membership, and everything has to be done in an ugly manner by the ugly members, who are not at all superstitious, as the membership is limited to thirteen, and the meetings begin at thirteen minutes to seven and close at thirteen after eight every Friday evening.

. . . .

As the Xmas holidays approach the boys yearn for home, as it is on occasions of holidays of this kind, that the soldier boy thinks most of his friends, family and social ties at home, and feels his own loneliness. But he has a peculiar way of adapting himself to circumstances. Everybody is wondering where Christmas will be spent, in Cuba, in Georgia or at home.

Everybody is kept in suspense, anxiously awaiting every day's developments in the settlement of our trouble and the prospect of an early movement to Trinidad, Cuba.

After the embargo around our camp is raised, enlisted men will be granted furloughs of 4 days, but this will not justify a trip of over 600 miles from Macon to Virginia. Many of the boys speak of spending the holidays at home, but owing to the short allowance of time, few if any of them will avail themselves of the opportunity to visit the Capital of the Old Dominion.

Ham

"Black Man," Sixth Virginia Infantry, U.S.V., Camp Haskell, Ga., December 13, 1898; from Richmond Planet, *December 24, 1898. "Black Man," always more outspoken than the* Planet's *other regular correspondent in the Sixth Virginia, takes the occasion of the regiment's release from arrest to condemn Colonel R. C. Croxton and other white officers for all the problems encountered by Virginia's black volunteers.*

Sir:

Last Friday afternoon, after having been under arrest in quarters for twenty days, cut off from the outside world, and for a portion of that time deprived of the privilege of buying a newspaper or receiving our mail, the Sixth Virginia Regiment, U.S.V. Infantry was released from under arrest. Was ever such an indignity perpetrated upon men who were brave and patriotic enough to offer their service to their country when her flag had been insulted and an attempt made to sully her honor? The true inwardness of this cowardly incarceration of more than eight hundred of Virginia's loyal sons will not be known until the Sixth Virginia is mustered out, and the men and officers free to express their opinions and tell the real cause of the trouble in the regiment.

.   .   .   .

To begin with, Lieutenant Colonel [R. C.] Croxton is the sole cause of all the trouble. Not being contented with his position and pay as a second lieutenant in the regular army, at the beginning of the unpleasantness between Spain and America, he sought promotion in the volunteer army. Being a Virginian, and having been detailed as a military instructor in several of the military academies in the state, the surest means of elevation and promotion lay through the Virginia Volunteers.[1]

When the President accepted the services of the first and second battalion of Virginia infantry, Col. Croxton was placed in charge of the partial regiment. Peevish, fretful and irascible by nature, he was more so upon recovery from the sickness immediately preceding his taking command of the regiment. Knowing that he was an army officer, his harshness to both men and officers was from the first looked upon as a part of military discipline . . . and despite the oaths and general "cussing," for which the officers came to after every regimental parade, his will was law, and no one dared question it. This was at Camp Corbin. When we reached Knoxville [Camp Poland] the same thing continued, and fault, nothing but fault was to be found. . . . At three grand reviews before Gen. [J. C.] Breckinridge, before General [Russell A.] Alger and before Governor [Asa] Bushnell [of Ohio] and staff,

[1] Richard C. Croxton, a lieutenant in the First Infantry, U.S.A., was detached from his unit in the regular army in 1897 to serve in the office of Virginia's Adjutant General, where he was in charge of ordnance. Appointed commander of Virginia's black regiment, Croxton was commissioned Lieutenant Colonel in the volunteer army. Once the Sixth Virginia was mustered out in 1899, he returned to his unit in the regular army and was promoted to Captain.

the Knoxville press was unanimous in its praise of the marching
and manoeurvering of Col. Croxton's Sixth Virginia Regiment.

But these reviews over, and the boys back in camp, no
commanding officer rode down the lines or passed through the
company street to cheer the boys nor commend them for their
soldierly bearing. No word of encouragement ever came when after
a stay in Knoxville of more than two months, when on the eve of
their departure, the press of the city makes special mention of the
gentlemanly soldierly conduct of the Negro soldiers, saying that
not one man in the two regiments (3rd North Carolina and 6th
Virginia) was arrested by the police force of the city nor figured in
the courts for disorderly conduct, drunkeness or the likes. With
such marks of approval by the White press, after four month's
service under colored officers, the commanding officer complains
of the efficiency of some of the officers and asks for a board to
examine into their capability and efficiency. Is there any sane
person, who for once believes that the "efficiency and capability"
of the officers was in question? No, someone saw an opportunity to
get white staff officers and others for association.

Well, they are here, and what is the result? Discipline, order,
respect for the commanding officer all thrown to the winds of
heaven! Who is to blame? Not the Governor of Virginia but the
Colonel of the regiment at whose hand the Governor was deceived.

.   .   .   .

The refusal of the men to give quiet acquiescence into the
appointment of white officers has turned loose upon the regiment
the flood gates of vituperation of the prejudiced southern white
press. . . . While these papers speak in bold headlines of the
"mutinous Sixth," they never speak of the knives, shears, and
razors stolen from the Sixth after they were disarmed. No, for this
was done by white soldiers. On the Sunday of our arrest, Col.
Somebody of one of the immune regiments assisted by a lieutenant

colonel and our commandant searched our camp for fire-arms and other weapons of defense.

Now as nearly every other man in the regiment is his own barber any number of razors and shears were found. Very few soldiers are without pocket knives, and so hundreds of those were taken for safe-keeping. . . . When our arms were returned on Friday, only about one third of the razors, shears and knives . . . were returned. But there is one thing, the long-bearded man is no longer a curiosity in camp.

.   .   .   .

The white officers are still here and as the commanding officer is anxious that they remain, every one is at sea as to whether he will keep his promise true, as to recommending the acceptance of their resignation and the appointment of men of color. Every preparation is being made to fit the command for foreign service, yet when the corps commander sent to Col. Croxton asking how many men could be furnished for service upon a moment's notice, his reply was 971, but that he had written to the Adjutant General of the Army asking that regiment be mustered out, because they have said they will not be willing to accept white officers.

There are many reasons to argue why not one of the officers should be white. First of all, the two battalions of Virginia have always been distinctively colored and efficiently commanded; again, the understanding was when we were mustered in that we were to have colored officers; experience has shown . . . that the efficiency of the regiment can be better maintained under colored officers than under white ones; that with all the officers colored, less expense will be brought upon the government.

Now, there are some who may ask how this latter may be brought about. Since the advent of the white officers, two large tents intended for the hospital corps have been brought into use as mess-tents for the officers, one for the colonel and his white officers, and the other for the colored officers. Before the advent of the white officers, the colonel took no thought of the comfort of the colored officers, so the officers purchased lumber and had their own mess hall built. This, the white officers did not do when they came, and thinking it too much like social equality to mess with colored soldiers, used the lumber which the government had bought for tent-flooring, to build their mess-halls, and later appropriated one of the large hospital tents as a mess-hall. Of course, the colonel saw it would not do to have the white officers only use a large hospital tent, so a requisition was made for a second tent, which the colored officers use.

When we reached Macon, it was found too distasteful for the white officers, to use the sinks used by the colored officers, so another sink for white officers was dug and housed in, that meant the needless waste of more than five hundred feet of dressed lumber. When colored lieutenants were detailed as regimental adjutants and quartermasters, they occupied the same tents with company lieutenants; not so since the colored officers have been relieved and white ones substituted, for the white adjutant and quartermaster occupy separate tents on the left of the colonel's tent. The colored officers have as their cooks hired men whom they brought from Richmond. The white officers have detailed men from the second battalion. The hostlers for the colored officers also came from Richmond and are also hired men. The white officers' hostlers are detailed from the second battalion, and these detailed men do no company duties, yet "white officers add to the efficiency of the service."

.   .   .   .

Black Man

"Ham," Sixth Virginia Infantry, U.S.V., Camp Haskell, Ga., December 13, 1898; from Richmond Planet, *December 17, 1898. "Ham" includes in his regular letter to the* Planet *comments on the racial discrimination practiced by white Georgians and on the unsettled state of affairs in Virginia's black volunteer regiment.*

[Sir:]

At last the 6th Virginia have been turned loose at least, to a certain extent. Last Friday afternoon, we mounted our own guard, and the Immunes who have been guarding us for three weeks have returned to their camp.

The first night our men were on was a miserable one. It was the coldest one we have experienced since being in the Sunny South. First, it rained, hailed and when we awoke in the morning the ground was frozen stiff and covered with an inch and a half coating of snow.

When it was known among the other regiments here that our boys had been freed, a mighty cheer arose . . . and its echoes reverberated through these Georgia pines in tones not heard since the Civil War.

Passes are being granted to enlisted men at the rate of 8 men per day from each company. The Provost Guard in town are very strict, and absolutely no soldiers are allowed in town after five o'clock.

. . . .

The 7th U.S. Cavalry of the regular army reached camp last Saturday. They have a full regiment of 1200 men and 1500 horses, a wagon train with about 150 mules. They are encamped at the race track in the Fair Grounds about half a mile from town.

. . . .

This morning Reveille was sounded at 5:30, the boys were given breakfast at 5:45, and everything put in readiness for the Grand

Review given for our Corps Commander, Maj. Gen'l [J. M.] Wilson, in the city at 9 o'clock. At 7 o'clock our command left camp for the long march to town. . . . Every man was in heavy marching order, with his rifle, canteen, haversack with lunch, shelter tent, poncho, and blanket rolled across from shoulder to waist. More than 7500 troops were in line, and it was truly a magnificent sight. . . .

It was a sight never before witnessed by the citizens of Macon, and the idea of 4000 Negro troops in line was something that they never even dreamed of before.

The boys created considerable favorable comment however. It is strange how these people regard the Negro soldier. One cannot go into town without being eyed suspiciously, and looked upon as something out of the ordinary; this applies to the colored as well as the white element. It is noticeable, so far different from the manner in which we were treated by all classes of citizens while we were stationed at Knoxville.

The secretary of our Y.M.C.A. was informed by the proprietor a Steam Laundry to which he had carried some linen to be washed that "this laundry is for the exclusive purposes of white people's work, and we do nothing whatever for colored people." On some of the street car lines, one car is set apart for the use of colored people.

I understand from reliable authority that in this neighborhood is a large workhouse, where colored girls and women are kept and forced to work in chain gangs, cleaning the public roads and doing all kinds of menial labor, with ball and chain around their ankles, for slight offenses.

Altogether from my personal observation, this state has created a very unfavorable impression in my mind, and offers very slight inducement to citizens of color.

Many of the boys are putting in applications for furloughs home during the [Christmas] holidays. Changes and incidents follow each other so rapidly in the affairs of this command, that it is unsafe to predict or even think what will happen next. While seemingly everything points to a long campaign in Cuba, and every preparation is being made therefor, beneath the surface, many significant currents flow to a probable early muster out.

. . . .

Ham

"Ham," Sixth Virginia Infantry, U.S.V., Camp Haskell, Ga., December 29, 1898; from Richmond Planet, *January 7, 1899. News of the imminent muster out of the Sixth Virginia prompts "Ham" to review the offenses committed against "Uncle Sam's black boys in blue" during their sojourn "in this pest hole of the South."*

[Sir:]

Uncle Sam has given the boys a handsome Xmas present—an order for the mustering out of the regiment. An inspector is here now going over the books and papers of this command preparatory to muster out. It was the most welcome present any of the boys received during the holidays. The 3rd North Carolina has also been mustered out. Just how long we are to remain here is hard to tell, but the boys yearn to put their feet on Virginia soil.

The boys are indignant that every box shipped them by loved ones at home has to be broken open at the guard house and anything of a mutilating nature confiscated and broken up.

. . . .

The weather here is very cold, and on Xmas day a few flakes of snow fell, but it is now clear and fair. We receive weather reports regularly and are kept posted on any probable changes in weather conditions.

One of our men, Private Elijah Turner, was shot and killed by a

street car conductor last Thursday. We are unacquainted with
the facts in the case, but the jury rendered a verdict of
"justifiable homicide" . . . and the conductor was released.
Ever since then our men have been restricted to their company
streets for fear of their going out to avenge their comrade's death.

Nobody was allowed to leave camp, even on pass until Monday,
when as a sort of Xmas present or indulgence, all drills were
suspended, when a few men from each company were allowed to
go to town. Could the men have gotten out, there is nothing they
could have done as all the pistols, knives, and razors have been
taken from them. Even our sentinels on duty at night in these
woods are walking around with empty guns. No balls with
which to protect themselves, the camp, the government property,
or nothing else.

Yet we are the bad people some of the prejudiced, lying
southern papers would have us appear. Nobody in our camp
has any weapon of any kind, for offense or defense, since we
crossed the abominable Georgia line.

Two men of the 3rd North Carolina were shot and killed in a
street fight in the town yesterday. None of our men implicated.

. . . .

Hasn't a week passed since we have been in this pest hole of
the South that some of Uncle Sam's black boys in blue, haven't
been "justifiably homicided," at least this is the only word that
seems to strike the minds of all juries who try cases for "killing
nigger soldiers," and we will thank God with all our hearts when
we are moved from the contaminating influences of contact with
these "Georgia Crackers," for they truly deserve the title.

Ham

"Ham," Sixth Virginia Infantry, U.S.V., Camp Haskell, Ga., January 3, 1899; from Richmond Planet, *January 7, 1899. In the following brief communication to the* Planet, *"Ham" expresses his great pleasure at the prospect of being mustered out of service.*

[Sir:]

Nothing definite is known here of the actual time, when this command will be ordered home for Muster Out, although that is the only topic of conversation between the men, and it seems from appearances that it will be a very short while, and the majority of the boys don't care how soon.

A large number of the boys are suffering from sore arms, nearly all of the members of the 2nd Battalion having been vaccinated during the past two weeks.

The Grippe has attacked nearly all of the regiments in camp, but fortunately only a few of our boys have it.

.   .   .   .

The paymaster is in town and the boys are anxious to see the "ghost" walk, which is the camp name for the paymaster, as nearly every body is broke, having spent their money during the holidays. We are to be paid off this week and it is expected that as soon as this is done the movement to Virginia will be commenced. . . .

Ham

"Ham," Sixth Virginia Infantry, U.S.V., Camp Haskell, Ga., January 16, 1899; from Richmond Planet, *January 21, 1899. The following letter from "Ham," written on the eve of the Sixth Virginia's departure for home, describes how the black volunteers retaliated against their white detractors in Macon by refusing to spend their muster-out pay with local merchants there.*

[Sir:]

The work of preparing muster out roll is progressing as rapidly as possible. The men are counting the days, between now, and the time when they shall be mustered out and returned to their respective homes. Everybody in camp with any clerical ability is kept busy . . . helping straighten out the different papers and books. . . . All of the companies have been physically examined by two army surgeons and this part of the work is practically completed.

. . . .

The Macon paper came out in an article this morning, as a sort of refutation of the different statements it has published against us, from time to time, saying our camp was kept in first class condition, our men orderly, and that they had been laboring under a false impression of the 6th Virginia, and that our men were well behaved, and had not given any more trouble than could be expected of other soldiers.

It may be done to influence trade and to induce our men to spend some of their money here, but we think the crackers are too late, as the men have thoroughly decided not to buy anything unless absolutely necessary.

. . . .

Ham

SEVENTH INFANTRY, U.S.V.

C. W. Cordin, Seventh Infantry, U.S.V., Camp Haskell, Ga., no date; from The Gazette *(Cleveland), December 17, 1898. Cordin, a resident of Ohio and a member of one of the so-called "immune" regiments of black volunteers, records his initial impressions of life in the South.*

Hon. H. C. Smith, Editor of the *Gazette*

Dear Friend:

I am improving rapidly and have been transferred to quarters, but it will be some time before I am ready for duty. Enclosed in this letter you will find a small piece of a tree which has a history. The Seventh and Tenth Immunes, Third North Carolina and Sixth Virginia, Afro-American regiments, are in camp about three miles from Macon. Between the camp and the city is a "public park" in which only white people are allowed. In this park was a tree on which six or seven Afro-Americans had been lynched, and it was common knowledge that the tree was kept for that purpose. Upon it was a sign reading: "D (for dogs) and niggers not allowed here." The Sixth Virginia being the first of our four regiments to arrive, saw the sign and learned the facts as stated above, first, of course. A squad of them made it their business to go to the park and cut down that tree, and when the park-keeper (white) came to remonstrate, limbs were cut from it and he was given a good thrashing. None of the boys were ever found out. Not being able to go to the tree myself, I have been unable to get you a larger piece.

Labor (Afro-American) per day brings here thirty-five cents. Cooks in private families receive five dollars a month. Other help less.

The engineers, and Second Ohio regiment (white) with whom I have talked, have no use for this part of the country or the people (white), and eight out of every ten ask why our people permit such outrageous treatment as they are accorded.

As soon as I am able I will send you more information.

Yours sincerely
C. W. Cordin
Cpl., 7th Immunes U.S.V.I.

C. W. Cordin, Seventh Infantry, U.S.V., Camp Haskell, Ga., December 21, 1898; from The Gazette *(Cleveland), December 24, 1898. Cordin explains how the black soldiers stationed at this camp in Georgia responded to local racial mores and criticizes President William McKinley for his efforts to conciliate white Southerners.*

Hon. H. C. Smith, Editor
Cleveland *Gazette*

Dear Sir:

The first battalion of the Third Engineers have gone to Cuba to prepare our camping ground.

Gen. [John C.] Bates, commanding the First Army Corps, held a preparatory review recently, getting ready for President McKinley's visit. In the corps are three white regiments and four Afro-American. The Macon Telegraph (white) had a two column write up of the review, which contained not a line in reference to Afro-American regiments.

An Afro-American and a white man had a fist fight recently. The former got a $75 fine and one year in the stockade (chain gang). The white man went free. Afro-American women are given like sentences on the slightest pretexts and have to serve in the stockade. I am told by members of my company who have seen them working that they have to do the same work that men do. Just before we came here the city authorities had a large

stockade gang (Afro-American men and women in chains) on
this side of the city digging a ditch. They don't bring out the
women any more, as the boys of the four Afro-American
regiments have made threats of releasing them.

There are dirty, low, white brutes down here that the devil
wouldn't have for a precious gift and it is to these also the
president has tendered "the olive branch." My God!

One of our boys had trouble with a big, burly brute of a
conductor (white) on one of the street car lines recently and was
set upon by other toughs (white) on the car at the time. Result:
—five shots have already been sent after that conductor and it
is only a question of time when he will be "got."[1]

C. W. Cordin
Cpl., 7th Immunes

*C. W. Cordin, Seventh Infantry, U.S.V., Camp Haskell, Ga., no date;
from* The Gazette *(Cleveland), January 14, 1899. Always sensitive to
the plight of black Southerners, Cordin records several examples of the
injustices and cruelties perpetrated against them by whites.*

Hon. H. C. Smith
Gazette

Dear Sir:

A member of the Sixth Virginia (private) was shot and killed
the 22nd Ult. by a street car conductor. The Afro-American

---

[1] Incidents involving the black volunteers at Camp Haskell occurred regularly on
the trolleys in Macon, largely because the soldiers refused to ride in the Jim
Crow "trailers" hitched to the trolleys. When the Negro troops first arrived at
Camp Haskell, the Macon trolleys apparently made no effort to enforce segregation in seating arrangements and added the Jim Crow trailers only at the insistence
of white citizens in the city. Reporting on the situation early in December, 1898,
a correspondent wrote: "It is very true that a few trailers have been put on, but
the negroes are allowed to ride in the front car just as if the trailers were not on."
Nevertheless, by the time the Negro volunteers left Camp Haskell early in 1899,

soldier wanted to ride in the front car and the conductor would not let him. Words ensued and the sequel was that the United States soldier was killed. What will be done remains to be seen. In consequence there has been no night passes issued for fear that vengeance might be wrought upon some miserable, low-lived Georgia "crackers."

I met an old man on his way home from town with his mule, his wagon and two sons, where he had been to take his last bale of cotton. He hailed me in a most pitiful manner and asked me if I would come and do something for him. He told me that the white folks were trying to wipe the Afro-Americans out "down home." This is his pitiful story: He runs a farm for a Mrs. Woodley; raised and delivered $470.70 worth of cotton and had drawn $14 per month in rations for nine months. In the meantime he had not drawn one-cent for anything else, and had furnished his own mules and implements. His children helped him. This morning this Mrs. Woodley presented him (William Lamar) with a bill of $16.20, telling him, if it was not paid by night she would take his corn (300 bushels). He dare not sell one ear of it. If he does he is liable to go to the stockade (chain gang) for a long term as no part of the corn is his until it is divided. No white person will lend him a cent and an Afro-American dare not. He could borrow from one white firm by paying 50 cents on a dollar, as the New York Loan Co. only lends to our people. Mr. Lamar has a wife and 13 children. He told me it was the truth that the white people try not to leave the Afro-American farmers one extra nickel. If you could only see the hundreds of poor, half-starved Afro-Americans walking into town on the morning of the 19th Ult to see McKinley you would believe it.

---

at least three black soldiers had been killed by trolley conductors in altercations prompted by the refusal of the soldiers to relinquish their seats in the "front cars." See *The Atlanta Constitution,* December 5, 21, 23, 27, 1898; *Macon Telegraph,* January 6, 8, 1899.

There is a rumor that the Immunes, seventh and tenth
regiments, and the Engineers are to go to Cuba in a few weeks.
Orders came from Washington that the Third North Carolina
will be mustered out soon. They have all "colored" officers
and yet 900 of the rank and file had in applications for discharge.

Macon has many Afro-Americans in business and who are
quite wealthy. Among them Mr. Henry Hammons, who has a
splendid business, theater, saloon and restaurant and pays taxes
on $10,000 worth of real estate.

The "boys" (Afro-American soldiers) made a fine showing
before the president, and although it rained, there was an
immense crowd. There was only one tune cheered and that was
"Dixie." The reception given by the citizens was a cheap affair.
The health of the camp is good. I will write your valuable paper
nothing but what is absolutely the truth.

I forgot to state what Mr. Lamar wanted me to do. He
thought as I was a U.S. soldier I could write a letter and give it to
him to hand to Mrs. Woodley and cause her to give him his just
dues and he did not believe me when I told him my letter
would do no good.

Fine weather prevails here and has for a week or more with
the exception of occasional rain showers such as you have in the
spring time. Don't need any fires in our tents and only one blanket
at night, and that is a little warm.

I took a walk in the country this afternoon and stopped at the
cabin of an old lady. While in conversation with her she said
that was where her master placed her when he freed her. He
gave her the cabin, a half acre of land and turned her over to
the county authorities. This fact gives her the privilege of going
to the proper county officials and getting one ticket gratis each
month, that calls for 75 cents in trade at any store she wishes to
trade at. She is charged double price for whatever she gets.

We are camping in the same place that Maj. Gen. [J. M.]
Wilson used when he ousted Jeff. Davis' cohorts. About a quarter

of a mile from the seventh regiment is the foundry Jeff had built
for the manufacturing of guns, etc.

In regard to the tree which was kept for lynching purposes and
which was cut down, I have learned something new to me from a
man who lives in sight of where it stood so long. One Afro-
American was hung on the tree by the name of Will Singleton,
who was caught in Alabama. The mob took him to their tree, first
cut out his ————; then hung him and shot him full of holes.
His ———— were taken to the city, put into a bottle and pickled
with alcohol. It was kept in Hurley's saloon on Avenue Street
(in a prominent place) until a few weeks ago, but was hid away
since on account of the presence of the soldiers. This is not from
one man but from a dozen or more reliable citizens. Only a short
while ago a white, burly brute named White, shot and killed an
Afro-American, because the latter saw fit to hold up for himself.
The white scoundrel and murderer has not been arrested as yet.
The Afro-Americans I have talked with claim the white people
treat them very good now, since the soldiers are here. One old man
explained: "Good Lawd! jess wait tell deys' all gone; den you'll
see hard times about heah."

I find from careful observations that our country people are not
lazy as claimed; they work just enough to keep body and soul
together because if they get more than that the white folks will
take it from them. They dare not go into a law suit, as justice is
not for them. Not half the Georgia crackers pay the wages they
promise. They will give their "colored" help 10 or 25 cents in
"driblets" and pretty soon claim they (the help) have been paid in
full. And if any words are passed, a crowd comes to the poor
Afro-American's cabin that night and he is whipped and
sometimes killed. . . .

The Macon Telegraph gave the four regiments (colored) a
four line notice out of a seven column write up and there were
only seven regiments in the parade. The much talked of spirit of a

united north and south is all bosh, as far as the south is concerned, and someday it will be known only too well in the North.

Wishing you a Merry Xmas and a Happy New Year, I am

Yours respectfully
C. W. Cordin
7th Reg, U.S.V.I.

C. W. Cordin, Seventh Infantry, U.S.V., Camp Haskell, Ga., ca. January, 1899; from The Gazette *(Cleveland), March 18, 1899. In his far-ranging commentary on race relations in the South, Cordin notes that whites are considerably more respectful of the armed black soldiers than of unarmed black civilians.*

Hon. H. C. Smith, Editor
Gazette

Dear Sir:

We have had warm rains all the past week, which have made the grass and foliage turn out green, as we all want to see it at home (in Ohio) in the spring time. The general health is good and all are in good spirits.

The hatred of the Georgia cracker for the Negro cannot be explained by pen. In every contemptible way do they show it to all except our soldiers. They are too cowardly to bother them to any extent. I have not heard of one soldier being insulted. Most of the boys who have no gun or revolver borrow one whenever they get a pass to town. Therefore, the white people have learned that the boys are prepared for unwanted insults. . . .

The penal institutions of the South include what is termed a stockade. Women (colored) as well as men receive long sentences to this place for trifling misdemeanors. . . . When a woman is sentenced to the stockade it is to hard labor. No laundry work or anything of the kind. She must take a shovel and pick, and work in gangs on the suburban roads and ditches. . . . If she don't keep up her part, the whip will help her along. About the last ten days or week of their sentence they are given the choice to work out the balance of their sentence or get a flogging. Not long since one girl, about 19, who had served her time up to five days, was given her preference to serve the balance or receive the flogging. She took the latter, so you can judge the severity of the former. If an Afro-American goes to an attorney he must pay the fee in advance, and rarely is there an exception. . . .

The Afro-Americans of Macon celebrated Emancipation the first week in January. A program was rendered at the First Baptist Church, the Tenth Regiment, U.S.V.I. band furnishing the music. At the A.M.E. Church, the Seventh Regiment, U.S.V.I. band furnished music. Although there were two factions celebrating, the day was well spent and large crowds were out. Before we came here, the people were taught by the cracker papers that we were hobos, toughs and thieves, and hence the better colored citizens have been afraid of the soldiers. But by exhibitions of true manhood and soldierly bearing we have won the respect of the best people. . . .

The muster papers are about all made out for the mustering out of the Sixth Virginia and Third North Carolina. They have commenced to turn in arms and ammunition. Next will be the examination. Col. Goodwin[1] is now division commander in the absence of Gen. [William J.] McKee. Lieut Col. [C. D.] Comfort is now in command of the Seventh regiment. All of our superior officers are fine men. Col. Comfort is not only liked but loved by the whole regiment.

I don't want to forget to tell you of the "election" that was held

[1] The "Col. Goodwin" mentioned here obviously refers to Colonel E. A. Godwin, the white commander of the Seventh Infantry, U.S.V., one of the "immune" regiments.

in Belden (Georgia) not far from here. The Macon Telegraph
spoke of it, saying the mayor got every vote that was registered,
except one, and that man was out of town on the day of the
election. Of course, the nominee was a democrat. The population
of the town is about one third colored. This is a sample of
elections in this district.

The statement that the North and South are "bound by ties of a
united nation, with common interest to all," etc., is not a reality.
It is a myth with only symptoms of reality for the sake of
aggrandizement. Should Providence bless us with a new
allotment of Joshua E. Giddings, Lovejoys and Charles Sumners
to cause all God-fearing people in all parts of the country to lend
their ears, hearts and wills to the cause of the down-trodden and
despised Afro-American in his humiliated condition in the south,
the feeling that is now dormant would be dominant. It would put
an end to the bug-a-boo cry of "down with Negro rule" and
Wilmington Massacres.[2] I must admit that there are some fine
white people here, glad to talk with us and treat us very nicely as
long as no other white person is near. Just let one come near and
you will be dropped like one drops a hot potato.

Among the many prosperous business firms among our people
here are Central City Drug Co., W. H. Bailey, manager. It is one
of the finest drug stores in the city and is prominently located
opposite the city building. J. M. Brown runs a fine grocery store
across the way. The race has reason to feel proud of these
progressive men. Yet many will discommode themselves to
patronize a cracker rather than them. . . .

The Georgia crackers, hereabouts have learned of my
Gazette articles and are looking for me—so I understand. If
they "find" me (and it is not difficult) one or more of them will
"cross the river" with me when they start to mob or lynch this

[2] The Wilmington massacre refers to the bloody race riot that occurred in
Wilmington, North Carolina, in November, 1898, in the wake of an impassioned
political campaign.

northern Ohio product. Meanwhile I am on my guard and a
walking rapid-fire battery.

Au revoir (not good-bye)
C. W. Cordin

*C. W. Cordin, Seventh Infantry, U.S.V., Camp Haskell, Ga., January
28, 1899; from* The Gazette *(Cleveland), March 11, 1899. In the following letter, Cordin not only describes his duties as a member of the
Provost Guard but also comments on the "deplorable" conditions of
Negroes in the South.*

Hon. H. C. Smith, Editor
Gazette

Dear Sir:

We have had fine weather until this morning, which has been
rainy weather, ending in a light snow that melted immediately.
The Second Ohio leaves in a few days . . . to be mustered out.
Company K (my company) and Company M have taken their
places as provost guards in the city of Macon. . . . Every man
in the two companies feel their responsibility and will by a very
little extra effort prove to the citizens of Macon that there are not
any here in the capacity of Tin soldiers, but gentlemen in every
meaning of the word, and will give to all the greatest respect
and demand the same in return. We are quartered in a large
four-storied building, have comfortable beds and mess quarters,
and are all quite satisfied with the change. We have not yet
entered upon our duty, but we feel equal to the task.

An Afro-American and a white woman were arrested in
Savannah a few days ago for living together (the law prohibits
intermarriage), tried and given $1000 fine each and one year on
the chain gang. The judge modified the woman's sentence and

gave her twenty-four hours to get out of town. In view of this
fact you would blush with shame at the privileges the white
southerner has, and those he don't he takes. It is one of the
common occurrences for a "colored" woman to be grossly
insulted, not only when they are alone, but even when she has an
escort. It is all the same, especially if the white southerner
happens to be drunk. The escort is afraid for his life. . . . The
true condition of the southern Afro-American is indeed deplorable.
They fear the white man about as much as the rat does a cat, and
have very few privileges such as we enjoy in Ohio. There is no
law here that a white man is bound to respect where our people
are concerned. The "Negro" is looked upon as menial servant,
with the epithet of "nigger" and "coon" and in return the whites
expect to be addressed as "marsa" and "misses." Our people in
talking to you and referring to the whites always say "Marsa"
and "Misses" so-and-so. How many of these people live and
keep body and soul together on one peck of meal, ten pounds of
salt pork and $6 a month is a mystery. No matter how large the
family is. Surely there must be a just God who will someday turn
his loving kindness on the Negro in the South.

The Sixth Virginia was mustered out Tuesday and took a special
train home. Quite a number of white merchants loaded up
wagons of goods and took them out to sell, but the soldiers had
been ridiculed so badly by the white people of Macon that they
would not buy a cent's worth, and now they [whites] blame the
war department. They think the boys ought to have stayed and
spent their money here. The Third North Carolina will be mustered
out Thursday. That will leave only two Afro-American regiments
here, the Seventh and Tenth U.S. volunteers, (immunes).

We were sorry to see the Ohio boys leave, as they have proven
to be our friends and several times have taken our men from the
police when they were about to be put under arrest for a trifle.
In one case a white man called one of our soldiers a vile name
and the soldier hit him in the mouth. A policeman placed the

soldier under arrest. A corporal and two men (Second Ohio) put in an appearance and demanded the release of the soldier and the demand was granted. Had it not been for the white soldiers he would have had a long sentence to work out on the chain gang.

The seventh regiment U.S.V. band gave a concert at the A.M.E. church last Tuesday evening and it was largely attended and passed off very nicely with the exception that many of the younger class of Afro-Americans of Macon do not know how to behave themselves.

Not a braver or more loyal regiment of men ever returned home from their country's calling than the Second Ohio. They stood by us. The Second Ohio will ever be remembered.

I am yours,
C. W. Cordin

C. W. Cordin, Seventh Infantry, U.S.V., Camp Haskell, Ga., February 5, 1899; from The Gazette *(Cleveland), March 11, 1899. Delighted by the prospect of departing from Camp Haskell and of leaving the "Georgia cracker" to "his own devilment," Cordin nonetheless fears for the safety of Negro civilians once the black troops are gone. According to him, Negroes were convinced that so long as large contingents of black soldiers were present in the area, whites had tolerated "many things they have not been accustomed to."*

Dear Sir:

Rainy weather continues and it is also very warm. Overcoats are articles on the thoroughfare.

Contrary to expectations, orders were received from Washington on the 3rd to muster out the Seventh and Tenth immunes, with 13,600 other volunteers. The Seventh will be mustered out about the latter part of March. . . . The Seventh has received and accepted an invitation from the citizens of St. Louis, Mo., through

Lt. Col. [C. D.] Comfort to a reception and jollification, and all
are anxious to carry out the project, as we will secure a special
train and not be insulted by being compelled to ride in the
abominable "Jim Crow" cars. Eight companies have signified
their willingness to go to St. Louis. . . . The offer was first made
by Mayor Zeighenheimer [sic] of St. Louis,[1] who is a whole-
souled man and loyal man, regardless of color, and the colored
people of the city never forget him when he comes up for office.
St. Louis is the mustering place of the regiment, and after the
affair is over, each company will leave for its mustering place.

Companies K and M are still on provost duty, and well are they
performing it, as the papers give us some good taffy for the good
order that has prevailed since we were put on duty. After 10
o'clock at night patrols are sent out to search all questionable
resorts for drunken or disorderly soldiers or soldiers without
passes. Sometimes we have to force our way into a house and it is
one of the bitterest of pills for the white keepers to swallow to
see us exercise the least authority with white soldiers. Our duty is
understood by the soldiers and gracefully submitted to. It is the
citizens who do the kicking, but they are allowed a limit, and if
necessary are turned over to the police, who have so far backed
up everything we have done. The Seventh will go home feeling
proud of its being in the service and earning for itself the good
name of being the best drilled and best disciplined of ten
immune regiments, and of having always left a good name
wherever it was stationed. I understand that Gen. [William J.]
McKee will go to Washington in a few days to endeavor to have
the order revoked in regard to the Seventh. The Sixth Virginia have
all been mustered out and have gone home. The Third North
Carolina finished mustering out the last battalion today, and
have all left. The Third engineers have all left for Cuba but one
battalion, and they will leave as soon as transport is made ready

[1] Henry Ziegenheim was elected mayor of St. Louis on the Republican ticket
in 1897.

for them. The Second Ohio will leave shortly and with the mustering out of the Seventh and Tenth, the Georgia cracker will be left to his own hellish devilment, and God help the mustered out soldier that remains behind and gets into the least trouble, for they will put him on the chain gang for keeps. The local Afro-American expects to catch the devil. This is the sentiment of most I have talked with. Everything has been peaceable and quiet since the soldiers have been here, and in consequence the crackers have had to take many things they have not been accustomed to, so when we are gone they will get even. This is their threat.

Richard's and Pringle's minstrels were here last night, with Billy Kersands as star, and played to a crowded house, and as is the custom when a "colored" show is given the house was privileged to the Afro-American except for the first four rows of seats in the parquet, which is reserved for white people on such occasions. The cracker was a minus quantity; otherwise it was one of the finest appearing and cultured audiences that I ever saw. The society of women in the south can not be equalled. To have had the pleasure of gazing upon such an august assemblage, and especially Georgia's fairest, is indeed a feast to be long remembered. By request a guard was furnished the show. Lieut. Campbell, a corporal, and ten men were detailed to duty. Eight-tenths of the male attendants were soldiers, white and colored, and not one whistle or boistrous noise was heard. In consequence the manager came down to the office and complimented us to our superior officers for the soldierly and gentlemanly manner in which we discharged our duty. . . .

A rumor is current in the morning papers the order mustering out the Seventh Immunes has been countermanded but that is hardly probable.

With a final wish to get out of God-forsaken Georgia, I am

> Respectfully,
> Corporal C. W. Cordin
> Seventh U.S. Vol. Inf.

C. W. Cordin, Seventh Infantry, U.S.V., Camp Haskell, Ga., February 14, 1899; from The Gazette (*Cleveland*), *March 18, 1899. In the following letter, Cordin continues his account of the racial insults encountered by Negro soldiers at Camp Haskell.*

Editor, *Gazette*

Dear Sir:

The mustering out of the Seventh and Tenth Immunes is proceeding rapidly, as some of the companies have turned in their guns and are standing examinations.

Excitement has been very high for a couple of days, and the present circumstances are critical—all on account of hatred for the Negro. The provost guard had occasion day before yesterday to arrest several disorderly soldiers (all colored) and as the provost squad (two men) neared the guard house with the prisoners, policemen (white) took them away. Reinforcements came and took them out of the patrol wagon, whipped one policeman, knocked several white men down and ended by taking the lieutenant of the police's gun away from him and beating him over the head with it. Soldiers outside the provost guard did most of this. The guard was summoned as witnesses this morning, and when they reached court in company with Lieut. Col. [C. D.] Comfort and several other officers, and a captain from the Tenth Regiment, who is a good lawyer, to their astonishment, charges of disorderly conduct and avoiding arrest were [placed] against them. The lieutenant colonel gave each in turn a fine recommendation, and on terming the defendants "gentlemen," the court and plaintiffs laughed and looked towards each other. The prosecuting attorney in referring to the several defendants, referred to them as that yellow man or that black s———of b———. We were dumbfounded at this. This happened in open court, too. When the proposition was made to bind over the defendants in the sum of $100 each, the prosecutor jumped to his feet in anger and said that it was foolish to think of putting "damned niggers" under less than $1000 bonds. Had the court stood by the custom prevailing here, he would have placed them under bond in the above sum. Being unable to get it, we would have landed in jail all night, but the judge listened to Lieut. Col. Comfort's talk. He guaranteed to have the men in court when called for. The men were allowed to return to quarters.

On the following day a policeman ordered a sentry off of a post in front of the provost guard house, to get an intoxicated soldier. The sentry answered the policeman that he would not do it, and for that the policeman raised his billy and came toward the sentry, who charged bayonets and called "halt." In an hour or so, the sentry, William Ford, private of Company K, and member of the provost guard was arrested and placed in the city prison. His trial was held the following day. As Ford did not have any white witnesses he was convicted on the testimony of the policeman and was given $25 (fine) and costs and 90 days on the chain gang. When the sheriff asked him to come along, he said: "Come on, you black s—— of b——." William hit the sheriff. This caused him to be arraigned on another charge and to be fined $125. In the first trouble (with the officer) Ford was right, as it was his duty to remain on the post until properly released by some officer of the guard. This so enraged the members of the guard of Companies M and K, and so many threats and low murmurings were heard by the provost officers, that they deemed it best to send these two companies back to camp which was done. After this occurrence, we were not needed, as an agreement has been reached by request of the city attorney that no provost be allowed to patrol the streets in squads on duty unless called out by the mayor or chief of police. No patrols were put on the street until 6 p.m. For several days we were denied passes outside of the building. The hatred and hellishness of the Georgia cracker is so deep and intense against the Afro-American that not even United States soldiers stand an iota of a show, and especially when we are not allowed to carry any ammunition. We are only permitted to carry it when on active duty, and then only two rounds.

The newspapers here have been complimenting the Second
Ohio (white) on every occasion. . . . On the other hand, the
most that could be said of the Afro-American regiments . . .
was said only too well with that old time southern poisonous
intention. Yet, when the Sixth Virginia was mustered out,
officers and men went immediately home like gentlemen and true
soldiers. The Third North Carolina did likewise. The merchants
were at both camps at the time [of] . . . the mustering out of
the two regiments with their wagons loaded with merchandise for
sale and not one penny's worth was taken. Not one word of
praise did the papers give the soldiers as a result. Far different
when the Second Ohio mustered out. The same merchants were
there with their merchandise galore to sell. Some had two-horse
express wagons, some had one-horse wagons, and some had "ye
ole mule," but they were "thar and thar" strong. For the fun of
the thing the Yankee (Second Ohio) stole a march on them and
stripped the wagons of everything from socks to trunks. They
got away with about $2500 worth of stuff, all the crackers had to
"tote" home was "hisself." The papers have not printed one
word of the affair for they are ashamed to. To read the
editorials in the Macon Telegraph you would think that all the
Second Ohio boys needed was wings. The police went to the
depot where they were all ready to take the train, and put two of
the boys under arrest. A lieutenant asked the police what they
intended to do and they answered that they were going to lock
the boys up. The lieutenant answered that if they did there would
be the hottest time in Macon they ever saw, and the police
turned the boys loose.

I will write again soon. Wishing your valuable paper continued
and greater prosperity, I am

Sincerely yours,
Cpl. C. W. Cordin
Co. K, 7th Immunes

Allen S. Peal, formerly of the Seventh Infantry, U.S.V., Columbus, Ohio, ca. March 15, 1899; from The Gazette *(Cleveland), April 8, 1899. Peal, a lieutenant of the black "immune" regiment recently mustered out at Camp Haskell, Ga., denies reports regarding the misconduct of the regiment but claims that the actions of whites were sufficient to "sow the seeds of rowdyism" among black soldiers.*

Dear Sir:

The following paragraph appeared in the [Columbus] Dispatch, a local paper, on March 10:

"The colored troops who, on muster out, are misbehaving in the South, are doing an injury far more than personal. Their rowdyism strengthens the prejudice against the race."

The writer of the above is undoubtedly misinformed at least. Beneath the so-called "rowdyism of Negro Troops" in the South is an ocean of unrevealed circumstances. The great cause of the open friction is the southern white man's stupidity or indisposition to leave off singing "all coons look alike to me" and its sentiment. As the Negro troops came from a comparatively free north to camp in the sunny south—not angels, but average mortals, they read with no smiles, "this place for blacks," "this place for whites," "no Negroes served here." They had met (thank heaven) a more discreet and a whiter man at their home— [a] man whose heart was more in harmony with his skin. Herein lay the birth of the so-called "rowdyism of the Negro troops." The least effort on the part of a Negro soldier to get the treatment his money demanded was the sure signal of the peculiar southern biped to cry, "Negro domination". . . .

What man loves to be mistreated and herded off indecently, indiscriminately because he is black or white? Reverse the conditions, place some arrogant, discriminating man over the white man of the south and "rowdyism" is merely a hint of what would transpire. I feel I have reason to congratulate the black boys in blue for the guarded conduct, ground down as they were

under ancient, barbaric customs of southern cities. I wonder at
the forbearance of the black heroes of San Juan and Santiago who
later endured with the rest of us the constant unprovoked and
utter disregard of any but an old-time cotton field "darkey." I
don't mean to argue the race problem, but if there be mitigating
conditions under which the white man justly mistreats the Negro
then there must be the same conditions to mitigate these outbreaks
of "rowdyism." For my life I can't blame any man for insisting on
decent treatment—it seems that liberty is a beautiful thing to be
cultivated in any but a Negro's heart. I believe no white man's
sincerity when he feigns to fear a Negro coming into his social
circle. As a race, we don't think of it. My mother's table is the
grandest I know of. But I believe we are right to insist upon our
civil rights and urge decent public treatment. When Negro
soldiers saw in Macon, Ga., a sign reading "No Dogs or Negroes
allowed in this Park," they tore it down; and in my mind they
did right to that spirit in which such people boast of running a
free, civilized country. That was no more "rowdyism" in
sentiment than the spilling of England's tea in Boston harbor. After
this park affair, all Negro soldiers looked hideous. The worst
street cars were too good for us. Southern chivalry was eternally
aroused. Why, very few of us wanted to harm anybody except a
Spaniard who might "have the drop on us." The merchants [in
Macon] did not want our money until near the last, when they
found we were possibly half human and that our money bore the
same old American eagle. A tailor would tell us, "Go back into
the rear and try on this coat. I can't take colored people's
measures in here but I'll bet I can fit you." "Can't try on the shoes
in here," says the smiling shoe man; "just can't let Negroes do it."
And out we'd go, some of us commissioned by the great father in
Washington to bear freedom to people beyond the sea. I
wondered while trying to hum "My Country 'tis of Thee"
whether America had any liberty to spare.

But most harmful to Negro troops was the yellow journalism of the South. To prove it was biased and prejudiced in its very heart I have newspaper clippings showing that the very coming of Negro troops was heralded with unfounded contempt which poisoned the public mind before they arrived. No disturbance occurred but what the puppet so-called journalism chronicled it, needlessly bold, trimming it with that effete style of "darkey," "culud gemmen," "dusky dame," and those terms which all true men of this new age hope have died with slavery. As noted a journal (generally fair with the Negro) as is the Atlanta Constitution—this paper often dealt the Negro soldier an unfair blow. I don't say maliciously but I know it was done. Its edition of February 28, 1899, had a bold account of "Negro Troops Rioting in Macon, Ga. on Muster Out."

This was a lie but it was hurled broad cast as an argument forever against the race. On the next day in the same Atlanta Constitution was one of the most beautiful accounts of the same regiment passing away as quietly as the proverbial Arabs.

I would justify no rowdyism among blacks or whites, but I despise thoroughly all sickly snobbish pen pushers who have "Negro fits."

The men that one day clubbed British soldiers have now passed into the paradise of America's patron saints. Conditions must change again—I hope with no blood. The white man [in the] south must handle more masterly the situation or this rowdyism will infect the whole region. I urge for the Negro simply passing respect. Every man loves that much liberty. I heard a few days ago the city prosecutor of Macon, Ga. declare that "I am going to show a nigger soldier that he is the same as any other nigger," referring to a Negro commissioned officer of the United States volunteer army. His harangue was filled with "that wall-eyed nigger" and such epithets uncalled for and slimy for a high official. These things sow the seeds of rowdyism. During this general abuse I chanced to observe among the spectators that heroic Negro, Lieut. [Alfred M.] Ray, who as a sergeant faced death and planted old glory amid a storm of Spanish bullets. I don't believe such words inspire a hero. Something is wrong. God in his time will right it. His justice will not sleep forever.

> Allen S. Peal
> Late Second Lieutenant, Seventh U.S.V. Infantry
> Mustered Out at Macon, Ga., February 28, 1899

THIRD ALABAMA INFANTRY, U.S.V.

W. A. Baker, Third Alabama Infantry, U.S.V., Camp Shipp, Ala., February 12, 1899; from Savannah Tribune, *February 18, 1899. Baker, a corporal in Alabama's black regiment commanded by white officers, maintains that many of the men in his unit are anxious to be mustered out since there are "no battles to fight."*

Editor Tribune:

Please allow me space in your valuable medium to say a few words in regards to the life of the boys in blue who are stationed here in camp. We came here from Mobile, Ala., last September and have been experiencing a very severe winter but the boys don't care much for the weather, for they made up their minds before enlisting in the 3rd Infantry, Alabama Volunteers, to face the hardship that belongs to the "brave."

A heavy snow fell last night and is falling now, the mountains surrounding us are covered with snow, six inches. Some of our boys have gone out this morning on a hunt and they expect to return with plenty of game.

Our neighbor regiment, the 4th Kentucky, has been mustered out of the service . . . finishing up on Saturday when they took the train and left for their homes.

There are only four regiments here now, viz; 4th Wisconsin, 2nd Arkansas, 2nd Infantry (regulars), 3rd Infantry, Alabama Volunteers.

All reliable visitors to our camp say ours is one of the best that they ever saw on their tour. Our camp is kept clean and tidy and the men who have charge of the sanitary work understand it to perfection. The stove we use in our tents is a novel and the boys are kept warm by them.

There is a great deal of rumor afloat that we will be mustered out. This rumor has no foundation . . . but a great many of us are anxious to get out of the service because we are tired of remaining in camp and have no battles to fight and a large number of [those] mustered out will join the regular army.

The officers of our regiment are doing all they can to have us well drilled soldiers. Next week our battalion will have target practice out at the range. . . . Company E is doing all they can to make the best score. . . .

There is a public rumor here and elsewhere that our regiment has been booked to go to Augusta, Ga., shortly after pay day, which will be on or about February 24th.

> Yours,
> Corp. W. A. Baker
> Co. E, 3rd Ala. Reg.

Chaplain T. G. Steward, D. D.

Major Joseph B. Johnson,
Sixth Virginia Infantry, U.S.V.

Corporal W. T. Goode

Colonel John R. Marshall

Major R. R. Jackson

Captain Jordan Chavis, Chaplain,
Eighth Illinois Volunteer Regiment

**Captain J. L. Waller,
Twenty-third Kansas Infantry**

**Captain W. B. Roberts,
Twenty-third Kansas Infantry**

Negro Troops Boarding Transports for Cuba, June, 1898

Third Section of Company K, Twenty-fifth Infantry

The Flanking Group Taking It Easy on the Return

The Scouts Halt and the Advance Passes the Word

The Reconnoitering Flankers Return the Fire

IV

THE IMPERIAL GUARDS IN CUBA

If we fail the whole race will have to shoulder the burden.
                                COLONEL JOHN R. MARSHALL,
                                U.S.V., 1898

With the collapse of Spanish authority in Cuba, the fate of the island was uncertain. A conspicuous lack of cordiality existed between Cuban rebels and American military forces. Many Americans, in fact, questioned whether Cuba possessed the capacity for self-government. In some quarters there was an obvious disposition to renounce the Teller Amendment and its disclaimer regarding any intention of annexing Cuba. Whatever the future status of the island might be, the United States assumed immediate responsibility for its government and administration. General Leonard Wood became military governor of Santiago, and fresh supplies of troops, including several "immune" regiments, embarked for Cuba to replace the weary, fever-ridden veterans, who were sent to Montauk Point, New York. Among those dispatched to the island as part of the occupation army were several Negro regiments.

The first Negro unit to take up garrison duty in Cuba was the Eighth Illinois Volunteer Infantry, an all-black regiment with a full slate of black officers, including Colonel John R. Marshall. The unit originated in the Ninth Battalion (Colored) of the Illinois militia created in 1895 largely as a result of the efforts of John C. Buckner of Chicago, a popular Negro politician and member of the state legislature. Buckner served as its commander until ousted on the eve of the Spanish-American War because of political differences with Republican Governor John R. Tanner. Out of consideration for the demand of Negro voters in Illinois, Tanner increased the battalion to regimental strength under the President's second call for volunteers and elevated Marshall, who was more politically acceptable to him, to the position of colonel. The new Eighth Illinois Regiment was mustered into federal service late in July, 1898, and sent to Cuba less than a month later. Although Negroes applauded Tanner for creating the black regiment, their enthusiasm was dampened by his treatment of so popular a leader as Buckner. Colonel Marshall in particular suffered from persistent criticism at the hands of Negroes who considered him an unworthy successor to Buckner and as a man unlikely to reflect credit upon Afro-American patriotism. The regiment, in fact, never completely overcame the effects of the political considerations involved in its creation and in the selection of its officers.[1]

The Eighth Illinois sailed from New York on board the *Yale* on August 11, 1898, and arrived in Cuba five days later. The regiment first pitched camp on a site near San Juan Hill where grim reminders of the bloody battle existed in abundance. After a few days here, the troops traveled by rail to their permanent headquarters in the town of San Luis. Colonel Marshall served as commander of the post and as military governor of San Luis Province. A detachment of the Illinois troops under Major Robert R. Jackson was stationed nearby in Palma Soriana.[2]

Shortly after the Eighth Illinois had established itself at San Luis, two other Negro regiments arrived in the town. One of these was the Twenty-third Kansas Volunteer Infantry. The organization of this regiment had figured in the political contest between Republicans and Populists for control of Kansas in the elections of 1898. Under the President's second call for volunteers, Populist Governor John W. Leedy, who was fighting for political survival, generated considerable support among Negroes by authorizing the creation of two black battalions with black officers. While

---

[1] *Chicago Tribune,* April 28, May 22, June 18, 19, 1898; *Illinois Record* (Springfield), April 9, May 7, 21, June 25, July 16, 23, 28, 1898; Charles Winslow Hall, "The Eighth Illinois, U.S.V.," *Colored American Magazine,* 1 (June, 1900): 94–103.

[2] The activities of the Eighth Illinois Regiment are chronicled in W. T. Goode, *The "Eighth Illinois"* (Chicago: Blakely Publishing Co., 1899); Regimental Records of the 8th Illinois Colored Infantry, Records of the Adjutant General's Office, Record Group 94, National Archives.

Leedy and the Populists assumed credit for organizing the black volunteers, the Republicans demonstrated their friendship for Negroes by exerting influence upon the War Department to have the two black battalions mustered into federal service as a regiment. James Beck, a Negro long active in the affairs of the Populist party, was appointed regimental commander by Governor Leedy. But the Republicans claimed that without their influence in Washington the regiment would never have been sent to Cuba as a part of the occupation forces. Whatever may have been the reason for the selection of the Twenty-third Kansas for service in the island, the regiment was indeed ordered there and arrived at San Luis about two weeks after the Eighth Illinois.[3]

The third Negro unit stationed in this town was the Ninth Volunteer Infantry, an "immune" regiment commonly called the Ninth Louisiana Immunes because most of the troops had been recruited in that state. The soldiers of the Illinois and Kansas regiments considered their outfits far superior to the black immunes, whose officers were white Southerners.[4] Obviously, the immunes possessed little of the sense of "being on trial" which characterized the units with complete rosters of black officers. The demoralization and lack of discipline among the Ninth Infantry owed much to the attitude and behavior of its white officers. "In the southern white officer's eye," a member of the Eighth Illinois noted, "the man who did the most grinning . . . and could dance the best and make the best monkeyshines was the best Negro soldier."[5] Even less impressive than the pride and discipline among the black immunes was their lack of immunity to Cuban fevers.

The soldiers of the three Negro regiments located at San Luis performed a variety of chores. One of their first assignments was to

[3] The Colored Citizen (Topeka), April 21, 28, June 2, 23, July 14, 21, August 25, September 1, 8, 15, 29, November 4, 1898; The American Citizen (Kansas City), June 24, July 1, 16, 1898; The Tribune (Wichita), November 5, 1898.

[4] For a history of the Ninth Immunes, see W. Hilary Coston, The Spanish-American War Volunteer (Middletown, Pa.: Mount Pleasant Printery, 1899).

[5] Goode, The "Eighth Illinois," p. 173.

take charge of the 5,000 Spanish prisoners of war interned in the town and to supervise their shipment back to Spain. For a time the black volunteers were on constant alert against bands of guerilla fighters who reportedly hid out in the nearby mountains. When the rumored attacks failed to materialize, the soldiers became less jittery and turned their attention to the task of assisting in the rehabilitation of San Luis Province. They constructed roads and bridges, repaired streets and plazas, and engaged in various projects designed to improve sanitary conditions. The black volunteers remained in Cuba for about six months and, upon being mustered out early in 1899, some of them volunteered for service in the Philippines.[6]

The departure of the black volunteers from Cuba did not mean the end of Negro soldiers' service in the occupation army. Early in May, 1899, the black cavalrymen of the Tenth Regiment who had distinguished themselves in the Santiago campaign returned to the island to perform garrison duty. Establishing themselves in a half-dozen stations in southeastern Cuba, the men of the Tenth Cavalry not only participated in the physical reconstruction of the country but also engaged in field activities against "insurrectos and bandits." Their prize capture was Troncon, the notorious bandit. In January, 1900, part of the regiment was transferred from Cuba to the Philippines; the remainder stayed in Cuba until May, 1902. The consensus among the black cavalrymen was that their garrison duty in Cuba was "the finest it [the regiment] had ever had."[7]

The following letters from Negro soldiers, both volunteers and regulars, who served in the occupation army in Cuba, reveal diverse reactions to the people and environment of the island. The soldiers seemed to have gotten along well with the natives and at least two dozen married "Cuban señoritas." Others became so

[6] Ibid., pp. 133–37, 197, 218; Theophilus G. Steward, *The Colored Regulars in the United States Army* (Philadelphia: A.M.E. Book Concern, 1904), p. 287.

[7] E N. Glass, *History of the Tenth Cavalry* (Tucson: Acme Printing Co., 1921), p. 39.

impressed by the economic possibilities of Cuba that they vowed to remain there permanently and encouraged other black Americans to join them. A few soldiers actually made investments in real estate and a captain in the black Illinois regiment purchased a sizable coffee plantation. Other black troops looked with disdain upon Cubans, whom they described as an incredibly filthy people, and upon Cuba, an "accursed country" which held no attractions for them. No matter how hard the lot of the black man in the United States, they found it preferable to life in Cuba.

The letters from some black volunteers indicated that, like other volunteers, their patriotic fervor gave way to homesickness and discontent after they had been separated from families and friends for several months. No less than other civilians hastily marshaled into military service, the black volunteers found it difficult to accept army discipline and the privations of Cuban camp life. Obviously they were no more immune to Cuban fevers than other Americans. They were inclined to blame their officers, whether black or white, for what they considered their sorry plight. The decline in morale was especially evident in correspondence from members of the Eighth Illinois Regiment, who became increasingly critical of Colonel Marshall. Their letters provided prime ammunition for Marshall's old adversaries in the Negro community of Illinois. Charges made by his men were used by his political enemies to confirm their claim of his unfitness for the position of regimental commander.

John R. Marshall, Eighth Illinois Infantry, U.S.V., Santiago, Cuba, August 28, 1898; from Illinois Record *(Springfield), September 3, 1898. Marshall, one of three Negro colonels in the volunteer army, makes his first report to Governor John R. Tanner of Illinois after the arrival of his regiment in Cuba.*

His Excellency, Governor John R. Tanner
Springfield, Illinois

Sir:

I have the honor to report the arrival of the Eighth Illinois Infantry, United States Volunteers, at Santiago. I arrived here with 1,195 enlisted men and forty-six officers. We have eight sick men, [the] others all right.

We are camped on the battlefield about two miles out. Dead Spanish soldiers are being burned on the hill about a quarter of a mile from us. Others are buried all over the place, some with their feet and hands sticking out, buzzards picking the flesh off their bones. It has rained ever since we arrived. One battalion, under Colonel [James H.] Johnson, left yesterday for San Luis, and I will leave this afternoon for the same place.

The regiment will stay there [San Luis]. I reported to General [Henry W.] Lawton. He said the First Battalion was the best, and made a better appearance than any of the volunteers. Their discipline was excellent, and he knew the regiment would take care of San Luis. The city is dirty. The stench is almost unbearable. The Spanish prisoners are being made to clean it. Chloride of lime is being scattered every where. No artist can picture the deplorable condition of the inhabitants. I am, sir, respectfully

Your obedient servant
John R. Marshall
Colonel Commanding

John L. Waller, Twenty-third Kansas Infantry, U.S.V., San Luis, Cuba, September ?, 1898; from The Parsons Weekly Blade *(Kans.), September 24, 1898. Waller, a prominent black politician and former consul to Madagascar who secured a captaincy in Kansas's Negro regiment, reports his initial impressions of Cuba.*

Sir:

The 23rd Kansas got ashore at Santiago at 8 a.m., September 1. We marched to the great Spanish (now American) warehouse where we waited all day for transportation by rail to our camp ground, San Luis, which is situated in the mountains twenty-six miles inland from Santiago.

I think God has made no more beautiful country than on which we are camped. It contains about 100,000 acres of the most fertile land, interspersed with rivers and creeks of running water which are alive with as fine fish as man could wish to catch.

More than 20,000 acres of this land has rested from the plow ever since [Antonio] Maceo drew his sword against Spain to liberate Cuba. This is one of the most beautiful bathing places in the world. There are about fifty natural bath tubs formed in the rocks, over which the water pours continuously.

Everything about Santiago and its harbor presents the strongest evidence of a fearful military struggle between the American and Spanish armies. Just over a hill, about a mile away, is the place where the "rough riders," 24th and 25th Infantry and 9th and 10th Cavalry grappled with the Spanish Army, and with thousands of other troops drove the Spanish army step by step from parapet to parapet, till the great victory was won and Spanish control in Cuba forever at an end. The 24th and 25th Infantry (colored) and Hood's Louisiana Immunes are now camped on the battleground.

A year's touch of American hand and civilization will make Santiago one of the greatest places for money-making in Cuba, because it sits in the midst of a rich agricultural and thickly populated country. We found the condition of the natives very greatly changed for the better by the help of the Americans. Hundreds and thousands of Cubans who were driven to the mountains and forests three years ago by the Spanish are returning to their former homes since the arrival of the American troops. They are fed and cared for by our government as carefully as are the soldiers of our own army. The Command of President McKinley for Spain to depart from Cuba has brought peace and comfort to the outraged Cubans.

John L. Waller
Captain, Co. C
23rd Kansas, U.S.V.

John R. Marshall, Eighth Illinois Infantry, U.S.V., Santiago, September ?, 1898; from The Parsons Weekly Blade, *September 24, 1898. Colonel Marshall, ever conscious that his black regiment was "on trial," assured Governor John R. Tanner that his men "will add glory to our race and honor to you who sent us."*

John R. Tanner
Governor of the State of Illinois
Springfield, Illinois
Sir:

I have the honor to inform you that the 8th Illinois Infantry, United States Volunteers, is now stationed at San Luis, and we are getting along fine. A good many of the men are sick with malarial fever, but none have yellow fever yet. We have eleven cases of measles. The water is very bad and the surgeon cannot get any ice. We have about thirty in the hospital and others in their quarters. No one is complaining. We are very proud to be here to represent Illinois. I know that our regiment is on trial and our race also. I think we will add glory to our race and honor to you who sent us. I assure you that you have the thanks of every man in the regiment. I expect another regiment here today from Santiago. General E. P. Ewers has been appointed brigadier commander, and will make his headquarters here. Companies E and F [of 8th Illinois], under the command of Maj. [Robert R.] Jackson, are stationed at Palma, about 20 miles north.

San Luis is a town of about 6000 inhabitants supported by sugar mills. There are about 4000 at Palma. The Cuban soldiers want to take possession of everything. They still carry arms, but do not come into the city armed. The people are very poor. They have nothing to eat and no clothes to wear. Children from 1 to 6 and 7 years of age go about the streets naked. I received 35,000 rations for them last week from the Red Cross Society. The first day I gave out 6000 rations and yesterday 1200. Anything from Illinois would be acceptable and highly appreciated.

You can not imagine the condition of the people. I found some so starved they could not stand up, and had to send food to them. Others are in the mountains near the city, starving to death. I also gave medicine to the sick, but we have nothing for them but quinine pills.

Our horses arrived from New York yesterday, with eighteen men, who got left there.

> Very respectfully
> Your obedient servant
> John R. Marshall
> Colonel, 8th Illinois
> Volunteers

W. B. Roberts, Twenty-third Kansas Infantry, U.S.V., San Luis, September 7, 1898; from The Parsons Weekly Blade, *October 15, 1898. Captain Roberts reports on the health of his men and vividly describes the devastation caused by revolution and war in Cuba.*

[Sir:]

I write you that you may know a few things about me and my affairs in this most peculiar place in the world. San Luis is the most peculiar I have ever seen or dreamed of. It is situated in a beautiful valley between the Serre Madre mountains, a unique town of about 4000 inhabitants, all Cuban and colored people, but all speak Spanish and we cannot understand what they say, only a few words.

.   .   .   .

We are camped on the outskirts of the town, just across the branch from the 8th Illinois regiment, and have met several of the officers and think a great deal of them. All are getting along nicely together. Our men visit back and forth and have a good time.

We have but little [sickness] in camp, most of what we have is bad colds and malaria. We have 24 men in the hospital but none seriously sick. It is impossible to keep from taking cold until a person gets acclimated. It is very hot in this climate and the nights are cool enough to sleep under blankets and it rains every day. Big dews fall at night. So you see the weather conditions are much different to anything we have been used to, but I [am] feeling fine, except a slight cold, and am trying to keep well.

There is no yellow fever here, but a good many cases in Santiago, there being there two hospitals for fever patients.

This country is five hundred years behind ours. Little dirty streets, with houses worse than our barns, made of bark from coconut trees which are the most common trees here. It is a sight to see our men climbing coconut trees after coconuts. . . . Will be ripe fruit here aplenty in about two weeks. Everything grows here—lemons, oranges, pineapples, bananas and all tropical fruits. We have plenty of lemons for lemonade. . . .

This is a great country of possibilities, but poverty reigns supreme. The fields are grown over . . . and are as wild as they ever were in the world. The people are pitiful sights, nearly naked and half starved little bony boys, girls, women and men.

We have seen no Spanish soldiers since our arrival, but evidence of war is everywhere—cannons, old Spanish ones, block houses or small forts on every hill and then some.

As I sit in my tent writing I can see two Spanish block houses within a quarter of a mile. The Spanish guns that were captured are being transferred to Santiago from where they will be shipped to the United States. I saw 20,000 Spanish Mauser rifles in a pile in Santiago when I was there the other day.

These people treat us as best they can and they do everything to make friends with us.

Our regiment has about 200 Spanish mules grazing on the hillsides near the camp, which are in our charge, and our boys have a time riding these little mules around and getting kicked by them.

This is no place for women, because there is no place for them to stay, but if we were in Santiago or any other place of any size we could accommodate the ladies, and it may be possible soon for us to do so.

As soon as it is possible, we officers have a plan to bring our wives here, that they may see the country and be with us, for this is a great treat to us to be able to see this country and people. It would be worth a fortune to anyone to be here awhile and see what I am seeing.

Santiago has many fine places, the remains of the Spanish aristocracy, now occupied as offices by the officers of the American army.

There is some talk of sending us to Havana but we don't know anything definitely about it, but I think it is a "black" dispatch, as there are all kinds of rumors here every day.

The barracks where the 8th Illinois is quartered is an old Spanish prison and there are all kinds [of evidence] of cruelty and butchery—beheading blocks all covered with human hair and dried blood, and pieces of rope still hanging from the old round rafters, where many a poor unfortunate Cuban has been hung. Old bloody blankets were carried out of the hospital department of that old crib of a barracks, where Cubans had been butchered, and burned by the American soldiers. Some of these sights are terrible. . . .

It is reported that there are 1500 Spanish soldiers in the hills about 65 miles from here and we may have a tie up with them any time, as they have been ordered to come in, and lay down their arms, but they have, as yet, refused to do so. Gen. [E. P.] Ewers, our commander, has given them till the 20th to report in here and lay down their arms, and if they do not comply, we will have to go out and bring them in; and these 2000 Negro troops here are the ones who can and will be pleased of the opportunity to do it. We hate the Spanish more and more every day as we see the result of this ten years' war and confusion, for they have made a barren tract out of a once fertile field.

It takes a letter fifteen [days] to reach you from here, for there is only about one mail liner a week out of this part of the island.

W. B. Roberts,
Capt., Co. F
23rd Kansas Regiment

Simon Brown, Twenty-third Kansas Infantry, U.S.V., San Luis, September 12, 1898; from The Parsons Weekly Blade, *October 22, 1898. In a communication to friends at home, Private Brown provides a ringing declaration of the black man's patriotism.*

Citizens of Oswego [Kansas]

Ladies and Gents:

As you all know, I, on the 6th day of July, 1898, left my home, my dear loving mother, sisters and brothers, and friends to come out here in this unknown country, in defense of the stars and stripes, under which you people are now living in peace. I did not volunteer to come here to be called a brave kid; but because I thought it my duty to defend the stars and stripes of my country, although it may cost me my life.

But friends, if such sad misfortune should happen to me, when I fall I intend to draw my last breath for the old flag under which I was born, which bears the colors, red, white and blue, better known as "Old Glory." I realized at the time when I answered the call of Gov. [John W.] Leedy for volunteers that I was subject to death at any moment by the gunshot of the cruel, cowardly Spaniards, by which I am surrounded. But nevertheless I am ready to die upon the battlefield defending our country, "Grand America," and the poor Cubans as well, because I am convinced that these people are of our Negro race, although they cannot speak the English language, but they have the complexion of our race.

We, the Kansas lads of the 23rd regiment, are willing to stay in the service here until freedom rings all over the island of Cuba. We mean to show the entire world that Kansas [has] none but valiant hearted soldiers. The Spanish soldiers are arrant cowards, when in battle, and they fire and then retreat. The American soldiers fire and advance, and continue until the battle is won or lost.

Now friends, the next time I write I will give you all the history of this country.

I am,

Respectfully
Simon Brown
23rd Kansas Regiment

W. B. Roberts, Twenty-third Kansas Infantry, U.S.V., San Luis, September 17, 1898; from The Parsons Weekly Blade, *October 15, 1898. Roberts describes a visit with the family of General Antonio Maceo, a mulatto leader of the Cuban revolution, whom Negro Americans held in high regard.*

[Sir:]

I write you again that you may know I am well and having as good a time as possible in this country. I have been around this town quite a good deal and have seen a great many of the sights as described by Consul [A. C.] Brice before his departure from Matanzas. You remember his description of the starving people, merely skeletons, walking around; homes of bark and clay with nothing in them but rags and sick, starved children.

Our camp is beseiged every day by women and children, begging for something to eat, and the condition of these poor people cannot be described. It would be the greatest pleasure of my life to be able to feed, clothe and administer medicine to these suffering people, and I know if the generous hearted, liberty loving people of Kansas could know the conditions of these poor suffering people in this end of the island, they would send clothes, food and medicine here for them; for, with all we have read and heard about Cuba and its suffering people, the half has never been told.

This town was once a prosperous farming center. It is 26 miles

from Santiago, with two immense sugar mills, which have not
been in operation for over three years, and the land that was
cane fields are now nothing but a broad plain between two
mountain ranges that are so tall you never see the tops except on
clear days, for the clouds are always below the mountain peaks.

The Cuban men are scattered all over the island in squads
and companies, armed, and will continue to be armed until the
last Spaniard has been transported from this island.

I was in town from our camp last night with . . . several other
officers of the 23rd Kansas regiment, and while there visited the
house where are living now the mother and two sisters of Gen.
Antonio Maceo, the great Cuban general, and they have his
photo. . . . With us was an interpreter, and they told us the
story of their lives and experiences during the war. It is something
terrible to conjecture, for among other things, they said the home
of the Maceos and where Gen. Maceo was born, was six miles
out from San Luis (and by the way, a party of us officers is
going out there in a few days relic hunting) and where they had
the most beautiful farm in this part of the island. A fine orange
grove paying them annually about $10,000; a lemon orchard
bringing an annual income of $5,500; 27,000 coffee trees
bringing in nearly $75,000; a fine farm or plantation raising cane,
a large sugar mill with a railroad running from here to the mill
on the farm; a fine house where the family lived and 36 houses
where the people lived who worked the thousands of acres of
land, and a prettier picture than the Senorita Teresa Maceo
described could hardly be imagined. But when the war broke out
in 1895, the farmer Maceo rallied around him his followers
and went into the field to free his country and his people, and as
we all know, struck the blow that interested our great country
and through her, Cuba became free. But Maceo was himself
betrayed into a Spanish trap and murdered, as was also three
brothers killed in the war. Spanish soldiers invaded this, the
province of Santiago, while Gen. Maceo was north in the province

of Santa Clara . . . and destroyed every Cuban house and farm in this whole province.

The Spanish burned the sugar mills and houses on the Maceo farm, cut down the orange, lemon and coffee trees, tore down the fences and in one day laid waste to everything around the once fine house of the Maceo family. They also killed over 800 mules and horses and a herd of nearly 400 cattle. . . . and this once proud family who were rich and educated are now living in a poor little thatch or bark and clay house with nothing to subsist upon, only what they earn by washing clothes for us American soldiers, and yet they are proud and do not complain, but are glad to say, "I gave all that my people might be free." And whenever the name of Maceo is spoken among Cubans anywhere they make signs and exclamations, for he is the Cubans' idol in this part of the island, and every one of them would help the family back to prosperity, but are so poor themselves that they cannot help themselves.

We as soldiers are well provided for; our sick list is small compared with the 8th Illinois, which is camped near us here in San Luis. We have only 27 on sick report in our regiment. . . .

There have been five deaths in the 8th Illinois, four dying from sickness and one killed by an accidental gun shot, but we have none as yet.

. . . .

W. B. Roberts,
Capt., Co. F,
23rd Kansas Regiment

Harry H. Ross, Eighth Illinois Infantry, U.S.V., San Luis, September 30, 1898; from The Freeman (*Indianapolis*), *October 22, 1898. Corporal Ross's letter reveals that a few weeks in Cuba tended to dull whatever glamor military service may have once held for him. He prays for deliverance from "this country of disease."*

To Editor of the Freeman

Dear Sir:

Seeing the pride your paper has taken in the interest of the colored soldiers I thought I would tell you a little about the Eighth regiment, Illinois Volunteers. Feeling satisfied that the American Negro points with pride to the state that gave us Lincoln, Grant, Logan and a governor, John R. Tanner, who thought so much of the African race that they represented them with a full colored regiment from colonel to private and the men appreciate all that has been done for them and have shown it by responding to the call to Cuba.

When we were called here to avenge the wrong of the Maine and to assist in freeing these half starved, half clad Cubans, our boys were only too proud to know that they had an opportunity to come and when we landed, seeing the condition of these people that are a hundred years behind the times, our young blood rushed through our veins and we were ready for battle. Let the worst come to us, but now that all is quiet; the storm is over; there is another picture that has presented itself and that picture is disease and death. Sir, when we bade our kind old fathers and mothers, sisters and brothers, wives and sweet-hearts good-bye, we were in the best of health but now it is entirely different for more than four-fifths of our men are sick with the dreaded malaria and fever. Why, when you go to a spring where the water is gushing from the base of a mountain, desiring to get a cool drink there, you fail, the water is warm for the earth is like a stove and it is impossible for one to stand the sun. When

you look from your tent you can see four men conveying a sick
comrade on this side and that side to the hospital and two more
in this and that direction assisting another and the two are almost
as feeble as the one they are assisting—then comes the trying
time, the question is such: we stay here and die or is the good
people of our homes going to pray for our deliverance from this
country of disease; how can we stay here and die without the
hope of our bodies coming home; how can we bear to know that
ever should we return we can only present to our sweet-hearts
and mothers . . . a wreck of humanity? The streets of the best
cities [in Cuba] are worst than our alleys in our country; the fruit
is full of fever and the water must be boiled so as to retain health.
Our officers and men possess the best brains and it should not be
wasted here. The men lay awake all night and [are] up before
day for they can not sleep for thinking of their loved ones at
home. If it was necessary for us to stay here and die at the point
of bayonet for our country's cause, we would say amen, but that
the war is over and we have nothing to do but stay here and suffer
this dreaded disease and heat, it is too much for us to stand. I
can't say any more now but do hope the day will hasten when our
boys breathe the free air of the land of their birth and can realize
that old and familiar song, "My Country 'Tis of Thee," for Cuba
is now free and we desire to be.

> Respectfully yours
> Corp'l Harry H. Ross
> Co. H, 8th Reg., Illinois Volunteers

*W. B. Roberts, Twenty-third Kansas Infantry, U.S.V., San Luis, October
3, 1898; from* The Colored Citizen *(Topeka), November 11, 1898.
Roberts describes an incident in which a hotel in Santiago, owned by a
white American, was prevented from drawing the color line against a
Negro officer.*

[Dear Parents:]

When we are in Santiago we are reminded so much of home.
There is a hotel there called The American, run by an American
who is from St. Louis, Mo. They try to draw the color line here in
Cuba. The first time I was there I went to that hotel with Capt.
[William H.] Hawkins of Atchison, who is very light in color.
They thought he was white so said nothing to him, but the
proprietor was going to stop me. He said his boarders and white
customers objected to eating with colored men and that he
could not afford to ruin his business by accommodating me, and me
an American army officer in full uniform; and you should have
heard me go after him. I told him I was an American officer and
had always associated with gentlemen all my life and [did] not
now propose to disgrace myself or my shoulder straps eating at a
side table or in a side room to please a few second class white
officers who never had money enough to take a meal in a first
class hotel until they became officers in the volunteer army of the
United States during the present war; I ask no special privileges,
but would have what was due me as an army officer or know
the reason why; that he need not think that we colored soldiers
who spilled so much of our precious blood on the brow of San
Juan hill that it might be possible for him and other Americans
to safely do business, and are standing now with bayonets on
guns as sentinels to protect them in that business, were going
to allow any discrimination on account of our color; and all I
wanted to know was whether or not he was going to feed me.
The dining room was full of officers and others, and you could
have heard a pin fall while I was talking, and while the proprietor

was finding something to say an officer whom I later found out to be Gen. [Ezra P.] Ewers of military district No. 1, got up from the table, walked over to me and grasped my hand and said: "Come, Captain, take my seat; and you, Mr. Hotel Proprietor, get it quick; and I don't want to hear any more of this d——n foolishness with these officers of mine!" And I was a little king there in about a minute. . . .

W. B. Roberts
Captain, Co. F., Twenty-Third Kansas

W. B. Roberts, Twenty-third Kansas Infantry, U.S.V., San Luis, October 7, 1898; from The Parsons Weekly Blade, *October 29, 1898. In the following letter, which includes various news items regarding black volunteers stationed in Cuba, Captain Roberts pays a tribute to the Negro troops of the regular army who took part in the Santiago campaign earlier in 1898.*

Editor, *Blade*
Parsons, Kansas

My dear old friend:

At last I write you. Ain't you scared? We receive your valuable paper with considerable regularity and it is always hailed with great delight by the boys of Co. F.

.   .   .   .

We have camped in or near this city three regiments—the 8th Illinois Inft., the 9th Louisiana Immunes, and the 23rd Kansas, all colored, and we are masters of the situation up here.

You need not think that because there is no active fighting to be done here that we have nothing to do, for we are constantly doing guard duty, and it is a battle for us to ward off these dreaded fevers and malaria, which has made such havoc in the ranks of United States troops, and we have to take medicine as a preventative. I never believed in medicine at home, you know, but here I am a great friend to quinine, and barrels of it is used by us soldiers on the island and we must take it or be sick.

The literature sent us by Prof. J. E. Johnson . . . [fulfilled] a long-felt want, for it is almost impossible to get anything to read, and the boys have arranged a library, and every book and paper taken out to [be] read must be signed for and returned. Chas. Carl is librarian, and the reading matter is much enjoyed, and the boys take [as] much care of it as they would a thousand dollar library in the United States.

The other day while in Santiago I met an old Parsons boy named Bart Brown. He said he lived in Parsons a good many years and knows all the old timers. . . . His father was in the meat market business . . . in the early days of Parsons. He gave me several relics from the battlefield of San Juan hill. . . . That is where the 9th and 10th Cavalry and 24th and 25th Infantry did such great fighting and proved to the world the Negro is the [greatest] fighter in the world. That same day I saw [Richmond] Hobson, the hero of the Merrimac.

All the Parsons boys send their best regards to you. . . .

    I am

               Your friend,
               W. B. Roberts,
               Capt, Co. F., 23rd Kansas Regiment

George J. Beard, Eighth Illinois Infantry, U.S.V., San Luis, October 21, 1898; from Illinois Record, *November 12, 1898. Though proud to be a member of Illinois's Negro regiment, Beard has grown weary of Cuba and longs to return to the United States.*

Mr. Charles E. Hall
Springfield, Illinois

My kind friend:

I have been writing about one to three letters a week home and as every letter that comes here from Springfield says I am dead, I have decided to write to everyone in Springfield from a bootblack to the mayor . . . and possibly some of them will reach there and they will find out at home that I am "a live one," both bodily and from a financial standpoint, which is a fact.

. . . .

The 8th Regiment is at the present time the whole show in this province. We are as well-drilled, and better, than any other Reg. I have seen drill. We have just been issued new clothing . . . and when we go out on dress parade it is a shame that the good people in Springfield could not see us. The 8th Reg. Band plays music that would make Prof. Lehman and the Watch Factory Band stand and say, "I didn't think they would do, but they have." If the President of the United States and the Secretary of War have not put us on this island and forgot all about us entirely we may have a chance to show everyone a dress parade that will be simply grand.

The health of the Reg. is fairly good. There are about 15 men sick in Co. H of Springfield and about the same number in several other companies but none are serious at this writing. Since we have been on the Island the 8th Reg. has lost about 6 men. . . . We [Company H] have been blessed with fairly good health and considerable wealth. . . .

The hardships we have endured since in Cuba are more than

enough to kill any man, but God in his kind wisdom has saw fit
to spare our lives. If we are kept here a year or two, mothers will
not know their sons, wives will not know their husbands . . .
for we will be living skeletons. . . . I certainly long to see the
old home once again, and I am going to live in hopes if I die in
despair. Oh, how I would like to be in the *Illinois Record* office
again setting type. I am very sure I would let all wars pass by
and attend to my work, for the soldier's life is not [what] one
would think it is. When a man dies here he is put in a pine box
and buried two or three deep in a Cuban grave yard and is soon
forgotten by all. I hope God will spare my life to see home again
and I will never leave even to go on an excursion to Jacksonville
(Illinois).

> I am
>
> Respectfully yours,
> Geo. J. Beard
> Co. H., 8th Ill., Vol. Inf.
> Military Station No. 1
> San Luis de Cuba

*"Three Privates," Eighth Illinois Infantry, U.S.V., San Luis, November
13, 1898; from* Illinois Record, *November 26, 1898. Disillusioned with
their assignment in Cuba, three privates complain bitterly about their
regimental commander, Colonel John R. Marshall, whom they insist has
not only mistreated the men but also consistently misrepresented their
attitude toward service in the island.*

Illinois Record
Springfield, Ill.

Dear Sir:

I thought I would write to-day for it is Sunday, and I haven't
anything to do. Things are coming to a lovely point; the men are

down on the Col. [John R. Marshall], and some of them swear
to kill him when we get back home. All of the sick men he wants
to go back to work before they are able; they are not dying fast
enough for him. He had a chance to let the Regt. go back home,
but the sight of that $291.00 [monthly pay] was too much for him
to let go by; he never made that much money in Chicago. He
has been sending letters that we like the country and the place
and that we send our regards. It is all wrong; the boys hate him,
curse him and if it was not for being in the army he would have
been dead long ago.

When the colonel was sick, he was like a baby; he wanted
this and that. When he got well he treated the boys like dogs.
We are not allowed out of the company street after 5 o'clock;
we have to stay in our tents. Our food at times is not fit for the
Cubans to eat, but we are compelled to eat it or starve. What
show have we? The worst is too good for us. I guess we will live
to leave our bodies on Cuban soil, for the remembrance of the
8th [Illinois Regiment] who once went to Cuba to make a
record for themselves, but were left behind. When the men left the
U.S., they gave up good positions and homes, parents, friends,
wives and children to come over to fight, but when they arrived,
they, instead of fighting, were made to do garrison duty and now
the officers believe in putting the men in the guard house and try
to take his money away. We are not regulars, we are vols. and
not only that we were a part of the state militia. Why are we
not called home like the other volunteers? Well, the others have a
pull and moneyed men behind them, so that the government had
to comply. But the 8th have none, that is the reason they are here.

When the men leave the barracks, they walk down to the
brook and wash, and go around the Cuban houses. You sit by
the door and the family sits around in a circle, and there you are.
You can't understand them, nor they you. When the boys get
back home, never speak of Cuba to them, for you might find out,
never go to war with a Col. like Marshall; he is too near white;

he is for number one; the rest can look after themselves. All the colored people can do in Chicago is to pray for our safe return. I could write more but if the Col. knew I wrote this I would not be in the ranks long enough to say good-bye.

Wishing you the compliments of the season for we have none.

Three Privates
[8th Illinois Infantry]

Frank Burns, Eighth Illinois Infantry, U.S.V., San Luis, no date; from Illinois Record, *December 10, 1898. In the following letter to a friend, Burns describes the "customs of the Cuban people" and mentions an episode involving black volunteers and the Cuban police which attracted considerable attention in the white press in the United States.*

Mr. James Young
Springfield, Illinois

Dear Sir:

It is with much pleasure that I write to you. I would have written sooner but for the inconvenience of getting writing materials. I received your kind words of encouragement and I was greatly lifted up. I cannot begin to tell you of my trip over here. It is true that we have many sick, and it is also true that we have had only nine deaths in our regiment.

If you were here you would probably laugh yourself to death at the customs of the Cuban people. They live in houses made of palm leaves and bark from coconut trees and they and their children, their horses, goats, chickens, hogs, dogs, cats, parrots, cows, lizards and furniture all stay under one roof and just as you have seen from photos the children go naked. The people use ox carts to transport whatever you wish moved, although one often sees a mule or horse hitched to a cart. When a person dies, a coffin is borrowed or rented, the corpse is placed within and hauled to the graveyard, where the coffin is opened and the dead body is dumped into the grave. The coffin is then returned to the owner and this is what they call fooling the dead.

There is much marrying among American soldiers and Cuban women. Three of the boys of our company have taken unto themselves Cuban wives already.

A cavalry of Cuban police came to San Luis on the 14th [of November] and had a misunderstanding which caused the Cubans to lose their captain and four men. The 9th colored Regiment [Immunes] lost one.[1]

Will Rollins of Co. G, Jacksonville, is one of the body guards of the Brigadier General as is also Belton Brown.

I have taken a new step in life since I left Springfield. On the 30th of October I was baptized with several other converts and I now desire your prayers. Chas. C. Hatcher was also a convert. With kind regards to all, I am

Yours,
Frank Burns
Co. H, 8th Illinois Inf. Vol.

[1] On the night of November 14, 1898, several drunken soldiers of the Ninth Immunes, a Negro regiment, stole a pig from a Cuban. Jose Ferrera, a Cuban policeman, attempted to arrest them, but they escaped. Later that night the soldiers returned to the scene and proceeded to shoot at Ferrera's house. In the general melée involving black troops and Cuban civilians which followed, Ferrera and several other Cubans were killed. The San Luis affair received wide publicity and reflected adversely upon all Negro troops stationed in the vicinity. Shortly afterward, the Eighth Illinois Volunteers, as well as other Negro units, were ordered to camp sites outside the city of San Luis.

*C. T. Walker, Ninth Infantry, U.S.V., San Luis, ca. December 15, 1898;
from the* Augusta Chronicle, *December 30, 1898. Walker, chaplain of a black regiment of "immunes," writes the following letter to a
white newspaper in which he describes the Cuban landscape in rhapsodic
terms, comments on the health of the black volunteers and the success
of his religious revivals, and pronounces Cubans incapable of self-
government.*

Editors, Chronicle

It may be of some interest to your readers to hear from this
part of Cuba. I left Augusta the last of November to join
my regiment, the Ninth United States Volunteer Infantry
[Immunes], as chaplain, having been appointed by President
[William] McKinley last July. I sailed from New York on the
steamship Berlin and reached Santiago, Cuba, after a voyage of
six days. The steamship was crowded with passengers for Ponce
and San Juan, Porto Rico, and Santiago, Siboney, and El Caney,
Cuba. Congressman [Ebenezer J.] Hill of Connecticut and
General [Leonard] Wood's wife were among the passengers.
The colored chaplain was requested to preach twice on the
Sabbath to the passengers and the dining room was crowded with
attentive listeners.

Congressman Hill spoke in the highest terms of ex-Congressman
[James C.] Black and of our present Congressman William H.
Fleming. There were 31 carpenters on board from New York en
route to San Juan, Porto Rico, to build barracks for soldiers.
They are to remain there six months.

We reached Santiago in the early morning, just as the king of
the day was coming forth in his chariot of burning gold to dispel
the darkness of the night. We entered the harbor, passed under
the guns of Morro Castle, alongside the famous Merrimac, and
entered the quaint old city by means of small boats owned by the
Cubans. The landing was very much like that at Joppa. The

Spanish and Cuban dialect reminded us of the famous Arabs of the Orient.

Santiago is older than St. Augustine, Fla., and everything about it except the American soldiers, wagons and mules is in keeping with its age. After 9 o'clock in the morning it is so hot you can scarcely walk in the streets. The lazy Cubans are lying around in the shade sleeping and dreaming how to cheat Americans by charging three prices for everything you might desire to purchase. Cooked eggs are ten cents apiece, and everything else in proportion.

I found my regiment to be 35 miles from Santiago, near San Luis, Cuba. The country through which I passed was the most beautiful I ever saw, not surpassed by Switzerland and Germany. The soil is rich, valleys are beautiful and fertile, trees loaded with coffee, oranges, cocoanuts and many other fruits, while the mountains are sky-towering and picturesque.

I have often heard the song that December was as pleasant as May, but never saw it illustrated until I came to Cuba. It is now the middle of December and the heat is so intense that men fall out of the ranks daily prostrated by heat, and are carried to the hospital. . . . There are five men in the hospital with fever, their temperature ranging from 102 to 104 [degrees]. In this same regiment, when camped on San Juan Hill, at Santiago, 800 were sick with fever at once.

Our government will have trouble yet with the Cubans. There are frequent spats between them and American soldiers. A fight occurred a few days ago between the soldiers of this regiment and some Cuban soldiers, in which five Cubans were killed and one of the soldiers from my regiment. A Cuban soldier was shot today in our camp quite near me, by one of our soldiers. The people of this island are not yet capable of self-government.

The dews at night are like rain; the days are hot like July in Georgia and the nights are cool. Palm trees and mahogany are plentiful. I have had a number of walking canes made from the wood taken from the old Spanish blockhouses to express to America.

For two weeks I have been conducting a revival meeting in our regiment, which has resulted in the conversion of nearly 100 men. A large number of them were bapitzed last Sunday morning in a beautiful Cuban stream. And more than 50 will be baptized next Sunday morning. If churches and schools are planted upon this dark island, much will be done for the civilization and Christianization of this long oppressed people. The writer is perhaps the first Negro preacher to administer the ordinance of baptism in this part of Cuba, and perhaps the whole of Cuba. I will sail for America in a few days and I hope soon to be in Augusta.

Yours,

C. T. Walker

George J. Beard, Eighth Illinois Infantry, U.S.V., San Luis, no date; from Illinois Record, *December 24, 1898. Beard reports on the various activities of the soldiers in his regiment and describes in detail the Thanksgiving dinner which they provided for Colonel John R. Marshall and his staff. But clearly such festivities did little to combat the homesickness of the troops.*

[Dear Sir:]

Although in Cuba, several of the members of the 8th Ill. Reg., who have organized themselves into a Christian band, known as the Christian Endeavor, gave a very nice dinner Thanksgiving Day for their Col. and staff.

Promptly at 1:30 the Christian [Endeavor] tent was crowded with guests from Col. John R. Marshall down to the private soldier. The long table was beautifully decorated with wild flowers, gathered in the mountains, and all the good things to eat that could be obtained in the Santiago markets. Mr. William Farmer acted as head waiter and performed his duties as well as the full-dressed head waiter in the States. After all the guests had been assigned their places at the table, and the invocation given by our Chaplain, Rev. [Jordan] Chavis, the guests were seated and began to devour the following good things to eat:

Menu

Pickles	Tomatoes, Rice
Roast Ribs of Beef	Lettuce
with Brown Potatoes	Boiled Ham
Fried Chicken	Sugar Corn
Mashed Potatoes	Peaches
Baked Beans—Boston Style	

Assorted Cake

Claret   Lemonade   Coffee

Cigars

The dinner was served without a pan being on the table, as the committee had secured dishes, and that is something that a soldier in Cuba, except the officers, never sees. After everyone present had satisfied the inner man, Corporal George J. Beard, who acted as Master of Ceremonies, rose and introduced Rev. Chavis, Chaplain of the 8th, who delivered an address of welcome to our guests, which was responded to by Col. John R. Marshall. Corporal [R. W.] Westberry then delivered an address, "The Non-Commissioned Officer" and Private John Smith of Springfield spoke on the "Private Soldier." Mrs. Waller, wife of Capt. [John L.] Waller of the 23rd Kansas, was present and added greatly to the occasion by several encouraging remarks after which the guests retired to their quarters, hoping to eat their next Thanksgiving dinner at their several homes.

The 8th Ill. has moved from San Luis[1] and are at present about
3 miles and a half from there at a very beautiful place which
has been named Camp Marshall. We can not see a house unless
we walk about two miles, but we are almost surrounded by
beautiful mountains and we walk around camp looking at the
high weeds which are being burned down and the cocoanut and
palm trees.

The Cubans come out and bring the boys their washing
and when they get tired of looking at the mountains we look at
them.

Several of the men in Company H have learned to speak
the Spanish language fluently and they act as interpreters for
those who have not been so fortunate as to learn it. If the people in
Springfield could hear Corp. A. L. Morgan and Chas. Ross
talking to these Cubans they would think that they had studied
the language at some college; they talk so fluently.

The other evening I was down at the depot in company with
Noah Williams when the train steamed in from Santiago. As the
tip had been given out that there would be mail in that evening,
we went to meet the train. I saw my comrade who belongs to the
8th [Illinois Regiment] and who is acting [as] mail man, get off
a rusty looking passenger coach and as I did not see him with any
sacks, I thought we were not going to get any mail that evening,
but later he opened a cattle car where there were two mules, ice
and other freight, and much to my surprise I saw about twelve
sacks of mail. That was the first time in my life I ever saw mail
carried in a cattle car, but strange things do happen in Cuba.

The general health of the reg[iment] is fairly good, about
eight or ten in each company being in the sick book. In Company
H the sick are Frank Ford, dropsy; Reuben Williams, Corp.
[Charles] Ross, Harry Dickens, Amos Meredith, Frank Vernon

---

[1] Following the disturbance created in San Luis on November 14, 1899, by
the Ninth Immunes, all three Negro regiments were removed from the city. The
Eighth Illinois established camp about three and a half miles from the city.

and a few others, malaria fever; but I think they will all get well.

Every member of the 8th Reg. Band has got a new nickel plate instrument that shines like silver. The instruments bear beautiful engraving and the cornets are trimmed with gold. The band now looks simply grand.

It is rumored about the 8th [Illinois Regiment] will go to Tampa, Fla., in forty days, but I doubt it as it hardly looks possible that we can have any such good luck.

Well, I think that the 8th Reg. will be home sometime between this and 1900, and when we do come home I hope the girls will not make fun of us for we will be very green as we have been living about in the woods for so long.

Corporal Geo. J. Beard,
Co. H, 8th Ill. Vol. Inf.

"Committee of Vigilance," Eighth Illinois Infantry, U.S.V., San Luis, January 4, 1899; from Illinois Record, *January 21, 1899. This letter from a group of dissatisfied soldiers in the Eighth Illinois is a bitter indictment of the regiment's officers, especially Colonel John R. Marshall, "the man with a white face and a black heart and hand."*

To the Editor of the Springfield *Record:*

The New Year is now upon us in this accursed place, and scarcely has one set of indignities passed and another is upon us under the present regime of the great "I am." Yourself and the general public must know and shall print the inequities being practiced upon your patriotic sons who came here to do battle for humanity and God, and whose bravery and courage has been plainly demonstrated by their valour and noble acts in responding to a countries call when oppression was staring our country in the face. We not only came at a countries call in strict obedience to our beloved president Wm. McKinley, but we enlisted, took the

oath, were mustered into the U.S. Vols. over riding the
persuasions of mothers, wives, sisters, brothers and sweethearts,
walked over their advices, wading in their tears in our mad rush
to aid and be instrumental in making the first page in the
Afro-American history of the world, nor can those at home across
the deep blue sea, where the happiest moments of our lives were
spent, say as of old, "I told you so." Can those who at the very
beginning of the outfiting of this Regt., the 8th Ill., pleaded and
implored the Gov[ernor] of our beloved state, not to commission
the man with a white face[1] and a black heart and hand to the
position of Colonel [John R. Marshall], desert us, and will the
fearless, vigilent and much appreciated editors of *The Record,* at
this critical moment, turn a deaf ear to those who are the victims
of this abuse and inhuman treatment at the hands of this human
being, who are under him according to law, but above him in
principle, integrity and manhood?

You will and must know, dear ones in America, that what is
now coming to your public notice are facts worthy of your
keenest consideration, and comments, for hearts long, long ago
has bled by night, and mourned by day for home and a breath of
free and pure liberty.

I will run open my gun, place a bomb in it and let it burst so
the public and well-wishers of Christian humanity can see the
intrigue, chaos and ever abhorring deception, with which this
monster of decency and virtue overrides and rules your loved ones
in Cuba. I will first call your attention to the so-called benefits
that have been given for our aid and assistance, and while I
positively know I am right, and 1200 men including the few
honest men on the staff, will someday verify as the truth, I want
to say with perfect honor, many ladies in various cities
throughout our state have been misled and made blockheads of

---

[1] Colonel John R. Marshall was a mulatto whose complexion was so light that
some claimed he could have passed for white. His critics often referred to him
as "too white" or as "the man with the white face."

by those scheming individuals, who are now eating the fat of the land and their coalbins and flour barrels are full to the brim with goodies that was bought from the receipts of the various receptions, balls and entertainment given under the auspices of the Regiment's name, and we poor devils longed for and looked forward to the coming of the special visitor and courier sent to provide Xmas and Thanksgiving turkeys for us.

He had done his duty with integrity and he too has been victimized and made a "Jug Head" of by those who sent him. He brought over enough canned peaches to give each company sixteen cans and enough Bents soda crackers to allow two-thirds of a box for each company for Xmas dinner.

A question of information to the public:—Does sixteen cans of peaches constitute a full box of peaches and will sixteen cans feed 103 men for one meal in a peach pie or cobbler and would that cause an expenditure of $1000 cash and netted profit from the Benefit given at the First Regiment Armory [Chicago] to buy medicines, eatables and other necessities? If those peaches and crackers cost $833.50 per box of sixteen cans, when twenty-four cans constitute a box, then we'll all be satisfied, knowing that we dined so costly and ate so much fine food at the hands of such a grand committee as was set up to administer to our wants or necessities. Jno. R. Marshall knows all about this.[2]

Now let me tell you something, and be profitted by it. The hospitals are in a most deplorable condition, under Major Dr. [Allen A.] Wesley, the other mogul in the political regimental arena, and to prove this, write to any man in Company G and get the facts that I now break to you.

Private Frank Richardson of Jacksonville, Ill. was taken very

[2] The charges made in this letter are not easily substantiated and some are obviously exaggerated. But in the case of the funds raised by various black organizations for the benefit of the Eighth Illinois Regiment, their expenditure did indeed create considerable controversy among Negroes in Illinois. The charge was often made that these funds were never used for the purpose for which they were intended.

ill with the never ceasing malaria fever [and was sent] to the
hospital. He was sent after being in his quarters sick for a period
of nine days on medical treatment of salol and quinine. He was
very ill when taken there and from the effects of fever settling in
his lungs, consumption set in and he was recommended for an
honorable discharge with his transportation, subsistences and
allowances for clothing (not drawn) and at once to be sent
home. This was done through the strenuous efforts of Dr.
[Charles S.] Sunday,[3] the attending physician at the Hospital
from the 23rd Kansas. Dr. Sunday is what every sick man knows
that has gone to the hospital as an efficient and educated doctor
and a gentleman, kind and generous in his ways and a father in
care and indefatigable worker among the stricken of both the
23rd Kansas and 8th Illinois. Since he has resigned from his
Regt. a white Cuban doctor has been installed in his place. A
more deplorable state of affairs exists. Dr. Sunday was almost
forced to resign because of the lion attitude of Dr. Wesley.

Well, poor Frank Richardson gradually sank deeper and
deeper, his strength failing daily until his death relieved him of
his terrible tortures. His medicines were so strong and his strength
so wasted that the whole roof of his mouth was ate out from the
effects thereof, and when death had claimed his body it was made
known that for weeks prior to his death his honorable discharge
and money had been here and Col. Marshall, "as he is called,"
would not approve his papers, because it would affect the
strength . . . of the regiment, and of course without a full quota
this regiment must be sent home and another [sent] to take our
place. That and no other reason, with the exception of those
demagogues drawing fat salaries, which they do not deserve, kept
that black hand of his from signing the papers that would have
perhaps saved some mother's darling and some poor girl's
intended husband. Just think of it; ponder over it and on your

---

[3] Dr. Charles S. Sunday was Assistant Surgeon of the Twenty-Third Kansas
Volunteers.

knees and at your work send up a silent prayer to God that he
may hasten the time when the Sec. of War [Russell A.] Alger
will call us home and out of the hands of this, our human
persecutor. To say more of this is to still further deal with the
man or object while in Springfield.

Gov. [John R.] Tanner issued an order to Marshall that unless
the recruiting would reach its maximum in three days we would
be sent to our various homes. Marshall made promises to political
heelers and claim grabbers that if you will bring so and so many
men by such and such a time, I will make you captain, sergeant,
corporal and so on. Many jumped at it and on the last Sunday of
last July, forty men were brought in by an individual, and when
he found out he had been duped by Marshall he told the men to
get away and they went, and on that night the whole
non-commissioned staff of the old Ill. Nat'l Guard, known as the
9th Battalion, were armed and told to frighten the men, should
any of them try to make an escape, or to shoot and make them
stay and take the oath so that he might get his commission as a
Colonel.

Furthermore, this Regiment is composed of boys who are
under age and whose parents have never given their consent to
him [Colonel Marshall] that they might become soldiers, and he
had them enlisted and made soldiers so he could profit in his
purse by it. Oh! for a pen! a ceaseless pen, a fountain of perpetual
ink, a page of paper large enough for the world to read and know
these horrible facts, but truths.

Then again, in the examination; that was a fake. A man was
put first on the scales, weighed, measured and passed to the lung
tester, thence . . . for the inspection of the urinary organs. A
form was gone through, such as work your fingers nimbly, high
jumping. . . . Plenty of old men, so crooked in their knees until
they looked like a weather beaten shingle, toothless, as stiff as a
poker, blind in one eye and bald headed passed as good an
examination as young robust men. . . .

These deficiencies on the part of the medical advisors and hurried way in which they put through the men without consideration for the future welfare and health of the Regiment, make it a crime, yes, a black crime against them and also deception to good law and military discipline. If you burn your candle a few moments after . . . [taps], or should you not hear a command from our haughty officers, standing far away in the distant with his head erect so that the blanco Cuban Senorias or Senoritas will or would be impressed that they are Jay Gould; if you make an error, to the guard house you go; next the summary court gets you and no evidence will save you. A snug slice is deducted from your salary and you are sent from camp, near and in sight of old San Luis. There is a road being graded there and you shovel and pick in the hot sun at heat of 80 ° to 93 ° . . . . Marshall says, "Done enough; come up higher," and that will be after many days. This he calls local or primary punishment.

At this day when we are having peace, there is another mode of punishment; the "Hanging Act" and the "Spread Eagle." The Hanging Act is a rope suspended from the ceiling of the guard house. When a prisoner is brought in he is searched and of course relieved of his little change, which goes to help the poor.(?)

If there is a murmur the suspended rope is placed around the two thumbs; you are then drawn up to the ceiling so that your toes may barely touch the floor and the whole weight of your body is upon your thumbs. Imagine the pain.

The "Spread Eagle" is accomplished by placing a man on the ground (face downward), the arms extended and made fast to stakes or tent pegs and the limbs the same way. Every twelve hours the sentry, posted to watch you, asks if you are ready to comply with the order of the court martial. If you say yes, you are then released, only to be driven in the sun to the shovel or pick, to the water wagon, or to dig sink holes. Think of this in the time of peace and under these men.

Capt. C. L. Hunt of Co. C and Capt. [William T.] Jefferson [of Co. D] are noted for this novel method of punishment and this is inflicted before you ever have a trial. Is this justice?[4]

Please insist upon your Senators and Congress[men] to call us home at once.

> The Committee of Vigilance
> 100 Privates Strong

"One Hundred Privates," Eighth Illinois Infantry, U.S.V., San Luis, January 12, 1899; from Illinois Record, *February 4, 1899. Like other letters which purported to chronicle the misdeeds of Colonel John R. Marshall and the officers of the Eighth Illinois, this one made the front page of the* Illinois Record, *a Negro newspaper in Springfield, whose editor was Marshall's most persistent critic and political adversary.*

Mr. Editor
Illinois Record

Dear Sir:

The good people of the State of Illinois and the world at large must and shall know what a lasting disgrace is now being put forward by the officers of the 8th Illinois. To begin with, Sergeant [George L.] Patterson, of Co. F. of the Regt., stationed at Palma, where two co.'s, E and F, garrison the city armed, was killed in November and a very poor investigation was instituted which gave evidence that lurking Cubans, lazy, indolent scoundrels, who had been fed, nourished and clothed by our sympathetic men at Palma, laid in wait and gleaning an opportunity to quarrel with Patterson and in the melee did shoot and kill the sergeant. This was a shadow thrown upon the

---

[4] Although the records of the Eighth Illinois Regiment contain no evidence regarding the punishment mentioned in this letter, they do reveal that the regiment had an unusually large number of courts martial.

regiment, and [so as not] to make the matter noticeable, his
name was carried over on the payroll for two successive months
and the honest officers of his company divided the pittance (his
salary $21.60) among themselves, for cigar and whiskey money,
until the month of January when, of course, the paymaster's
department must publish the current expense incurred during the
fiscal year, giving in detail deceased, disabled and those
discharged. It was at this juncture that a discovery was made that
someone had been signing for Sergeant Patterson and he being
dead two months. Now an investigation is going on and we, the
8th Regt., must wait for our pay for the month of December until
this investigation is over, and the commander of the regiment,
[Colonel John R.] Marshall, to keep the men in patient spirits,
has caused this rumor to be circulated, that our payrolls from
various companies were missent . . . and that other payrolls
would necessarily have to be made out before we could receive
our pay . . . which we really need because our mothers, sisters
and others who are dependent upon us to a certain extent, need
what is due them each month. Of course, it takes time for an
investigation . . . so that while the companies are under the
impression that new rolls have been made out and sent to
Santiago they would not murmur and would write home to loved
ones in America. Why? Because brother wrote it to me, or my
husband said so in his letter; but do not let the public and loved
ones be so basely deceived, because it is from no other cause than
the one herein stated, that we are made to wait for our money. A
shame, a lasting shame and a beastly disgrace, but of course the
black-handed villain cares only for self, consequently we suffer as
we have at the hand of this John R. Marshall, proteges and his
accomplices, money changers and debauchers. We know that this
can't survive much longer, for as Marshall and his pace-makers
are a set of self-made men, I must say and truthfully confess that
they are self-made, and a dirty job of it too was the making, for
God had nothing to do with their making. To prove this look you

into this and ask the mothers who now mourn for their dear beloved sons who[m] they thought heedless and rash in going to war without their consent but mark you these boys were forced to come and kept under guard that these men could profit by it in their purses, and by an assumed title which they now bear at the expense of your tears and the sufferings of your sons 2700 miles from you where a shortage of everything is prevalent, except intrigue, political spoilation and personal gain. Ah! yes had we been called home three months ago we would, as many have said, been lionized as heroes of the late Hispano-American War, but by having been held here by whom? Marshall who has disgraced the Negro race and public decency. He has had the audacity to write Senator William L. Martin[1] of the 5th senatorial district, a man whom we voted for and whose cause we advocated. Yes, letters from all grades of the officers, from Colonel down to the 2nd lieutenants, have been sent to him, asking him to use his influence in having the next General Assembly make an appropriation so that the 8th Ill. will or can have a place in the National Guard of the State, and all be mustered into the state service as soon as we are mustered out of the U.S. service, under present officers from colonel down. . . .

Oh! My God, such an appeal I hear coming from the ranks. No! No!!!. Ten thousand times ten thousand No. We would not muster into a Sunday school or Salvation Army for fear that Marshall might get into it.

A private in the regular army receives as his monthly pay $13.50 . . . a corporal $15.50, a sergeant $18.00 to $25.00.

We are in this fever stricken land away from all civilization, fed upon slimy native beef, old tomatoes, rotten potatoes that are shipped from the states and when they reach us the devil himself can't bear the odor; flour that was packed for the soldiers of the Civil War of '61 to '65; flour that our bread is made out of is full

---

[1] William L. Martin, a native of Missouri, was elected in 1898 to the seat in the lower house of the Illinois legislature formerly held by John C. Buckner.

of small white worms, and beans full of weavers, hominy musty. Now there is your portion of existence, and if you are stationed here in this island, God save your soul.

You can't talk to these people, you can't visit them, they have no churches except the Roman Catholic Cathedrals in Santiago and they cost you more than $13.50 per month to get the priest to pray your soul across the valley of Hades and Purgatory. No schools are in this western province, except one just established in San Luis by the U.S. What will you do but forget all you ever knew and become an ape or gorilla which some of us have come to favor.

To verify all that has been said in this letter, I will give you the proceedings of the last General Court Martial: One, Guilhame, private, sentenced 18 months hard labor and a forfeiture of all pay . . . confinement at the Santiago barracks; one Bridgett, private, 8 months and $10.00 per month, hard labor at the Santiago barracks; one Sergt. [William H.] Hill, twelve months hard labor, forfeit of all claims against the U.S., place of confinement, Santiago Barracks. Oh Lord, save these men from that eternal death, for they will never come out alive, and what were their charges? They got paid off, drank a little Cuban booze and hollered "Hurrah for the brave 8th Regt." They were bound, prodded with bayonets and kept in prison 31 days, then a one-sided trial came and this was the decision, as I have told you.

Write to Santiago to these men, to Sergt. Hill of Co. A, and you will know the horrible truth from his own pen. It has become a constant thing recently, and from the order of John R. Marshall our food is and has been one thing ever since we have been here and you know we must tire of bacon, beef, and beans, beans, beans.

The good Lord sent an Angel in the person of Capt. [John L.] Waller's wife, an American woman who made pies, and would bring them to our camp to sell to the men. No sooner did Marshall discover it than she was ordered from the camp of the

8th Regt., thus depriving the woman whose husband was the Minister to Madagascar, appointed under Harrison's administration and reappointed under Cleveland, when the French took him prisoner to Paris because of his popularity with the natives.[2] This little woman has been the loyal, true and honest wife for years undergoing many and many privations to help the man she loves, and who to her is that which no man can put asunder. This was her effort to help herself and help the boys by a morsel of good food, and the villian orders to fire if she insisted on coming each day. Now what do you think of that?

You can't buy a drink of whiskey, chew of tobacco, a stamp . . . in the camp limits but what that he (Marshall) gets a rake off from the Cubans for all they sell. This is as true as God is in Heaven.

The last act now in progress is a number of officers' wives are supposed to be on the way here to the paradise of the world, and these officers have taken another spell of grab fever. They have taken every tent not in actual use, every tent pole and piece of plank to fix up these women, when they should not be allowed in camp. The officers should rent houses down in San Luis and not rob the privates of the beef and other things. They are supposed to pay their own board and other expenses from their fat salaries.

Let the columns of your fearless paper herald these facts, until mothers, fathers, sisters and wives [will] not go to any more

[2] John L. Waller, born in 1850 in New Madrid, Mo., spent most of his adult life in Kansas where he became prominent in Republican politics. In 1891 President Benjamin Harrison appointed him consul to Madagascar. Relieved of his post in 1894, Waller remained for a time on the island to look after lands on which he had earlier acquired options. During the period following his tenure as consul he got into difficulties with the French authorities in Madagascar, presumably over his violation of the censorship regulations. Waller apparently insisted upon sending out letters describing the "horrors" of French rule on the island. He was arrested and ultimately sent to a prison in France. For the voluminous diplomatic correspondence on the Waller affair, see *Papers Relating to the Foreign Relations of the United States, 1895* (Washington: Government Printing Office, 1896), pp. 251–396.

benefits, for no benefit do we get from any entertainment given under the auxiliary, said to be working in our behalf.

We are yours for God, Truth and Humanity.

ONE HUNDRED PRIVATES

"Committee of One Hundred," Eighth Illinois Infantry, U.S.V., San Luis, no date; from Illinois Record, *January 21, 1899. The following letter, which was one in a series of communications that claimed to represent the views of a hundred privates in the Eighth Illinois, reviews the history of the regiment and indicts Colonel John R. Marshall as a rank opportunist and demagogue.*

Editor, The Record:

You are aware of the fact that Gov. Jno. R. Tanner commissioned the 8th Regt. (colored) with what he supposed was the right material for his inheritance to the seat of Senator when the seat of Hon. [Shelby] Cullom or [William] Mason would become vacant;[1] but "know ye" and all the state of Illinois that never was there a more abominable set of demagogues, with one or two exceptions, set at the head of human beings than those men in sheep's clothing commissioned at Springfield, August 12, 1898 by Gov. Tanner. I will give you what no one else has dared do for fear of summary or general court martial.

We, the 8th Regt., 1380 men strong, were ordered to break camp Aug. 7th, for Santiago de Cuba, to relieve the suffering and emaciated 1st Ill. Reg., Ill. Vols. who could no longer stay in that cess pool and fever climate.

The hostilities had only preliminarily ceased and our country

[1] When Governor John R. Tanner substituted Marshall for Buckner as commander of the Eighth Illinois Regiment, Buckner's allies charged that the governor was "playing politics" with the patriotism of black voters in an attempt to win their support for his forthcoming campaign for the United States Senate.

was to be satisfied in her claims or to resume her destruction of Spanish tyranny and misrule. We of one accord, with one heart, came to defend what? The Cubans? No! To defend a flag that does not defend us? No! To lay our lives as a sacrifice upon the altar of the malarious and slimy climate for the sake of being in the first colored regiment commissioned from Colonel down with Negro officers? No! But to break down that abominable assertion made by the Associated Press that the Negro would not fight, that he was a coward and did not deserve a place in the volunteers. We left our homes humble as they are, wives, mothers, sisters and friends, to say nothing of us who left life-time situations which we can never take up again, to help break down that infernal race prejudice and to have a page in history ascribed to us. That is what we came to this, the Hell-hole of the Island, for. We cared not for the Mauser bullets, cannister and grape shot. We feared not the treachery of . . . [the Spaniards] nor the traps or trenches of El Morro. It was a fearlessness inspired by those we love dearest of all on earth, to better their living and [to] secure equality and equity before the bar; social distinctions and civil rights from intrusion, lynch law, Jim Crow cars and a pure recognition of the ballot box.

You will not forget the first blunder made by the ignorant portion of this regiment when they made a charge upon you and would have done you bodily harm, because they were excited to wrath by the mouth and mouthpieces of him [Governor John R. Tanner] who gave them prestige as superiors.[2] You will in the near future see those who advised and assisted in that cowardly and dastardly act, hovering at your feet for mercy, for having

---

[2] Governor Tanner labeled as traitors those Negroes who said he "played politics" in selecting officers for the Eighth Illinois Regiment. In a speech to the black volunteers encamped at Springfield, on July 9, 1898, he specifically lashed out at the editor of the *Illinois Record,* James H. Porter, who was present in the audience. Excited by Tanner's remarks, the soldiers rushed toward Porter, who fled from the camp barely escaping bodily injury.

long since prayed to Almighty God to send death rather than be kept here.

I will give you an outline of the voyage from New York on the Yale.

The B[altimore] and O[hio] Railway landed us in Jersey City, Aug. 11th, '98 at 3:20 a.m. We were hurried over to New York where we were put aboard the Yale transport for Cuba. On that boat the indignities from that ship's crew together with that of our own officers was most abhorred and despicable. We were exposed to the hurricane deck of that boat and we laid our bodies down at night upon the nasty, filthy, wet deck to be aroused in the morning by the crew who came along with a fire hose . . . to do what they call scrub or "dog watch duty." Exposed as we were to the slush and spray of the rolling sea, the wet deck beneath our feet which soon became muddy because of our walking to and from one place to another to avoid the incessant and torrid rays of the sun, in our wet and damp clothes and denied the poor shelter or enclosure that we might have secured had it not been for an order, issued from the officers who were to lead in the battle, that none but commissioned or shoulder strap officers should pass beyond a certain point.

Our food was scarce and simply awful; we were, of course, on traveling rations and a shortage of that added to the kind it was . . . and supposed roast beef which is not only unsavory and unpalatable but ruinious to the linings of the stomach; a poison of nitric acid, fatal and poisonous to the system, that but few experienced and extraordinary physicians can eradicate. Such was our food for three days on the briny deep, for the sick and weak who were deathly ill at times, from the motion of the vessel. Finally, with persuasion and an enormous exchange of our traveling rations, the steward was induced to let us have some fresh beef which was . . . boiled so that the children of Hades could not have masticated it. At last Cape Maysi was sighted on

Sunday evening, August 15th, and one of our comrades was so elated at the sight of land that he threw overboard a five dollar bill he held within his grasp.

Monday we lay off Santiago near the shadow of Forte El Morro, not far from where [Richmond P.] Hobson sank the collier Merrimac. At noon we were launched in small boats and taken out in the bay to board vessels of smaller tonnage than the Yale to take us into Santiago, where, since the day of our landing we have been subjected to all kinds and sorts of indignities, exposure and ill treatment.

The much dreaded fever soon sailed in upon us and sad was the day and hour when this monster of human life places a firm grasp upon American white or black. To-day you are ill, tomorrow your sunken cheeks, thin hands, and weak system speak for you, that the bone yard will claim another victim and retire a soul from suffering.

The hospitals, both field and general, are taxed to their capacity and the medical treatment is what no one who has been there, can commend. This is the way you are examined: Well, Joe, what's the matter? Oh Dr. I'm so sick; Let's see your tongue and feel your pulse; Hump! Umph! Err'er Steward, give Joe 4 Q's and a little phenaecetine. Next! Bill. What ails you? Doctor, I've got a bad, sore leg. Let's see your tongue. Hump! Umph! Steward, give Bill six Q's and a little phenaecetine, and soon. Quinine may be good, but you ought to see those who are sick and have taken the Q's ordered them. One Brad Humphrey went crazy from the effect, and one J. D. Turner, now discharged, and by this time in Chicago, lost his hearing completely. Now since they have quit the use of these accursed Q's or quinine, things are a little better.

The food at the hospitals is horrible, although the great benefit was given at the 1st Regt. Armory at which our helpers and guardians and beneficiaries netted a snug sum of $1000.00 that we might have a morsel of good food, and who were so precise in the division of their earthly spoils they sent a courier here to see that we [would] get it. Yes, get what? The leavings of what the U.S. Commissary is bound to issue us and not one thing have we gotten in the way of . . . benefit, neither the sick nor the well, for this very morning at the Hospital de Militaire, breakfast consisted of dried saltpork of the saltiest kind and hard tack. Even the jellies, wafers and ginger ale sent by the Red Cross Society have been denied the sick in the place under Major [Allen A.] Wesley's care, and appropriated to the use of those in charge. Only one man can be looked upon as having an interest in the sick, and that one is Lieut. Gustavus A. Newells, who is now acting Asst. Adj. Genl., the highest honor yet given any colored officer of the 8th Reg. He is a man, a soldier and a gentleman, and the general public in Chicago, Springfield and other cities who have subscribed funds to help us, should take warning, and when those subscription lists are presented to them, not to subscribe one penny nor to assemble in the halls and trip the light fantastic toe and aid by their admission fee those who have and are now speculating on us here in the field awaiting the kind and almighty consideration of the 55th Congress of the U.S. to call us home. Better that the pulpit, press and influential individuals take up this matter, and with us, send a prayer to Jesus the Redeemer and Savior of Mankind to redeem us from the hands of tyrants and money changers, such as Christ drove out of the temple and such as we will drive out of existence when home again.[3]

The coal bins have been filled this winter from the money derived from speculation upon the 8th Ill., and demagogues are patting fat purses and drawing better salaries than ever before in

---

[3] The charge that funds raised by various Negro organizations for the men of the Eighth Illinois were siphoned off by the commissioned officers was the source of much controversy in the black community of Illinois.

their lives and playing Whist and sitting in the shade secluded from the torrid sun while the poor privates suffer indignities, court martials and even the taking away of sums, five, ten and twelve dollars, for missing roll call, which is frequently called when the mist and damp fog is so dense that the 1st. Sgt. can scarcely discern his roll paper.

Publish this on behalf of humanity and spread it broadcast in Chicago and elsewhere that some vigilant committee may see that these intrusions are righted and that those who have written such flowery letters home and have intercepted mails and deprived soldiers and privates of liberties due them from the code of laws governing the U.S. army may suffer as the persecutors of Sampson in the days of old, and may these political aspirants and debauchers who have even said to the Cubans, "We are the great Generals, Colonels and Captains and those are my slaves". . . [also suffer].

Now in my closing remarks to the general public I will say, we have suffered this long without benefit derived from the pretenders of charity in our name and scorn them. Be you not misled by them, but for God's and humanity's sake, appeal to Congress to get us home before the rainy season of '99 or else you will have no need to send us a benefit nor anything else but coffins that we may not have to be buried in the covering of our dog tents as was poor Saul Smith who was shot by a sentry.

These and other facts will be made public when we are home, for the penalty of this letter is . . . Leavenworth, Kansas for two years.

I will praise Major [John C.] Buckner . . . and others who were influential in raising that grand, ever memorable celebration to our honor, but everlasting torture to those who feasted upon our Xmas and Thanksgiving turkeys and warmed their chilled heels and toes by the coal bought with the money that was to have given us turkey, cranberry sauce and pie, yes pie, here in Cuba on these two occasions. You can tell all who ask you, we really had turkey cut out of a side of a hog and sauce from sugar cane for our Xmas dinner and Thanksgiving breakfast.

In the words of the Negro ditty: "Let us bring our clothes back home. If you have turkey just send us the bone. When you drink beer we will be satisfied with foam, if you'll let us bring our souls back home."

The Committee and Privates of One Hundred

George J. Beard, Eighth Illinois Infantry, U.S.V., San Luis, February 21, 1899; from Illinois Record, *March 11, 1899. Beard, a former employee in the office of the* Illinois Record, *notes one important source of the restlessness and discontent in the Eighth Illinois when he remarks, "We came here to fight and not to clear up ground for these Cubans."*

To Editor of *Illinois Record:*

We are still on the noted Island of the Southland and there is but one question in every man's mind and that is when are we to go home? The rank and file of this regiment is certainly tired of Cuba. I have been informed by good authority that there have been several meetings held in Cook County and other parts of the State of Illinois for the purpose of petitioning the War Department to retain us here until the weather gets warm in the States. Those good people may have the best interest of the 8th regiment at heart, but we prefer to return to the great State of Illinois and breathe that pure air once again as some contagious disease is liable to start here at most any old time and sweep us off the earth.

When we were in Camp Tanner [Springfield, Ill.] and the order came to go to Santiago de Cuba, and relieve the First [Illinois Infantry] that were suffering from the dreaded fevers and other diseases, peculiar to this climate, no one sent any petitions at that time to hold us in the States, and all who are afraid that the men will die if they come home during the cold weather will do the 8th Reg. a favor to just think and keep their thought to themselves.

The 19th of Feb. was the day we were to start for America, but we are still here and no one knows when we will start. We are faring as well as one could expect here in this climate; we could not meet a much more sudden change in being brought home in the dead of winter than we meet here every twenty four hours, for at the noon hour it is about 90 in the shade and very little shade to be found, and at night from 2 to 6 a.m. we have everything else but frost and it is cold enough for that at times. Some mornings about 6:30 they call it a fog here but I call it a young rain and about 8:30 the mist clears away and the sun appears; the mercury goes to its original stand, 90 in the shade. So you can see how utterly impossible it is for any of us to enjoy good health.

Everything is expensive here. It is almost impossible to get a paper of any kind . . . and the men are as eager to get a paper fifteen or twenty days old as you would be to get the fresh morning paper. We are entirely shut out from the outside world, only to be kept on this island longer than any other volunteer soldiers that came for the same cause that we came for. We are not tired of serving our country's cause, and if it was tomorrow or any other time we were ordered to the front line there would not be one that would shrink or weaken. We came here to fight and not to clear up ground for these Cubans, but came to make them free and avenge our country's wrong and give them a chance to do their own work. And now that we have assisted in accomplishing our aim we do not think it is fair that we should stay here, away from our families, homes and sweethearts and possibly catch these dreaded Cuban diseases, which will only wreck our bodies and impede our future happiness.

Private C. C. Early of G Company was shot in Santiago by a Cuban police during a quarrel.

Well, I must close, hoping by the time you receive this letter we will know when we are going to start for the States.

Respectfully yours,
Corporal Geo. J. Beard
Away Down in Cuba
Co. H. 8th Ill. Vol. Inf.

W. C. Warmsley, Ninth Infantry, U.S.V., San Luis, May 19, 1899; from The Bee (Washington), June 17, 1899. Warmsley, a black physician on duty with an "immune" regiment, extols the opportunities open to Negroes in Cuba.

Mr. G. W. Jackson
Washington, D.C.

Dear Friend Jackson:

I may visit the United States now and then, gaze once more upon the monument at Washington, again visit the Capitol Building and white house, converse with my many friends and acquaintances and again enjoy their proverbial hospitality, but to make the States my home, never!

I am seated in the office of an old Spanish hospital, alone, and where thousands of soldiers, Spanish and Americans, have no doubt died. You can see, therefore, that I have an excellent opportunity for study and reflection.

I am surrounded with palm and banana trees and beautiful landscape scenes on the edge of this small town of San Luis, with its population of 4000, nearly all of whom are anxious for me to leave the army and practice medicine here. Santiago is 20 miles from here. I visited there yesterday. Its population is about 50,000, the majority of whom are colored from a Cuban point of view. There is not a colored doctor here at present. In fact, I am the only colored physician on this end of the island, but I do not feel lonesome one iota.

I have quite a number of masonic brothers in Santiago who are quite loyal to me. One of the white physicians here (Santiago) is making from $6,000 to $8,000 per year. I am told that I could make more than this if I would quit the army and locate in Santiago.

The businessmen (colored) of Santiago say they would like to have one million colored men of education from the States. The colored here, unlike those in the states, are loyal to each other and honest to a fault. They will support a colored man in whatever business he undertakes.

We need doctors, lawyers, teachers and merchants. A small capital is needed to get one going in business. The Spanish language is easily learned. There is a gold mine here for a colored dentist. In order to practice medicine here one must become a member of the Academy of Surgeons.

Yes, the whites are prejudiced against the jet blacks; but prejudice, unlike the American article, is not so bitter.

I hope and trust that the educated colored men of America will come over here. Tell them not to fear the fever, but come. The opportunities for business ventures here are excellent. A doctor would make a fortune soon in any of the Cuban towns on this end of the island. The towns near and around Havana are too near America, but on this end the professional colored man would be idolized. I know from simple experience. One could get rich in Santiago teaching English.

I suppose you will not give up your "sure thing" to come, but do everything in your power to encourage intelligent young men of our race to come.

W. C. Warmsley
A.A. Surg., U.S.A.
Dept. of Santiago de Cuba

John E. Lewis, Tenth Cavalry, Manzanillo, Cuba, December 30, 1899; from Wisconsin Weekly Advocate *(Milwaukee), January 18, 1900. A black cavalryman on garrison duty in Cuba urges Negro Americans to emigrate to the island where their economic advancement will not be obstructed by "the color line."*

Editor
Wisconsin Weekly Advocate

Just before our departure for the States I will write you once more. I am very glad to state that the health of the regiment is good and it is with regret that I state that we will return to Texas. I did not care to return to the States until late spring, and [hoped] that we would be stationed [in the] North, but such is not our fate. I am tired of being in the South and receiving such treatment as we have generally received in the South, for that section I can pass by, and I am sorry to state, Mr. Editor, that our recruiting officers have not been as careful as they might have been, for the last recruits our regiment got since the war have not been up to the standard. Give us men who are an honor to the race. Such recruits . . . joined the regiment at Chickamauga Park, Georgia. No better boys ever shouldered a gun than those boys fresh from schools or factories of the South and East; and they proved their valor upon the battle field, for a good soldier is very obedient, no matter how harsh discipline is; and when they were discharged it was with regret that the older soldiers saw them go; but of course as long as everything remains as it is in H Troop [Tenth Cavalry], it will be hard to keep a good class of men. It takes months of hard training to make a soldier, not always abuse and to keep from them what is justly due a soldier —which I shall state more about in my next letter. The troops are expecting to leave here within the next three or four days and I am afraid that many will suffer from chills and fever as they did when they returned from Cuba in '98. Then it was summer. Give me Cuba rather than any section of the South that I have ever been in, and I hardly know of one Southern state that I have not been in. Here . . . a man is a man for what he is worth. The great Cuban, Gen. [Jesus] Rabbi[1] (a Negro), stopped over on his way from Bayamo to Havana, Cuba, and it was surprising how the Cubans turned out to do homage to that black Cuban general. It was the best of people who turned out. There was no color line drawn there. He is a noble looking man of about 40 years of age, 5 feet 9 inches high, weighs about 170 pounds, of a dark brown complexion; a goatee and mustache and of very pleasing manner. He it was who the Spaniards dreaded most next to Gen. [Antonio] Maceo and offered fifty thousand dollars for his head, dead or alive, and at one time it seemed as though our troops would have trouble with him; but it passed over. It was during the payment of the Cuban soldiers last July. General Rabbi did not want to give up his arms, but at last they came to an understanding and the Cubans delivered up a few arms, and there is no doubt that they have thousands of arms hidden out. Cuba, if everything remains at peace, should be the home of the colored man. Here you have everything to come for; it is not far from the States; and I am sure that if Bishop [Henry M.] Turner[2] and other prominent colored men should go to Cuba, they [Negro Americans] would go to Cuba, not far away to Africa. It does not require much work to farm, and it is just as healthy, with proper sanitary conditions, as America. This place was in a terribly filthy condition; no wonder people died of fever and other diseases so fast. Then Americans who came to the island eat too much of its fruit. It is impossible for them to eat

[1] Lewis is referring here to General Jesus Rabi, a black Cuban associated with the rebel leader, Calixto Garcia. General Frederick Funston described him as "one of the most striking men I have ever seen." Following the collapse of Spanish rule in Cuba, Rabi served for a time as a forest inspector in the civil government established by the United States.

[2] Henry M. Turner, senior bishop of the African Methodist Episcopal Church, was born of free parents in South Carolina, attended Trinity College in Baltimore, and served as a chaplain to a black regiment in the Union Army. By the 1890's he was the leading exponent of the back-to-Africa movement among black Americans.

this without having the fever, and the mango which is so tempting after being in the sun after falling from a tree twenty minutes, is about a sure case of yellow fever. Keep out of the rain as much as possible until you are acclimated. Your chances are just as good as the native for health. Mr. Editor, you find the colored man in all kinds of business and trade; all colors working together in the greatest harmony. I have heard a great deal against the Cubans, but could the American Negro say as much, and not submit as the American does, to about everything: and I only hope the time will come when they will call a halt and strike back; and if our general government don't protect you, protect yourself. There have been Americans who came to this island and tried to . . . draw the color line, but the Cubans would not submit to such treatment and cleaned up the place; and if they will only take lessons from the Cuban, America will then be the land of the brave and free and not until then. It is only a question of time when it will come, if the South is not more just to the American blacks. It is with regret that we are about to return to the States and to the South, but thank God my time is not long to remain [in service] and when I soldier again my regiment or troop will never be stationed in the South. I cannot risk all and receive no credit and [have] about all my rights taken from me because I am black.

.   .   .   .

My next letter will come from Texas. The boat has just arrived to take us back to dear old America after doing garrison duty for eight months. Everything is in readiness to leave and it is with regret, as I have stated before, to leave Cuba. So I will write you again just as soon as the opportunity presents itself. So I bid you good-bye.

Respectfully yours,
John E. Lewis
H Troop, Tenth Cavalry

FIGHTING IN THE PHILIPPINES

The [Filipinos] are hospitable to a fault, and they have too the full color sympathy, and appear to entertain a decided fondness for colored Americans, many of whom having come to Manila with the colored regiments, have married handsome Filipino belles.

CHAPLAIN THEOPHILUS G. STEWARD, 1901

I was struck by a question a little [Filipino] boy ask me, which ran about this way: "Why does the American Negro come . . . to fight us when we are much a friend to him and have not done anything to him. He is all the same as me and me all the same as you. Why don't you fight those people in America who burn Negroes, that make a beast of you. . . ?"

WILLIAM SIMMS, 1901

Our racial sympathies would naturally be with the Filipinos. They are fighting manfully for what they conceive to be their best interests. But we cannot for the sake of sentiment turn our back upon our own country.

COLORED AMERICAN, 1899

237

For several years prior to the arrival of Admiral George Dewey in Manila Bay in April, 1898, the Filipinos under the leadership of Emilio Aguinaldo had been rebelling against Spanish rule. At first the rebels hailed the American forces as deliverers from Spanish tyranny, but gradually they came to understand that the American promise of a free Cuba did not imply a free Philippine republic. On orders from President William McKinley and the War Department, American military forces in the Philippine Islands avoided any actions which might intimate recognition of rebel authority and Philippine independence, and in the treaty with Spain, signed in December, 1898, the islands were ceded to the United States. Determined to resist the new masters as vigorously as they had the Spaniards, Aguinaldo's forces resorted to war and early in 1899 launched what Americans termed the Filipino Insurrection. This bloody, brutal war proved more costly for the United States than the war with Spain.[1] The affair in the Philippines produced few heroes and little military glory. In fact, its moral and ideological costs were high. Atrocities and outrages perpetrated by American soldiers appeared embarrassingly reminiscent of the methods used by "Butcher" Weyler in Cuba which had so incensed the American people a few months earlier. The idea of employing military force against a people striving for independence proved especially troublesome for the American conscience.[2] But however troubled

[1] For a general account of American involvement in the Philippines, see Leon Wolff, *Little Brown Brother: How the United States Purchased and Pacified the Philippine Islands at the Century's Turn* (Garden City: Doubleday, 1961).

[2] On the anti-imperialist movement, see Fred W. Harrington, "The Anti-Imperialist Movement in the United States 1898–1900," *Mississippi Valley Historical Review,* 22 (September, 1935): 211–30.

this conscience may have been, the war against the Filipinos dragged on. The capture of Aguinaldo in 1901 finally broke the back of their resistance and by the end of the following year the United States had made good its claim to the islands.

From 1899 to 1902, approximately 70,000 American troops were used in the campaign to crush the Filipino rebellion. Among these were sizable contingents of black soldiers from all four regiments of the regular army and two full regiments of black volunteers recruited specifically for service in the Philippines. In mid-July, 1899, the first Negro troops—companies of the Twenty-fourth and Twenty-fifth Infantry—arrived in Manila; during the next two years other units of these regiments, as well as those of the Ninth and Tenth Cavalry, were dispatched to the islands.[3] In the fall of 1899, the War Department recruited two regiments of black volunteers, known as the Forty-eighth and Forty-ninth Infantry. In response to the clamor for black officers then echoing through the Negro community, the Department decided to select the company officers for these regiments either from black regulars who had distinguished themselves in Cuba or from Negro soldiers in state volunteer units with impressive service records. The Forty-eighth and Forty-ninth Infantry began arriving in the Philippines early in 1900 and remained there until the expiration of their commission a year and a half later.[4]

Distributed among army posts throughout the archipelago, the

[3] The activities of Negro regulars in the Philippines between 1899 and 1902 are chronicled in the Regimental Records of the 24th and 25th Infantry and 9th and 10th Cavalry, Record Group 94, National Archives; see also Rienzi B. Lemus, "The Enlisted Man in Action, or the Colored American Soldier in the Philippines," *Colored American Magazine,* 5 (May, 1902): 46–54; "Record of the 24th Infantry," *Manila Times,* June 29, 1902; information regarding both Negro regulars and volunteers in the Philippines appears throughout *Annual Reports of the Department of War, 1899–1900,* House Document 2, Parts 4–8, 56 Congress, 2 Session, and *Annual Reports of the Department of War, 1900–1901,* House Document 2, Parts 2–5, 57 Congress, 1 Session.

[4] *The Bee* (Washington), September 2, 9, 16, 23, 30, 1899; *Colored American* (Washington), September 16, 23, 1899; Regimental Records of the 48th and 49th Infantry, Record Group 94, National Archives.

black soldiers, both regulars and volunteers, participated in military operations from northern Luzon to Samar, five hundred miles to the south. Constantly on the move in pursuit of the elusive insurrectionists, they trekked across towering mountains, sweltering jungles, and balmy coastal plains, encountering along the way a variety of native inhabitants ranging from the Tagalogs to the dwarfish Negritos. Of the marches undertaken by Negro troops, none was more daring or spectacular than that by the men of the Twenty-fourth Infantry under Captain Joseph B. Batchelor, who walked from Cabanatuan to Tuguegarao.[5] The black soldiers rarely engaged the insurgents in full-fledged battles comparable to El Caney or San Juan Hill, because the war in the Philippines did not involve that type of combat. But the sniper fire and hit-and-run tactics of Aguinaldo's forces were just as deadly as the methods of more conventional warfare. This is not to say, of course, that black soldiers participated in no large-scale engagements, because the encounters with the insurgents at O'Donnell, Iba, Botolan, and various other points could scarcely be classified as minor affairs. Yet much of the service they rendered was the kind which "did not get noticed." It normally centered around activities such as "guarding the lines of communication, interior guard duty, scouting, escorting supplies, guarding work parties constructing works, and keeping the peace in captured towns and laying the foundations of civil government."[6]

When Negro troops first arrived in the Philippines, the natives viewed them with awe and fear, as an "American species of bete noir." A common reaction was: "These are not Americanos; they are Negritos." But quickly their fear turned into friendliness, and their awe into admiration. Filipinos came to accept the black American troops as "very much like ourselves, only larger," and

[5] This spectacular feat is described in William T. Sexton, *Soldiers in the Sun: An Adventure in Imperialism* (Harrisburg, Pa.: Military Service Publishing Co., 1939), pp. 215–19.

[6] *Manila Times,* June 29, 1902.

gave them the affectionate appellation, "Negritos Americanos." Most of the Negro soldiers reciprocated their good will and in many instances quickly established a bond of racial identity with their Filipino "cousins." It was generally agreed that in towns and districts "garrisoned by colored troops the natives seem to harbor little or no enmity toward the soldiers and the soldiers themselves seem contented with their lot and are not perpetually pining for home."[7]

The presence of black troops in the Philippines prompted widely disparate reactions among whites there. The *Manila Times,* a white journal consistently friendly toward black soldiers, claimed that they had "created a distinctly favorable impression" during their tour of duty in the islands, in spite of disparagement by those "who do not believe in enlisting colored men." The same newspaper also insisted that "in smartness of dress and general military appearance they have easily stood first among the regiments that have done garrison duty in Manila." In full agreement with this view, the city's chief of police especially commended the Twenty-fourth Infantry for its exemplary behavior, asserting that no regiment stationed in the vicinity gave the police so little trouble.[8]

Most white Americans in the Philippines did not echo such praises. Particularly disturbing to the whites were the close ties of friendship which developed between the "Negritos Americanos" and the Filipinos. "While the white soldiers, unfortunately, got on badly with the natives," the correspondent Stephen Bonsal reported, "the black soldiers got on much too well." White military

[7] Ibid.; see also the testimony of General Robert P. Hughes in *Hearings before the Committee on the Philippines of the United States Senate,* Senate Document 331, Part 1, 57 Congress, 1 Session, p. 647.

[8] *Manila Times,* November 17, 1899, January 17, July 15, 29, 1902; for a different assessment of Negro troops see John Foreman, "The Americans in the Philippines," *Contemporary Review,* 86 (September, 1904): 395; Archibald Coolidge, *The United States as a World Power* (New York: Macmillan, 1908), pp. 73–74.

personnel came to suspect that black soldiers had more sympathy for the Filipinos' aspirations of independence than for American policy regarding the islands. A few white officers complained that the racial identity established between the Negro soldiers and the natives had resulted in a color line which discriminated against whites.[9] Apparently William Howard Taft, the first civil governor of the Philippines, shared some of these concerns. He felt that the black troops "got along fairly well with the natives . . . too well with the native women" and the result was "a good deal of demoralization in the towns where they have been stationed."[10] It was Taft who was credited with engineering the withdrawal of Negro troops from the islands in 1902 "out of their regular turn."[11]

Though white troops feared and resented the rapport between their Negro comrades and the Filipinos, their overt expressions of racial prejudice did little other than strengthen that relationship. Writing about American forces in the Philippines in 1900, Frederick Palmer insisted that color was a crucial factor and that if a man was non-white, "we include him in a general class called 'nigger,' a class beneath our notice, to which, so far as our white soldier is concerned, all Filipinos belonged."[12] From first-hand observation in the islands, Major Cornelius Gardner of the Thirtieth Infantry lamented: "Almost without exception, soldiers and also many officers, refer to the natives in their presence as 'niggers' and the natives are beginning to understand what the word 'nigger' means."[13] The *Manila Times* became so agitated

[9] Stephen Bonsal, "The Negro Soldier in War and Peace," *North American Review,* 186 (June, 1907): 325.

[10] Quoted in Philip W. Kennedy, "The Concept of Racial Superiority and and United States Imperialism, 1890–1910" (Ph.D. dissertation, St. Louis University, 1962), p. 96.

[11] Bonsal, "The Negro Soldier in War and Peace," p. 326.

[12] Frederick Palmer, "White Man and Brown Man in the Philippines," *Scribner's Magazine,* 27 (January, 1900): 81.

[13] *Hearings before the Committee on the Philippines of the United States Senate,* Senate Document 331, Part 2, 57 Congress, 1 Session, p. 884.

over the mischief done by the widespread use of the term "nigger" in referring to black soldiers and Filipinos that it called upon Americans to banish the word from their vocabulary.[14] But as Negro troops could testify, no such banishment took place.

Throughout their tenure in the Philippines, Negro soldiers were subjected to insults and discriminatory treatment by their white comrades. The men of the Twenty-fifth Infantry had scarcely landed in 1899 when, as they marched into Manila, a white spectator yelled: "What are you coons doing here?"[15] White troops not only refused to salute black officers but also delighted in taunting Negro soldiers by singing, "All coons look alike to me" and "I don't like a nigger nohow." Although attempts to enforce the color line sometimes became incredibly complicated, such as in Manila's numerous brothels, black soldiers were barred from "white only" restaurants and barbershops which proliferated in the wake of American occupation of the islands.[16] Such treatment obviously enhanced the appeal of Aguinaldo's propaganda directed at the "colored American soldiers" and helps explain the relatively high rate of desertion among Negro regiments. Black soldiers who deserted to the insurgents not only received high-ranking military commissions, but more important, they also enjoyed the "supreme respect" of their "colored kinsmen."[17]

The following letters from Negro troops present a view of American military action in the Philippines substantially different from that provided by white observers. Their correspondence reveals a welter of ambivalent attitudes toward the Filipinos, themselves, their status, and their part in the effort to thwart

[14] *Manila Times*, November 17, 1899.

[15] Several Negro soldiers answered: "We have come to take up the White Man's Burden." Quoted in Mary Curtis, *The Black Soldier or the Colored Boys of the United States Army* (Washington: Murray Brothers, 1915), p. 41.

[16] *Manila Times*, August 26, 31, October 4, 1899, May 11, 1900.

[17] Bonsal, "Negro Soldiers in War and Peace," p. 326; *Manila Times*, July 9, October 15, 1901.

Aguinaldo's bid for Philippine independence. The letters of Negro soldiers clearly indicate that they appreciated the irony and contradiction inherent in their position as enemies of a "colored people" striving for freedom in distant Asiatic isles.

The idea of taking up the white man's burden in the Philippines elicited varied responses among black soldiers. At one extreme were those who shouldered the burden with a zeal worthy of the most fanatic proponent of Anglo-Saxonism. Their treatment of Filipinos often resembled that accorded Negroes in the United States by whites. At the other extreme were those black soldiers repelled by the idea of taking up the white man's burden against another "people of color" and thoroughly sympathetic to the Filipinos' demand for freedom. From this category came those who deserted to the insurgent cause. The majority of Negro troops shied away from either extreme and attempted to come to terms with what seemed to be contradictions in their role as defenders of white supremacy. Most Negro soldiers simply viewed their assignment in the Philippines as a duty expected of them as American citizens. The more introspective of them hoped that a creditable performance of that duty would help black people in the United States to achieve more of the fruits of first-class citizenship. Yet they never lost sight of the similarity between the predicament of the black man in America and the brown man in the Philippines. What troubled many of them was the idea that, by shouldering the white man's burden in the Philippines to prove their own loyalty and patriotism, they were put in the position of suppressing freedom for the Filipinos, with whom they had ideological and racial ties. This dilemma bred all kinds of ambivalence. Whatever the attitude assumed by black soldiers in the Philippines or however convoluted some of their rationalizations, according to one Negro editor, their individual perspectives were conditioned by "the wrongs we have suffered" in the past.

Rienzi B. Lemus, Twenty-fifth Infantry, La Lanio, Philippine Islands, September 22, 1899; from Richmond Planet, *November 4, 1899. Lemus reports on the activities of the first contingents of Negro troops to arrive in the Philippines.*

Dear Editor:

Doubtless my letter has hardly reached you yet, but since then I have been to the other companies and to the 24th [Infantry] and found out that all the boys were anxious for their people at home to hear from them; they are so busy they haven't time to write. . . . I went over to the 24th [Infantry] the other day and found quite a number of Richmonders. They were glad to see me, but very busy preparing for the movement soon to begin.

The other night our outpost challenged what was supposed to be an armed body of Filipinos approaching, but upon examination it was found out they were a scouting party, composed of Co. C and G, 24th Infantry. . . . We wouldn't allow them to go any further that night as they were cold, hungry and tired.

. . . I learned they had been out since 6 a.m. and had marched and made the ascent of the East Mountain range and from its summit had discovered a body of Filipinos drilling on extended order, such as used only in fighting. Upon descending and making for that point, the soldiers they had seen before were peaceful citizens planting rice, they having turned so upon the approach of our soldiers by concealing their arms in the dense underbrush.

.   .   .   .

Gen. [Arthur] MacArthur is still pushing his campaign with his usual vigor. During the past week he has been busy. Clearing rebels out of the territory already taken. The

Government and Gen. [Elwell] Otis are very lenient on the
people. Every day hundreds of people pass through the lines.

. . . .

A Corporal and a private of the 16th Infantry are sentenced to
be shot for robbery and assault on a sixty year old native woman.
He was caught in the act and tried by military court which
passed the above-mentioned verdict. Every time we get a paper
from there [United States], we read where some poor Negro is
lynched for supposed rape. In this case there was no Negro in
the vicinity to charge with the crime and the law has had its
course.

. . . .

Rienzi B. Lemus
Co. K. 25th Infantry

*M. W. Saddler, Twenty-fifth Infantry, Manila, Philippine Islands, ca.
September, 1899; from* The Freeman *(Indianapolis), November 18,
1899. Troubled by the prospect of fighting men of his "own hue and
color," Saddler provides a rationale for the Negro soldier in the Philippines by insisting that his primary aim is to augment his "standing among
American soldiers and add another star to the already brilliant crown of
the Afro-American soldier."*

[Sir:]
Nothing of a historical nature has been experienced since my
last letter. Everything is hustle and bustle; great preparations are
being made, and everything indicates a hard campaign in the
near future. Officers and enlisted men of my regiment are
undergoing rigid training, mentally and physically. Our greatest

aim is to maintain our standing among American soldiers and add another star to the already brilliant crown of the Afro-American soldier. I am not a correspondent by profession but am willing to keep my people informed in regards to our arduous Orient duties. We are now arrayed to meet what we consider a common foe, men of our own hue and color. Whether it is right to reduce these people to submission is not a question for the soldier to decide. Our oath of allegiance knows neither race, color nor nation, and if such a question should arise, it would be disposed of as one of a political nature by a soldier. There is one great desire among the colored soldiers now-a-days that did not exist probably a decade ago. That is to be represented in the file as well as the ranks. As the situation now stands, we moisten the soil with our precious blood, stain the colors with our oozing brains, only to make an already popular race more famous. Many of the intelligent heroes of the ranks would probably give their undivided attention to military training if there was an open avenue to a commission from the ranks and many inspired youths would cast their lot with us and display courage on the fields of battle. The Afro-Americans are represented in these islands by two thousand sable sons, as a Manila paper puts it "Greek against Greek" and in the usual old way we are here as an experiment. But experimenting with the colored soldiers has always added another laurel to support my assertion. I point with pride to the 54th Massachusetts, the regular army in the Indian campaigns, the 9th and 10th Cavalry and 24th Infantry at San Juan Hill, the 25th Infantry at El Caney and before Santiago. The latter regiment in which the writer had the honor to exercise military skill and face cannon balls. The honors of the campaign in the Philippines are to come. Military maneuvering and fighting between civilized colored men is not recorded in history. The results of black regiments against black regiments are not known. The coming campaign is indeed one of an experimental nature. The Filipinos, in my estimation, are far superior to the Cubans in every degree, though Spanish rule has made them treacherous, but they are trying to carry on a civilized warfare, and for an American to fall a captive to them does not mean present death as the case of the Spanish prisoners in the hands of the Cubans. I am thoroughly convinced that if these people are given home rule under American protection it will finally result in absolute independence.

M. W. Saddler
Serg't. Co. K, 25th Inf.

C. W. Cordin, Twenty-fifth Infantry, Manila, October 15, 1899; from The Gazette (*Cleveland*), *December 2, 1899. Cordin, formerly of the Seventh Volunteer Infantry (Immunes), describes a skirmish with the Filipino insurgents.*

Editor, *Gazette:*

Times are getting pretty warm around these diggings . . . as the rebels are trying to get to the water works where the Twenty-fourth are stationed, and also to Manila. The Twenty-fifth are stationed on the outskirts. The Twenty-fourth have had a couple of pretty warm scraps and some minor skirmishes. The Twenty-fifth had one or two little skirmishes at Caloocan and La Luma. One in particular, at La Luma, I want to describe . . . as I was on outpost at the time, about a half a mile from the company, doing picket duty. On October 9, a few moments after one o'clock p.m. we noticed a file of queer looking people coming out of the bamboo woods, and as about 200 Chinese coolies had been carrying bamboo from these woods to our lines, to build our supply road, we did not pay much attention to them as they were dressed just as the Chinese coolies are. All at once they threw out their skirmish line. As

the body of men did this another body to their left marched
out of the woods as skirmishers, and before we could send
word to the company, the insurgents opened the battle, and it
seemed as if every bullet came towards us two lonely men. In a
moment's notice we were down in our trenches that are near our
picket tent. We must work, and this is where our target
practice came into good play. We worked like demons. These
men came out and reinforced us, and for about an hour we kept
them from advancing. At the end of that time Company B came
out to our outpost on the left, volley firing. This made the
Filipinos sick and they soon scampered to the woods. We lost
ten men killed and one wounded. I don't know how many were
killed on the other side as they carry away their dead and
wounded. They have two men to one rifle. I am going to tell
you, friend Smith, there is lots of difference in looking a man in
the face when you are shaving him and looking him in the face
when he is throwing lead at you. The next day three companies
went out on skirmish looking for these people but could see
nothing of them, although we went ten miles south into the
interior. It is the prettiest country with fruits of all kinds in
abundance. These people never could be starved out, for nature
gives them a bountiful supply at all seasons of the year.

I had the pleasure of saluting and shaking hands with Major
John R. Lynch (the only Afro-American paymaster in the
volunteer or regular army) a few days ago in Manila. He is well
and enjoyed his trip here very much. The Filipinos in Manila
are rapidly becoming Americanized in a great many ways.
They are now wearing shoes and stockings. Manila is beautiful
and full of interest. . . .

.   .   .   .

As far as I can note from casual observance, I should class the
Filipinos with the Cubans. They are intelligent and industrious,
and although some of their habits are unclean, their clothes are

always spotless and neat. They are eager to learn American
ways and customs, and even [if] they don't understand, would
rather have one speak English to them as they think they can
learn quicker that way. They are friendly and hospitable. . . .
There are here some of the best mulatto people I have ever
seen in my life. They are handsome. It is common for the
women to wear their hair hanging down, and when they pass
anyone on the street, they have to take hold of it and get it out
of the way of the passerby as the American ladies do their
dresses. The ladies wear no hats. A good deal of the business
is done by the Filipinos but the major part is done by the
Chinese. The United States has lots of trouble catching the wily
Cheno. He is prone to steal and smuggle. We caught two the
other day and fined one $700 and other $500 in gold. I guess
this will help to break it up. Well, I hope my friends enjoy
this letter. I will write more next time. I understand we will be
here about ten years. The volunteer regulars, of course, will
have a chance to get away. When the war is over, I shall make
trip to Hong Kong if nothing happens.

C. W. Cordin
Co. B, 25th Infantry
U.S. Army

*John W. Galloway, Twenty-fourth Infantry, San Isidro, Philippine
Islands, November 16, 1899; from* Richmond Planet, *December 30,
1899. Galloway's record of conversations with Filipinos reveals the extent to which an "affinity of complexion" existed between them and the
Negro American soldiers stationed in the islands.*

Dear Mr. Editor:

We received the copies of the *Planet* sent to us at this point.
You can imagine how much we appreciated them when we had

not seen a paper of any kind for weeks, and as for an Afro-American paper, I can not remember when I last laid eyes on one. The address of Mr. [Booker T.] Washington is the talk of the camp. Since coming here the boys' bosoms have expanded greatly. Their ideas have indeed broadened. They all say in chorus that Mr. Washington's ideas are destined to revolutionize America educationally, and as to the Negro, we feel the depth of his advice and feel the path of action outlined by him is the only practical one for colored youth.

Since dropping you a few lines from El Deposito, we have been constantly on the jump. First, at San Fernando, then Mexico, Santa Anna, Prayal Cabial, San Isidro. Advantage was taken of these "hikes" to study the Filipino and the Filipino question from the point that follows.

The whites have begun to establish their diabolical race hatred in all its home rancor in Manila, even endeavoring to propagate the phobia among the Spaniards and Filipinos so as to be sure of the foundation of their supremacy when the civil rule that must necessarily follow the present military regime, is established.

I felt it worth the while to probe the Filipino as to his knowledge and view of the American colored man that we might know our position intelligently. What follows is a condensed account of the results. The questions were put to the intelligent, well-educated Filipinos so you may know the opinions are those of the sort who represent the feelings of the race, and may be taken as solid.

Ques. Do the Filipinos hold a different feeling toward the colored American from that of the white?

Ans. "Before American occupation of the islands and before the colored troops came to the Philippines, Filipinos knew little if anything of the colored people of America. We had read American history in the general, but knew nothing of the different races there. All were simply Americans to us. This view

was held up to the time of the arrival of the colored regiments
in Manila, when the white troops, seeing your acceptance on a
social plane by the Filipino and Spaniard was equal to, if not
better than theirs, (for you know under Spanish rule we never
knew there was a difference between men on account of racial
identity. Our differences were political.) began to tell us of the
inferiority of the American blacks—of your brutal natures, your
cannibal tendencies—how you would rape our senioritas, etc. Of
course, at first we were a little shy of you, after being told of
the difference between you and them; but we studied you, as
results have shown. Between you and him, we look upon you
as the angel and him as the devil.

Of course, you both are Americans, and conditions between
us are constrained, and neither can be our friends in the
sense of friendship, but the affinity of complexion between you
and me tells, and you exercise your duty so much more kindly
and manly in dealing with us. We can not help but appreciate
the differences between you and the whites."

Interview of Senor Tordorica Santos, a Filipino physician. By
the difference in "dealing with us" expressed is meant that the
colored soldiers do not push them off the streets, spit at
them, call them damned "niggers," abuse them in all manner
of ways, and connect race hatred with duty, for the colored
soldier has none such for them.

The future of the Filipino, I fear, is that of the Negro in the
South. Matters are almost to that condition in Manila now.
No one (white) has any scruples as regards respecting the
rights of a Filipino. He is kicked and cuffed at will and he dare
not remonstrate. On to another interview.

Ques. How would the Filipinos view immigration to any extent
of American colored people to their country? How about
conditions between them, living side by side?

Ans. "Of what I have seen of American colored people, as
exemplified in their soldiers, I am very much impressed with

them. This in the light of present conditions, when they have little opportunity to show themselves to us in a social way . . . is very encouraging.

"I have very little knowledge of what the American government will do with us in case they elect to hold us as a colony. I have heard that all confiscated lands will be opened for American colonization under some homestead law . . . but I had not counted the effect it would have upon us. . . . We are accustomed to look upon American relations on any basis, other than that of Filipino independence, as inimical to us. But since American sovereignty is inevitable and American colonization is a probability, I unreservedly believe that all my people would look very kindly upon your people as neighbors. What we are resisting is effacement. Contact with whites to any extent in whatever way we accept them means that to us. The colored people, being of like complexion to our own, the evolution that would come to us through contact would not be so radical, can be viewed in an entirely different light from contact with white people. In your country you are used to moulding all nations and races of white men into one— white Americans—that forms an example of what I mean. The same condition would obtain between you and my people, they would become good Filipinos.

"I wish you would say to your young men that we want occidental ideas but we want them taught to us by colored people. In the reconstruction of our country new ideas will obtain. In American political and industrial ideas we will be infants. We ask your educated, practical men to come and teach us them. We have a beautiful country and a hospitable people to repay them for their trouble. Our country needs development. Unless an unselfish people come to our assistance we are doomed." Interview of Senor Tomas Consunji, a wealthy Filipino planter.

I wish to add, before closing, that . . . our young men who

are practical scientific agriculturists, architects . . . engineers, business men, professors and students of the sciences and who know how to establish and manage banks, mercantile businesses, large plantations, sugar growing, developing and refining . . . will find this the most inviting fold under the American flag. Cuba does not compare with the Philippines. Another thing, too, when they secure missionaries and teachers for the schools here, see that they get on the list. They must be represented here. White men have told them we are savages. We need to be in evidence to convince the Filipinos of our status. I do all in my power to picture ourselves to them in a good light, but positions of influence among them is what will tell. They extend to us a welcome hand, full of opportunities. Will we accept it?

Yours truly,
John W. Galloway
Sgt. Major,
24th U.S. Infantry

C. W. Cordin, Twenty-fifth Infantry, Manila, November 18, 1899; from The Gazette (Cleveland), February 3, 1900. Cordin comments on the life of black soldiers in the Philippines and on their relations with the native inhabitants of the islands.

Editor, *Gazette*

It is with the greatest pleasure that I now write you. I am in good shape at this writing. Campaigning is very hard work here, as we have to put up with being thoroughly drenched most of the time. We have been making trips in the country every day for a few weeks but have seen nothing so far. The volunteers have come and relieved us. We have been to San Fernando and Engiles and Sattoliav. This is a fine country in the interior.

Fruits are abundant. As we go further in we find distress general. As the rebels leave they destroy everything they have time to destroy. The First Battalion is now at San Fernando and the Second is on the "hike." The volunteers were quite amusing when they came to relieve us. They thought some of us were natives. On hearing this, three of us went over to visit them the next morning, and the first tent we came to, there were eight or nine men in the tent, and one man was standing outside. He asked us some questions and we answered "meo no entaends." He looked at us with a funny expression on his face, and went around the tent. Then, some fellows from the inside yelled, "Say, what in the h—— is the matter? They've got us surrounded haven't they?" That was too much for us and we had to laugh. After they found out we were from the Twenty-fifth they invited us in and made it very pleasant for us. Much is said of the Filipino, pro and con. I have observed them carefully . . . associated with them, and have some very warm friends among them. I can say this much, they are immensely "human." They have peculiar traits and customs. They are ridiculed by many newspapers and globe trotters, simply for lowering them in the eyes of the world. As they understand the American just so rapidly do they become more friendly. I have attended several parties and I was made to feel perfectly at home. There is one trouble and that is in conversation. I like to talk Spanish so that I can add to my store. But they want to talk American for the same reason. These people are industrious and thrifty, and delight in wearing clothes spotless and white, patent-leather shoes, and fine skirts with foil on the inside of pants. Then he is dressed up. There is much of interest to be seen here. . . . I wish you a merry christmas. I am yours,

C. W. Cordin
Co. B, 25th Inf.

Patrick Mason, Twenty-fourth Infantry, Corregidor, Philippine Islands, November 19, 1899; from The Gazette *(Cleveland), September 29, 1900. Mason's brief letter reveals the ideological difficulties of a black American soldier in the Philippines for the purpose of taking up the "white man's burden."*

Editor, Gazette.

Dear Sir:

I have not had any fighting to do since I have been here and don't care to do any. I feel sorry for these people and all that have come under the control of the United States. I don't believe they will be justly dealt by. The first thing in the morning is the "Nigger" and the last thing at night is the "Nigger." You have no idea the way these people are treated by the Americans here. I know their feeling toward them [Filipinos], as they speak their opinion in my presence thinking I am white. I love to hear them [white Americans] talk that I may know how they feel. The poor whites don't believe that anyone has any right to live but the white American, or to enjoy any rights or privileges that the white man enjoys. I must stop. You are right in your opinions.[1] I must not say much as I am a soldier. The natives are a patient, burden-bearing people.

Patrick Mason
Sgt., Co. I, 24th Infantry

[1] In its editorials, the Cleveland *Gazette* took a strong stand against American annexation of the Philippines and suggested that under American rule the Filipinos would receive the same treatment accorded Negroes in the United States.

P. C. Pogue, Twenty-fifth Infantry, Bamban, Philippine Islands, November 24, 1899; from The Gazette *(Cleveland), February 3, 1900. In the course of relating the feat performed by the Negro soldiers at Fort O'Donnell, Pogue mentions the placards which Filipino insurgents addressed to black soldiers. Such placards, in appealing to color, attempted to win the support of Negro troops for Aguinaldo's fight for Philippine independence.*

Editor
Cleveland *Gazette*

[Dear Sir:]

It has been some time since I wrote you, and at this writing I send the details of the second engagement of the Twenty-fifth Infantry. The banner capture so far on the isle of Luzon was made on the morning of November 18 by three companies, E, H, and K, of the Twenty-fifth infantry. Although little attention is paid to it by the white soldier I am determined that the friends and relatives of the Negro soldier shall know of it. Capt. [H. A.] Leonhauser, acting major, with three companies made a night march from Bamban, 25 miles to Fort O'Donnell, surrounded the place and captured the entire rebel garrison, consisting of seven officers, 200 men, 345 rifles, 10,000 rounds of ammunition, four tons of supplies, a large quantity of documents relating to the movements of the rebel forces. One Filipino [was] killed. No loss of Americans.

The pamphlet or placard, I gave you an account of in my last letter . . . was written by Aguinaldo himself. Col. Bell of the Thirty-fourth Volunteers[1] captured several hundred copies of them in Mabalacat.[2] They were packed in bundles of 100 each, and were addressed to the Twenty-fourth Infantry

---

[1] The Colonel Bell mentioned here obviously refers to Colonel J. Franklin Bell of the Thirty-sixth U.S. Volunteer Infantry.

[2] One of the placards addressed "To the Colored American Soldier" stated: "It is without honor that you are spilling your costly blood. Your masters have

(colored), our brother regiment. The proclamations were burned except a few which were kept as souvenirs. Colored Americans are just as loyal to the old flag as white Americans and it will always be so. Nothing can be heard from the Twenty-fourth Infantry, but reports are that they are having very bad luck. Hoping that it is not so, I will close, sending you enclosed a copy of "Aggie's" [Aguinaldo's] pamphlet. I remain yours,

P. C. Pogue
Co. K, 25th Inf.

C. W. Cordin, Twenty-fifth Infantry, Manila, January 7, 1900; from The Gazette *(Cleveland), March 17, 1900. Cordin gives an account of several engagements between the black regulars and the Filipino insurgents.*

Editor, *Gazette:*

On the fourth inst. a scouting party from Co. B. was sent out to reconnoiter the foothills. The enemy being located, the party returned and reported their find. Enough rations were drawn for two days and extra ammunition, and at seven o'clock on the morning of the 5th, B and L Companies and a detachment from Companies E and K with Capt. Linhauser [*sic*][1] in command were on their way to Thonge, the enemy's stronghold. We followed a good sandy road for about four

thrown you into the most iniquitous fight with double purpose—to make you the instrument of their ambition and also your hard work will soon make the extinction of your race. Your friends, the Filipinos, give you this good warning. You must consider your situation and your history, and take charge that the blood of . . . Sam Hose [a Negro lynched in Newnan, Georgia, in 1899] . . . proclaims vengeance." Quoted in *Richmond Planet,* November 11, 1899.

[1] The name of Captain H. A. Leonhauser, Company K, Twenty-fifth Infantry, was often misspelled, even in official communications.

miles and arrived at a sugar mill and were ordered to rest until
daybreak. When that hour arrived, the march was then resumed
in single file across a rice field about one mile, then we arrived at
the thick underbrush of which the foot hills abound in plenty. We
kept the trail despite many obstacles and difficulties. Underbrush
had been filled on either side and as we desired to get through
and make as little noise as possible, we had to be very careful. On
we went in single file and silently under the guidance of Capt.
Linhauser, Lieutenant Merlin,[2] Co. B, Lieutenant Schenk,[3] Co. L,
and a detachment from H, T and M Companies. But a surprise was
to come and it did. Never did bullets rain thicker and faster . . .
our officers and men not only stood the fire from the right,
front and left of us, but charged a hill 250 feet high, thick
with prickly briars and underbrush. To walk up was an
impossibility. We crawled on one hand and knees with the gun
in the other hand. How we got up that hill so quick under heavy
fire . . . I can never tell. Too much praise cannot be given
our gallant officers who led the charge and the men who
followed. I must not forget that Lieutenant Merlin, Co. B, was
the officer to discover the insurgents' hangout the preceding
day with his scouts. When we got up on the hill, the insurgents
had gone, took to their heels and left their breakfast. I was
the seventh man on the hill. I have already told you the height
of the hill. Its top is about five acres in extent. After charging and
running them away from their stronghold, we did hasten back.
Geo. Washington of Co. B, 25th Infantry, died the next day.
Five American prisoners, captured in September [1899] were
held here, and when the first round was fired into their outpost,
these American soldiers, without trial, without friend, without
chance to pray even, were made to get down on their knees and a

[2] The reference here to a Lieutenant Merlin is obviously incorrect. The officer
was undoubtedly Lieutenant Carl A. Martin.

[3] The name of Lieutenant William T. Schenck is another instance in which mis-
spelling was frequent.

volley was fired into them. One fell over dead. The rest were surrounded. One tried to run away but was wounded. The soldiers took turns carrying the stretchers. After the wounded were cared for, the march home was commenced. The rear guard set fire to all the buildings of the insurgents' camp. The next day the wounded were sent to Manila under escort. Two of the prisoners were yet alive.

On the morning of the 7th, about 1 o'clock while all were peaceably asleep and dreaming of home . . . a fierce raid was made on Motalokie[4] by the insurgents. There was only one company there, which was L Co., 25th, and a small detachment that had gone there . . . with rations. The outpost immediately drew in and notified the company that the enemy was coming and firing. L Co. laid low to give them a warm reception. They came. After getting pretty well in town they began cheering at the top of their voices as they thought the Americans had vamoosed. When within a few hundred yards of the Americans a deadly fire was opened upon them, and soon they were scampering in all directions. Not an American was hurt. Two dead Filipinos were found, and a good many hats, some of them full of holes and some of them full of hair and blood. It is not known how many men were killed, as no matter how badly pressed they are they seem to carry away their dead and wounded. We left San Pedro, on the 11th, for Angeles, where we stayed three days, coming to Manila and embarking for Subig where we now are. Right in the mountains, cocoanuts and bananas are plentiful here. The boys are having lots of fun climbing the trees and knocking off

[4] Like a few other place names used in these letters, that of Motalokie does not appear in *A Pronouncing Gazetteer and Geographical Dictionary of the Philippine Islands* (Washington: Government Printing Office, 1902), which has been used to identify military stations and Filipino towns. Rather than speculate upon whether the correspondents committed errors in spelling or actually encountered villages by the names they used, the editor has retained the spelling of place names as they appeared in the letters.

green coconuts and drinking the milk which is excellent. Boating and bathing are the chief pastimes. Scouts went out yesterday and when least thinking about the enemy were fired on from intrenchments. The boys immediately fell to the ground and went to work, and in a few minutes, had put the devils on the run. One company from the 46th Volunteers came across a band of insurgents and had a scrap, getting two men wounded. The insurgents are supposed to be pretty thick here. The general health is good. We are getting plenty to eat and getting along very nicely. In one of my letters I see you made a mistake saying ten men were killed. It is not so. Please correct it. One man died from heart trouble and had been in the service for twenty-seven years.

Yours respectfully,
C. W. Cordin

Theophilus G. Steward, Twenty-fifth Infantry, Manila, January 19, 1900; from The Gazette *(Cleveland), April 21, 1900. Even more interesting, perhaps, than Chaplain Steward's observations on Filipino labor is his description of rounding up "a few white soldiers for disrespect."*

[Dear Sir:]

On leaving Wilberforce (University) for my long journey westward into the east, I could not realize the work before me. . . . It is difficult to think of myself nine thousand miles or more from home; and meeting people frequently who have come here by way of New York. . . . As I look upon this rich island of Luzon and see it teeming with life and industry, I am impressed with the idea of the curse of labor. . . . Here is the place in all the world to see people work. Labor, labor is the curse of the

Orient. Asking a girl who toils all day in a cigarette factory making one thousand paper plagues, how much she was paid for the day's work, her answer was "una peseta," equivalent to ten cents in our money and yet the people of Manila are better paid, and are living better now than ever before. . . .

. . . .

The condition of the laboring man is simply horrible. This morning I went out to Paranaque for the purpose of meeting my son, Captain [Frank R.] Steward, but when I got to the head-quarters of his regiment, I learned that he had left an hour earlier to go out on a three day's march with his company. He has two lieutenants and about one hundred men in his company, he being commanding officer of the expedition. Some time ago both Captain Steward and Captain [Emmanuel D.] Bass passed the night at my temporary headquarters in Manila. Captain [Edward L.] Baker of L. Company, commands the post in the little town not far from here, and is making for himself a fine record. The regiment is a good one and the men are strong and healthy. The colored soldiers are making for themselves a fine reputation among the Filipinos, and no one has a disrespectful word to say of them except some renegade American. I have found it necessary to round up a few white soldiers for disrespect since I have been here. In every case I have succeeded in bringing them to terms in the shortest sort of order. I was coming away from a hospital one Sunday and the corps man failed to salute me. I turned and followed him to the office and said to the steward: "Who has charge here?" He arose, and saluting promptly, replied, "Major Keefer, sir." "I want to see that young man," said I. "Call him." He did so, and the man came up and saluted as humbly as need be. I gave him a word of instruction, and that cured everybody around the hospital. The other day three volunteers riding in a hack (Forty-third volunteers) passed me as I was riding in the other way and indulged in some vile cursing at my expense. They did not know me as well as they thought they did. I ordered my driver to turn and follow them, and soon overtaking them, I ordered their driver sternly to halt, a command which he obeyed instantly. I then got out of my carriage and read them a lecture, they denying they had said anything disrespectful and begging me to let them pass on. I subsequently reported the affair to their colonel, not desiring any action to be taken as I had not sufficient proof; but it helped them. So, I have found it necessary to be a little exacting and have tightened up the reins around me a little. We have a Christian Endeavor Society in Manila. I was out to my regiment a few days ago. They have just made another move, coming down from the interior by the railroad and spending a few hours in Manila and then leaving by boat for Subig on the West coast north of Subig Bay. I am expecting soon to be with them permanently.

Chaplain T. G. Steward
Twenty-fifth Infantry

Michael H. Robinson, Jr., Twenty-fifth Infantry, Iba, Philippine Islands, ca. February 1, 1900; from The Colored American *(Washington), March 17, 24, 1900. In the following letter, which was published in two installments in this Negro newspaper, a black infantryman describes several encounters between his regiment and the Filipino insurgents.*

[Dear Sir:]

I will attempt to give a correct account concerning the movements of that part of the 25th Infantry now in the Philippines. The regiment had accomplished nothing of special note, until after our arrival at Bamban, Nov. 15th, since then we have had a very interesting time indeed. The most important features of the regimental campaign being: the capture of

O'Donnell Nov. 8th, Iba Dec. 9th, Botolan Dec. 8th, Fort
Camansi Jan. 5th and the defense of Iba Jan. 6th.

On the morning of Nov. 16th, an insurgent Captain approached
No. 2 outpost bearing a white flag and he made [the] Corporal
in charge understand that he desired to surrender. After having
been taken before Col. [A. S.] Burt, who treated him with all
respect due his rank, he consented to lead the command into
O'Donnell where he claimed was a force of nearly three hundred
insurgents. The 2nd battalion was ordered to prepare to start for
the insurgent garrison. They left Bamban, that is the 2nd
battalion did, marched all night and until 3 a.m. the next
morning, went into camp near a bamboo village . . . rested a
few hours, and moved on, about 3½ miles further. Here the
Insurgent Captain gave the information that we were near the
insurgent outpost. We surprised and captured [the] outpost
without firing a shot. . . . No one was injured on either side.
Our capture consisted of 150 prisoners . . . 200 Remington and
Mauser rifles, 10,000 rounds of ammunition, 50 ponies, 20 bull
carts and hulls, a great quantity of rice and sugar. Destroyed a
reloading outfit, after which the battalion started on the return
march. The Manila papers spoke of the capture of O'Donnell as
nearly equalling Washington's surprise of the Hessians at Trenton.

Our commanding officer was ordered . . . to send the 1st
battalion from Bamban to several towns of importance on the
coast of the China Sea, a distance of 75 miles overland.
Accordingly we left Bamban Dec. 3rd., 10:45 a.m. After four
days of difficult marching over a very precipitous range of
mountains known as the Zambales, we arrived before Botolan on
the afternoon of Dec. 8th. . . . We began the advance upon
the dawn. Nothing occurred until within 900 yards of their line;
at this point they poured volley after volley in our direction but
without effect. We continued the advance . . . [and] the
insurgents began to falter. We began our advance now by rushes,
that is a part kneeling to fire while the others advance under the

cover of the same successively. When about 200 yards it was
noticed the firing on their side was growing weaker each moment.
"To the charge" was sounded . . . and . . . we dashed
through bamboo fences and Botolan was ours. Insurgent loss
was 19 killed and wounded. Not a man was injured in our
command. Captured a large number of prisoners, and
antiquated smooth bore muzzle-loading guns, a number of rifles,
bolos, bows and arrows. The garrison strength of this town was
said to be 700 men. Company F under Lieut. H. C. Clark,
marched through town and to the sea, about 1½ miles distant,
being the first company to view the same.

After a rest, we started the next morning Dec. 9th about
4:00 o'clock, toward Iba, about 3 miles distant, marched within
easy reach of the above town, and were in trenches on either
side of a bamboo bridge to protect the advance of scouts and
Company M, who were to form the firing line proper. . . .
Just at the first peep of dawn the insurrectos opened up on the
scouts and Company M, and things were lively for quite a while.
The rear companies were now ordered to cross the bridge. As
we moved towards town, the firing could be heard only at
intervals and in a few moments ceased altogether. The insurgents
could now be seen retreating in every direction, leaving 14
dead and wounded. The capture consisted of 8 insurgents;
liberated 15 Spanish prisoners who had been held by the rebels.
. . . Company F left town about 11:30 a.m., after having cooked
breakfast and returned to Botolan, where they remained until
joined by the rest of the battalion, Dec. 11, 6 a.m.

The entire command immediately started for Subig, a distance
of 32 miles, principally along the coast. After having passed
through 17 barrios or small towns, we arrived in Subig, December
12, at 7 o'clock p.m. Remaining here a few days, we returned to
Botolan, December 20th, were relieved the following morning by
M Company and sent to garrison Iba.

On the morning of January 6th, 1900, Iba was attacked by

800 bolo and 600 rifle-men, making a grand total of 1400. The insurgents surrounded the town, leaving the road leading to the ocean open, giving us a chance to retreat, but we, however, being strongly positioned cared not for the opportunity. One of our outposts was cut off and were compelled to hide in the grass until after night. Five o'clock sharp they began firing from all sides; we were quartered in church, jail and warehouse, forming a triangle. They attacked the scouts in the warehouse but were repulsed again and again. Those who were in the rear of the jail gave yell after yell and their trumpeter blowed the charge, but instead of the charge being made at this point, those who were about 400 yards south of this position charged the church expecting to catch us unawares, but were driven back quickly. The firing kept steadily on until daybreak and when it became light we could see insurgents on all sides like bees; the officers could be seen trying to urge their men on but they seemed to falter under the deadly fire of the Krags. . . . At this juncture in the engagement Captain O'Neil[1] took a squad of F Company to see if he could drive them back far enough to allow the scouts to come out of the warehouse. When outside these men fired a volley in the air and charged; as they did so, the scouts took advantage of the momentary stampede among the insurrectos and rushed out. Now all hands got out in the open and things began to resemble a slaughter pen, bolo men armed with long knives being encouraged by their officers, tried to stand, but were shot down; but finally those who could took to their heels, carrying and dragging many of their dead with them. . . . In the road in the rear of the scouts' quarters where the final charge was made, men were piled one upon another, dead and wounded. It was an awful sight, one not easily forgotten, but it was fight or die with us, for things were exceedingly desperate for awhile.

Our commanding officer remarked after the fight, concerning

[1] Joseph P. O'Neil was a white captain in the Twenty-fifth Infantry.

the coolness of the men, saying it surpassed anything he had
ever seen of its kind. Not a man shirked his duty and acted as if
at target practice, firing carefully and accurately . . . and even
making comical remarks concerning the appearance of the
insurgents. . . . I am exceedingly thankful that I can say not a
man was injured on our side. . . . These boys feel that they have
avenged the cowardly murder of our friend and comrade,
William Shepard, who was murdered several days previous to
the fight, while bathing, by ten bolo men. We received this
information from a Cheno spy employed by our command.

I could say much concerning the capture of Fort Camansi
but fearing to consume too much . . . space . . . I will only
say that it was a very difficult and perilous undertaking. We lost
one corporal and a private was badly wounded, and the insurgent
loss was 12 killed and wounded; and before leaving the hill
all of the houses were burned.

In conclusion I will say that we of the 25th Infantry feel
rather discouraged over the fact that the sacrifice of life and
health has to be made for a cause so unpopular among our
people. Yet the fact that we are American soldiers instills within us
the feeling and resolve to perform our duty, no matter what the
consequence may be as to public sentiment. Those who are
thoughtful do not attempt to discuss the "why" concerning the
enlisted man. We have been warned several times by insurgent
leaders in the shape of placards, some being placed on trees,
others left mysteriously in houses we have occupied, saying to
the colored soldier that while he is contending on the field of
battle against people who are struggling for recognition and
freedom, your people in America are being lynched and
disfranchised by the same who are trying to compel us to believe
that their government will deal justly and fairly by us.

Hoping that you find space in your valuable paper for a
portion at least, of this article. Though the attempt be but a

feeble one, I trust it may serve . . . to convey the meaning
intended. I am

Yours obediently
Michael H. Robinson, Jr.
Co. F, 25th Infantry

*F. H. Crumbley, Forty-ninth Infantry, U.S.V., Zapata Bridge, Luzon,
Philippine Islands, February 7, 1900; from* Savannah Tribune, *March
7, 1900. Captain Crumbley, a black volunteer officer whose previous
military experience included service in the Georgia militia and the regular army, expresses his enthusiasm for the Philippines and for the Filipinos, who were "very friendly to the Negro soldiers." Crumbley urges
black Americans not to delay in making preparations to emigrate to the
islands.*

[Sir:]

The gallant 49th Infantry arrived at Manila on January 2nd,
and after a few days camp in the city was ordered out on the
firing line where we have been kept constantly on the alert
expecting and scouting the country looking for the rebel forces
which are nowhere to be found.

A few robber bands supposed to be the fragments of the
disbanded army are reported to us now and then and companies
and detachments go out daily from the different points occupied
by our regiment and sometimes encounter them. Several have
been killed and a dozen captured.

The troops enjoy excellent health and are anxious for active
service. The affairs of the island from a military standpoint, a
time of an insurrection, is held well in hand by the Governor
General and the lines are well guarded.

On January 7th quite a victory was won by our forces, south

of our camps, killing many, capturing quite a few with but slight injury to the army of occupation.

The Americans should, and would if they but knew the extent of the value of these islands, feel a great pride in our national acquisition. It is a mistaken idea many have that it is a burden to us; ere long when they shall know better, when peace has been declared and the commercial machinery of the islands is put into operation again, improved by American skill, the people of the country will raise their voices in praise and thanksgiving to the Congress and Cabinet of the United States for having adjudicated so wisely the Spanish-American War in liberating millions of people of Cuba, Porto Rico and the Philippines.

This is a beautiful country. The province of Manila has an area of 264 square miles with a population of over 400,000. The city by the same name is the Capitol of the Philippine Archipelago, and has a population of 155,000. It was founded in 1571; it is a well fortified city. . . . All around the city are a number of forts and block houses of Spanish design. In every direction one turns are seen great Catholic Church buildings with four to six bells in each steeple which ring out daily. . . . The streets are very narrow and the center of the city is as busy as any of your prominent streets in business sections. The postal service is being established by General [Elwell S.] Otis, but in the maritime provinces . . . the arrivals and departures are uncertain. . . .

To the south [of Cavite] about two miles is the region known as Tierra Alta. Here are many villas, being a splendid place for foreigners to recuperate. The natives in this district are perfectly friendly and anxious for a restoration of order. Gen. Otis has established the courts and is giving every encouragement to the natives. His efforts along this line are highly appreciated by the educated classes who have implicit confidence in the ability and purposes of our government to give them protection of life and property and emancipation from the heavy taxes imposed by church and state under Spanish rule. It is only the ignorant and robber classes that the rebels have as followers and they are rapidly disbanding.

It is perfectly safe to state . . . that the Commanding General has the situation here fully in hand and is rapidly restoring order among a people who have been in a state of rebellion the past sixty years. He is fully entitled to the confidence and respect of all Americans.

No man is a competent judge of the conditions here unless he has been here and studied the situation, and not even then, when he is overly jealous and influenced by selfish and mercenary forces. The natives are very friendly to the Negro soldiers, and since it will soon be the purpose of the churches and Christian agencies to send missionaries to this island, the young colored men and women of Christian education who desire to labor among an appreciative people ought to be selected to come as missionaries with spelling book and Bible; they should not wait till the field is covered by others but should come in the front ranks and assist in developing these people. Then, too, there are every openings here for the Negro in business, and room for thousands of them.

The A.M.E. Church, the A.M.A., the M.E. Church and the State Baptists would do well to send young men and women here as soon as possible.

F. H. Crumbley
Captain, 49th Infantry
U.S.V.

W. H. Cox, Jr., Forty-eighth Infantry, U.S.V., Manila, February 14, 1900; from Richmond Planet, *April 14, 1900. In the following letter, Cox expresses pride in the reputation acquired by a black volunteer regiment recruited specifically for service in the Philippines.*

Editor:

The 48th Infantry, U.S.V. arrived here safe on Feb. 4th, 1900 after a thirty-seven day trip across the great Pacific Ocean and China Sea, with only six men in the hospital. We disembarked the next morning and marched directly to La Loma church . . . and separated into companies, each independently upon the firing line, where the 10th Pennsylvania and the 20th Kansas regiments had such a fierce battle with the insurgents, and where Brigadier General [Frederick] Funston won such a noble reputation for himself and the 20th Kansas Regiment.

Since we have been stationed here we have made only a very few captures. But still we are very proud of them.

Well, I must say that our regiment (the 48th) is bearing the name of being the finest disciplined regiment on the island and our Commander (Col. W. P. Duvall) has the honor of bearing the name of the most gentlemanly officer that is stationed here and when we go out anywhere, we are looked upon as members of the Regulars.

And another record that the 48th has broken (and thank God that a Negro regiment under Negro officers has that honor applied to them) it was the first regiment of a foreign country that has ever paraded the streets of Yokohama, Japan[1] under arms, and the first chorus of Negro singers which has ever appeared in that city. We have a chorus of 500 singers, composed of members of the said regiment that has made for themselves

[1] The transport which took the Forty-eighth Infantry, U.S.V., to the Philippines put in port at Yokohama, Japan.

a reputation that will live in the minds of the people of Yokohama
and Nagasaki, Japan, and Manila, P.I.

. . . .

W. H. Cox, Jr.
Sergeant, Co. I
48th Inf., U.S.V.

*S. T. Evans, Twenty-fourth Infantry, San Nicolos, Philippine Islands,
March 30, 1900; from* The Recorder *(Indianapolis), May 19, 1900. In
the following letter to a friend, Corporal Evans tells of his experiences
on the firing line in the Philippines.*

Mr. Bonus Temple
Indianapolis, Ind.

Friend B. Temple:

Your letter of December was received some time ago and found
me in good health, but I have been sick quite a good deal since
I have been on this island. Temple, words cannot tell you the
hardships I have been through since we have been here. I have
been in nine battles and have escaped injury in all of them, but
it is no telling how long it will be before one of those
Remington bullets [finds] its way into me; but I am living in
hopes that I will return to the States just as I was when I left.
Temple, the first fight I was in I was not on to the way the
Philipinos did their shooting, but it did not take me long to catch
on to them. They just stick their heads up and fire away,
without taking any aim at all; whenever they hit anyone it is
haphazard. I have got so used to hearing Remingtons whiz by
my head that they don't excite me a bit. On the 7th of
December we laid under one of the heaviest fires for three hours

that any man was ever under, and we never had but five men
wounded. They were in their entrenchments and let us get within
200 yards of them before they opened fire on us. We were
marching in columns of four at the time when they raised right
up out of their trenches and poured a volley into us. We had
no more shelter than is on your parlor floor. We deployed and
fired at them, making them keep their heads down while some of
us crawled up close to the river bank, where the most were
entrenched and poured volley after volley into them, but our
work was not very effective because we were too low down.
We were on the river bank and they were so well entrenched
that they knew we could not get at them, so we had to swim the
river to flank them. There were eight of us, and [when] we made the
charge on them you should have seen them. We killed fourteen of
them outright and wounded thirty more. The Sunday before,
December 3rd, up in the mountains, they opened up on us at
about one thousand yards. It just gave us time to get right.
H Company went to the right and we flanked them; we killed
nine of them that day and wounded quite a number. I heard old
soldiers say they never saw young soldiers lay up to the firing line
like the recruits in H Company in all their lives. I wish you
could see us when we are going to have a fight. Temple, how is
it that you did not get a commission in the volunteers. I was
looking for you all the time but you did not show up.

Corp. S. T. Evans,
Company H, 24th Inf.

T. H. Wiseman, Twenty-fifth Infantry, Castillejos, Philippine Islands, April 13, 1900; from The Freeman *(Indianapolis), June 23, 1900. A black infantryman whose unit had been engaged in building telegraph lines reports on the health and activities of Negro soldiers stationed in a mountain district.*

Sir:

Things are about as quiet as could be expected here. We are still occupying Castillejos. Nothing of importance has occurred. Our telegraph line continues a success and it is now complete to Manila. We are having lots of sickness among our troops, mostly chills and fever. One example of how despondent this state of affairs renders our boys is Corporal Reefus Scott of Co. K, 25th Inf. on the 1st of March. He had been feeling very badly for some time and on this day, worse than usual. A detachment of Co. K went to Subig, 5 miles [away], to draw rations. While there, Corporal Scott decided that he could get better treatment in Manila, so he stayed behind when the detachment left. Taking a native . . . canoe he started alone for Balanga, en route to Manila, there being no boat at Subig. While on his way out about 20 miles from Subig, he was attacked by natives in boats and after firing three times his boat overturned resulting in his capture. The natives carried him ashore a prisoner, and took him near Balanga, a city of considerable size, forty miles from Manila on Manila Bay. After a day or two they began to trust him around almost alone. Taking advantage of the carelessness of his captors, he one day made his escape arriving within our lines on the 18th day of March, where some of our boys saw and talked to him. He was received by the 32nd Vol. regiment, not much the worse for the adventure. Our medical treat[ment] is not just what it should be. We are now in the hills and it is very inconvenient for sick men, yet we have lost very few considering what we have to undergo. A scouting party from Co. K. went into the hills, acting on information received by the

officers, from natives where there was supposed to be a company
of insurgents. They arrived there only to find 15 men on
outpost, the main body having just left. Our party was
rewarded by recapturing an American who had been held
prisoner by the insurgents. . . . Our Colonel visited all
companies several days ago. The 25th Inft., 8 companies, is now
garrisoning ten towns. We are scattered all the way from Subig
to Santa Cruz. This leaves very small detachments in some
towns, our rations being forwarded from one town to another.
Our duty is hard but it is done cheerfully. We all look forward
with dread to the swift coming rainy season which means mud
and mosquitoes. Well, we are fully acquainted with these posts,
the natives for the most part having ceased fighting, until they
gather their crops. When this is completed, out on the war path
they come in all their blue paint, then instead of the peace and
quiet which now reign, it will be much combat.

                                    T. H. Wiseman
                                    Co. K, 25th Infantry

*Edward Brown, Twenty-fourth Infantry, Cranglen, Philippine Islands,
April 14, 1900; from* The Recorder (*Indianapolis*), *June 9, 1900.
Brown notes the habits and customs of the Negritos which distinguished
them from other inhabitants of the Philippines.*

Dear Friend:

I received your letter and those papers and was glad you sent
them. Those were the first papers I have seen since I have been
here. A newspaper from the States is worth 25 cents over here. We
are up here in the mountains, where you can hear or see nothing
but wild Caribous, deer and ponies. We eat both the deer and
Caribous, but not the ponies; we haven't come to eating horse
flesh yet. This is a fine little place. The people up here are different

from the other natives. They are called Negritos. They don't
wear any clothes but a gee-string and are strung from head to
foot with brass band. They don't understand anything. They
carry a knife called a bolo, and are a very mean people. They
live on rice and dried fish. They are ruled by a president. They
never stay in their huts at night, but go into the mountains,
returning about 4 o'clock in the morning. They make fine cigars.
You can get about fifty for four clackers, which equals one cent
in our money. The government has about 400 working the
road between here and San Jose and pay them $1 a week and
their chow-chow; and they eat every hour. The soldiers are all
doing well. They would have better health if they would let that
beno alone. It is a drink that the Filipinos make. Poco Tempo.
Tell my friends that I am just the same as a Filipino.

Ed. Brown
24th Infantry

*Arthur E. Peterson, Forty-eighth Infantry, U.S.V., Sanopan, Philippine
Islands, May 3, 1900; from* The Colored Citizen *(Topeka), November
9, 1900. Corporal Peterson, on patrol duty three hundred miles from
Manila, reveals in the following letter much about the nature of the war
being waged in the Philippines and expresses admiration for the people
known as Igorrotes.*

[Dear Mother:]

My company is stationed at this place some three hundred odd
miles from Manila; in fact, the whole regiment is somewhere in
the vicinity. We are right in the heart of the mountains, and
we have to patrol all over them every day, day after day, climbing
mountains. Now, mountain climbing is not what it's cracked up
to be, even under favorable conditions, but when it comes to
climbing out here, where someone is shooting at you from behind

a tree, or a stone, it is a mess. And, of course, the sun is boiling hot and to make things worse I am on guard every other night; that is I only get about three nights' sleep a week. And even those three cannot be termed sleep, because someone will fire a shot during the night and then there will be no more sleep for me that night. But even so we manage to get along all right and keep good health. My health is excellent but we have a few sick men in the company. They are suffering from dysentery. That is the disease that does more toward killing men than the enemies' bullets do and I am taking care not to get it. I am very particular about what I eat and drink and that is the main thing.

The inhabitants of these mountains are called Igorrotes. They are only semi-civilized and wear no clothes, only a gee-string. The women wear a little apron about three inches square in front and, of course, they are a sight. But of all that, they are the most moral people I ever saw. Our civilized brethren and sisters in the states could learn something in that line. They eat everything. One of our pack mules died last night and this morning they were skinning and eating it. They eat dogs and anything else that they can get, so you see what kind of subjects they are. Some of them are nice looking. They are light brown, with coal black straight hair.

They raise a great amount of tobacco and every[one] smokes, women, children and men, all have a cigar in their mouth from morning till night. They also raise cotton and sugar cane in great quantities. They are something like our North American Indian. The women do most [of] the work. The men lie around and smoke. They build their houses and make most everything out of bamboo. They have no tools, but a knife—a great, big, heavy, unhandy thing called a bolo, but they can use it to perfection. Just think of building the shacks without a single nail in the whole business. It is truly wonderful.

When we were coming up here marching in the hot sun, each

man carrying seventy-five pounds of baggage, not counting gun and ammunition, there were two companies of us, about two hundred men. On the second day we struck a pretty hot pace and went thirteen miles without a rest or halt. The men just fell out like bees, and when we did stop, I believe there were 48 or 50 men left standing, and they are men too; if they were not, they never would have been in the army. When you see, 150 big, strapping young fellows fall out like that you can imagine how it was. I did not fall out. In fact, I did not feel very much fatigued. I could have gone further.

.   .   .   .

Arthur E. Peterson
Corporal, 48th Regiment

[*Unsigned*], *Negro soldier in the Philippine Islands, no date; from* Wisconsin Weekly Advocate (*Milwaukee*), *May 17, 1900. A black soldier, probably belonging to the Twenty-fourth or Twenty-fifth Infantry, insists that the abuse of Filipinos by white American troops is the cause of the insurrection.*

Editor, New York Age

I have mingled freely with the natives and have had talks with American colored men here in business and who have lived here for years, in order to learn of them the cause of their (Filipino) dissatisfaction and the reason for this insurrection, and I must confess they have a just grievance. All this never would have occurred if the army of occupation would have treated them as people. The Spaniards, even if their laws were hard, were polite and treated them with some consideration; but the Americans, as soon as they saw that the native troops were desirous of sharing in the glories as well as the hardships of the hard-won battles with the Americans, began to apply home treatment for colored peoples: cursed them as damned niggers, steal [from] and ravish them, rob them on the street of their small change, take from the fruit vendors whatever suited their fancy, and kick the poor unfortunate if he complained, desecrate their church property, and after fighting began, looted everything in sight, burning, robbing the graves.

This may seem a little tall—but I have seen with my own eyes carcasses lying bare in the boiling sun, the results of raids on receptacles for the dead in search of diamonds. The [white] troops, thinking we would be proud to emulate their conduct, have made bold of telling their exploits to us. One fellow, member of the 13th Minnesota, told me how some fellows he knew had cut off a native woman's arm in order to get a fine inlaid bracelet. On upbraiding some fellows one morning, whom I met while out for a walk (I think they belong to a Nebraska or Minnesota regiment, and they were stationed on the Malabon road) for the conduct of the American troops toward the natives and especially as to raiding, etc., the reply was: "Do you think we could stay over here and fight these damn niggers without making it pay all it's worth? The government only pays us $13 per month: that's starvation wages. White men can't stand it." Meaning they could not live on such small pay. In saying this they never dreamed that Negro soldiers would never countenance such conduct. They talked with impunity of "niggers" to our soldiers, never once thinking that they were talking to home "niggers" and should they be brought to remember that at home this is the same vile epithet they hurl at us, they beg pardon and make some effiminate excuse about what the Filipino is called.

I want to say right here that if it were not for the sake of the 10,000,000 black people in the United States, God alone knows on which side of the subject I would be. And for the sake of the black men who carry arms and pioneer for them as their representatives, ask them to not forget the present administration at the next election. Party be damned! We don't want these islands, not in the way we are to get them, and for Heaven's sake, put the party [Democratic] in power that pledged itself against this highway robbery. Expansion is too clean a name for it.

[Unsigned]

Walter E. Merchant, Forty-eighth Infantry, U.S.V., San Fernando de la Union, Philippine Islands, June 12, 1900; from Richmond Planet, *July 28, 1900. Merchant praises the "brilliant work" of the Forty-eighth Infantry, whose black officers were "stamping the lie to rumors that the Negro makes poor officers."*

Sir:

Allow me space in your valuable paper to say a few words about the 48th Infantry, U.S.V. (colored) that is doing such brilliant work in the Philippines. I must say brilliant work, for when regular army officers day after day, send out circulars congratulating colored officers of the volunteer service, that is enough to tell the world that somebody is doing noble work. For it is well known that the white officers . . . are deadly opposed to Negro men wearing the bars. It matters not how soon the war will end (of course after the war is over the commissions will be taken from the noble blacks as was done after the close of the Spanish-American War) the Negro captains and lieutenants of the 48th are by their bravery and daring vindicating the race and stamping the lie to those rumors that the Negro makes poor officers and for Negroes to accomplish anything in battle must be commanded by white officers.

The men of our regiments are proud of our black officers and will follow them where ever they lead.

. . . .

Every battle that the 48th Infantry has been engaged in they have come out victorious. Not one defeat is credited against them. Although they have been here on the northern line for 6 or 8 weeks, they have made some of the most important captures since the [beginning of] Philippine rebellion.

One of the most popular officers is Capt. James W. Smith of Xenia, Ohio, commanding Company D. Every command that has been given him since we have been in the enemy's country has been an important one. He has just returned from Sodipan, a small town among the mountains and the hotbed of insurgents, and at times he was left to guard the place and stores with only about 35 men, but he performed his duty well and brought back every man he carried there. He is ably assisted by 1st Lieut. J. H. Anderson . . . and 2nd Lieut. G. W. Taylor. . . . Lieut. Anderson is now Provost Marshal of this town.

. . . .

> Very truly yours,
> Corp'l. Walter E. Merchant
> Co. D, 48th Inf., U.S.V.

William H. Cox, Jr., Forty-eighth Infantry, U.S.V., La Trinidad, Philippine Islands, September 3, 1900; from Richmond Planet, *October 20, 1900. Cox reports the death of several comrades and in connection with the death of one, William Smith, delivers a moralistic lecture on the wages of sin.*

Hon. John Mitchell, Jr.

My dear sir:

Allow me a small space in one of your columns . . . to publish the following concerning the 48th Regiment from the

26th day of January, 1900, until the present time. Her work and
her victory.

Since this regiment has been out upon the firing line [it] has
for itself made a very fine reputation of which I must say that
the men as well as the officers will long remember in the future. It
has lost less men out of the regiment in action than any other
company of any other regiment, regular or volunteer, that are
on these islands.

I very much regret that I have to make known to the public a
number of men who are among the deceased. . . . Company H
lost 13 enlisted men who died from small pox and . . . typhoid
fever. Company K lost 11 enlisted men. . . . Company E lost
1 Corporal who was shot through the abdomen in an
engagement at Arringi. Company D lost 1 enlisted man. . . .
Many deaths were caused by being overcome by heat. Company
I lost 2 enlisted men. One died in Santa Mesa Hospital and the
other, Private Wm. Smith, died August 31, 1900, from Broncho
Pneumonia.

Smith was a man who lived a life of rottenness and dissipation.
He died in the Post Hospital. Acting Hospital Steward, George
Matthews, while undressing him after the Doctor . . . had
pronounced him dead, removed from his pockets a set of
dice and a deck of cards which were his idols until he died.
Two days before his death, he was excused from the hospital
and given permission to visit the barracks. . . . His idea was
to gamble and win some more money before pay-day which will
be sometime very soon. His remains were deposited in the
earth in a rough, undressed wooden box made by the Filipino
carpenter without any covering or lining.

. . . .

Our rations are getting very short and we don't know what
time the pack mules will be able to get here again with any
more rations, for the rainy season has set in, and it lasts . . .

90 days before it stops. It has been raining now 20 days and
there is little prospects of it clearing away.

I must stop now for I have to mount the guard every morning.
. . . I will try and write you more in a few days.

Hoping this may find space in your paper, I remain very
respectfully yours, sir

> Sergt. Wm. H. Cox, Jr.
> Co. I, 48th Infantry, U.S.V.

James Booker, Twenty-fifth Infantry, Masinloc, Philippine Islands, Sep-
tember 18, 1900; from Richmond Planet, *December 22, 1900. Booker*
reviews the activities of his outfit since its arrival in the Philippines in
July, 1899, and boasts that the insurgents have "never once had the
nerve to stand their ground when they were charged upon by the dusky
fighters." He also denies that American soldiers have committed depre-
dations upon the Filipinos.

Sir:

I have the honor to address you as to the present situation in
the Philippines. Two battalions of the 25th Infantry, colored,
arrived in Manila Bay on July 31st, 1899. . . . Since our landing
on the Island of Luzon we have executed some of as hard
and effective work as any other regiment in the Philippines,
also made some of the important captures of the campaign. . . .

We have participated in many warm engagements, losing
comparatively few men killed or wounded owing to the good
management of our officers, non-commissioned officers and men.

Wherever we have been stationed on the islands we have
made friends with the natives and they always express regret
when we are ordered from amongst them, especially if we have
been stationed near them for any length of time.

Our officers and men always make it a rule wherever we

are stationed to treat the natives with civility and we have always complied with this rule. We do considerable trading with the natives, always paying them for what we get. . . .

We treat them with due consideration, insurgent prisoners as well as peaceable natives; but whenever they show fight, they are greeted with a warm reception and they soon learn to their discontent what kind of fighting material, the seemingly peaceable black fighters of Uncle Sam's regular army are made out of.

We have been stationed in Zambales Province longer than in any other one place on the Island. We were the first U.S. soldiers to enter the province where we were met with strong resistance, but the Filipinos never once had the nerve to stand their ground when they were charged upon by the dusky fighters. They never have once scored a victory over the 25th Infantry. We had lots of trouble with the Insurgents during our first few months' stay in this province and had to recapture many of the towns we now occupy.

At one time we only garrisoned Subig, Botolan, Iba, and Santa Cruz; but we now garrison every town between Subig and Santa Cruz, a distance of 90 miles covering all of our territory, and I don't think it is any other two battalions covering the same territory on the Island. Before we split our company into detachments and commenced to garrison all towns between our immediate stations, we were frequently attacked by overwhelming forces which were mobilized in the towns unoccupied by Americans; but never once did they seem to have given up all hopes and since we have been garrisoning these towns with small detachments we have had very little trouble with them. The most trouble we have had lately is with the roaming bands of Ladrones (robbers).

We haven't a company in any one place along our route, except Iba, 25th Infantry Headquarters. The towns range from 8 to 10 miles apart, many less. We have not had any trouble with the natives in our territory for several months. We have killed, captured or forced to surrender the majority of the leaders in this province. Those who have not been dealt with . . . have sought other fields for operation. . . .

It is hard for them to mobilize any fighting force in this province or no where on the island can they carry any plan into execution without being intercepted by the Americans. The 25th Infantry has been stationed in the towns which we now occupy long enough to know hombres [who] belong to certain localities. Each detachment makes 2 or 3 trips per week so in that manner we get acquainted with the country and the people.

Whenever a strange hombre enters a town he is generally arrested and questioned. Sometimes he proves to be a deserter from the insurgent forces, sometimes a spy, and more generally coming in to surrender. Many insurgents are coming in daily under the Amnesty Proclamation issued by Gen. [Arthur] MacArthur, and if they continue to come in at the rate they have been it won't be long before the insurrection will be a thing of the past. Even now, 6 or 8 soldiers can penetrate the most secluded recesses of this island without fear of molestation. The robber bands are our greatest trouble. Many of them yet infest the island.

All the towns in our province have native policemen, in fact, I guess they are all over the island. They have proven to be of very valuable service to the Americans. They are always on the alert for any straggling insurgent or Ladrone. The better class of Filipinos are sick of the insurrection and are willing to help the Americans put it down. Some of Aguinaldo's leading followers have left him in his hopeless cause. This province is much quieter than a great many localities of the United States. According to newspaper reports, it took more troops to quell the riot at New Orleans,[1] La. than it did to put down the insurrection in Zambales Province.

[1] In July, 1900, a bloody race riot occurred in New Orleans. Robert Charles, a Negro who figured prominently in the disturbance, was hunted down and killed.

We were jubilant over the prospects of going to China a few weeks ago, but . . . our wise Excellency, the President, has restored peace, which he always does whenever his good and wise judgment is called into play. The 25th would like to have had China added to her list, but we will be contented with our past accomplishments; but whenever duty calls us we will not be weighed and found wanting. Our courage has won us fame; our moral principles and kindness have won us friends; our good workmanship and how to deal with the enemy have won us fear; our good discipline has won us praise from our superiors.

We have one of the finest Colonels in the U.S. Army. He is beloved and held in high esteem by all who are under him. We regret to think that soon he will depart from us, owing to him reaching the required age of retirement.

.   .   .   .

I have read a good many accounts, by discharged volunteers and regulars through the American newspapers, of depredations committed upon Filipinos by our men in the field, which reports are false. . . . The prisoners as well as the peaceable [natives] are treated with great consideration. Our officers take great pride in protecting [the natives]. . . .

If a person were to search the roots of these reports they could easily see where they originate. Some men came into the army for pleasure and some for adventure, but when they enlist and are presented their field equipment and commence camp life, their expectation of feather mattresses . . . ham and eggs, quail on toast and other such delicacies are not realized, they commence to cry to go home; they generally turn [out] to be chronic kickers and newspaper correspondents.

It seems as if they expect to campaign in a Pullman Palace Car. The American Army is better off without such men. . . . They should all be corralled up and fed on beeftea and chicken broth until they can be given back to their parents. . . .

Our doctors exercise the greatest precaution against contagious diseases and they see that a strict sanitary law is observed by soldiers as well as natives. All of the 25th are quartered in good barracks. Duty has been reduced 50 per cent and everything is going on in harmony.

I hope to write you again soon. Co. H as well as myself extend to you our best wishes for the success of your paper and the betterment of the condition of the Southern Negro. I remain

Respectfully yours
James Booker
Co. H, 25th Infantry.

P.S. I am a Virginian, [and] was born in Farmville, Va.; enlisted in Richmond, Va., March 11th, 1897; was discharged March 10th, 1900; re-enlisted March 11th, 1900, at Masinloc, P.I. and have been serving with Co. II. ever since I have been in the service. My experiences have been many in and out of the States.

Preston Moore, Twenty-fourth Infantry, Manicling, Philippine Islands, October 22, 1900; from The Freeman *(Indianapolis), January 5, 1901. A black infantryman who claims to have walked over 400 miles in the island of Luzon maintains that the Filipinos are "half-civilized" and characterizes the work of the American army as essentially "bush whacking and skirmishing."*

Editor, Freeman:

I beg space in your columns to say a few things of the Philippines to the many friends in the states. I am a soldier, sergeant in Co. C, 24th U.S. Infantry; sailed from San Francisco, Cal., June 22nd, 1899; arrived in Manila, P.I., July 24th, 1899. Receiving orders at once to move to the front, General [S. B. M.]

Young in command; taken station of Caloocan, P.I. The
country was flooded with water. We were in station for a short
time, then moved on driving the enemy in front, arriving at
Arzat on Oct. 13. Finding the enemy strongly entrenched we
had a hard fight. After the fight, we planted the Stars and Stripes.
The town is ours. There has been fighting ever since. The war
has been declared over, but bush whacking and skirmishing is
the work of the American soldiers. This might be called the
bloody field, from daily skirmishing. We could sweep the island
over and cease all fighting but the Americans do not molest or
destroy the commonwealth of the natives; take prisoners and
turn them loose, even on the battlefield. The natives have never
stopped their schools. In nearly every town there is one or two
schools in session. In this town I know of two rice bins
containing 11,000 bushels of rice; immense quantities of it are
in the town. The American has never oppressed the Philippino to
my knowledge; everything is free to the native, yet he fights.
With few exceptions the Filipinos are half civilized; their
education is very limited. In some of the large coast cities the
Filipinos go half naked; having a cloth tied about their body to
hide their shame, and all the rest exposed. They live chiefly on
rice, fish, sugar and fruits, and seem to enjoy life. All we see
of science tells of the past, that is of the Spaniards. The Filipinos
don't have any houses, they build shacks made of bamboo and
covered with grass. They sleep on the floor and cover with the
roof. They have no bedsteads or bedding, no knives . . .
they cook in dirt pots and use cocoanut shells for spoons. . . . .
Catholic religion prevails over the island. The church houses tell
of Spanish teaching and training, and are excellent buildings in
some towns. The cities on the sea coast, where all nationalities
are represented are fine, and have all kinds of modern geniuses
and sciences. One going to Manila would say it is a fine
country; so it is, but the people are not fine. Go into the interior
and you will see just what there is in the Filipino stronghold. I

have walked over 400 miles of the island, waded rivers, climbed mountains, and seen and know Luzon island. It is a very productive island and beautiful, and the United States need not be ashamed of it for its products are rich and rare.

We had hard fights July 4th, Sept. 13th and was attacked on the 15th. On Oct. 14th 6 men were killed and missing. I will write more next time.

> Yours truly,
> Preston Moore
> Sergt., U.S. Army

William H. Logan, Ninth Cavalry, Nueva Caceres, Philippine Islands, December 25, 1900; from Savannah Tribune, *February 16, 1901. A black cavalryman who was apparently among the American troops sent to China during the Boxer Rebellion, writes on a variety of topics including his Christmas dinner on the firing line in the Philippines, his cordial relationship with a former Rough Rider, and the need for Negroes to become educated.*

Dear Editor:

Will you kindly give me space in your precious paper to assert the following:

Merry Christmas to America! We will be as merry as possible. Christmas morn dawned clear and bright; no bad news to be heard. We had a soldier's field ration for breakfast, consisting of bacon, coffee and bread. We have some chickens in view and will have them for dinner, providing the Philippinos don't get bad on our hands; if they get bad we will have to take two shares of bacon and bread to go to the front. I hope that they will not start nothing today, but if they will I wish they would wait until after dinner. . . .

. . . .

After you march a day over here you will make the soft side of a mahogany board for a bed; this lad with his raincoat said when he was in Alabama that he hated a colored man but since the Spanish-American War he loves a colored man. He was in the Rough Riders. He said he would never forget the day when the colored 10th U.S. Cavalry charged San Juan Hill and saved his life. He said to me the only way I can show my love for a colored man tonight is to let him cover with half my raincoat. He and I covered our heads to keep the mosquitoes from eating us up.

I have now been across the continent and around the world from the eastern to the western shores from Cuba to New York, and in my travels, I see that one needs an education without which you are not what you might be. So all fathers and mothers and teachers who read this will please try a little harder to make the younger ones study harder. At the walls of Pekin, China, I saw some of every nation in the world and the colored race may have many of them bested. The world was against China. The mint was charged—in other words the soldiers charged the mint. The Japanese soldiers found many gold bricks. Well, time will not allow me to say any more at the present time.

I remain respectfully yours,

William H. Logan
Troop A, 9th U.S. Cavalry

*David J. Gilmer, Forty-ninth Infantry, U.S.V., Linao, Philippine Islands,
no date; from* The Colored American *(Washington), January 19, 1901.
A black captain, in his letter of farewell to the people of Linao, attempts
to dispel the idea that "all white men are unfair to the Negro races."
This curious document points up the anomalous position which Negro
soldiers occupied in the war in the Philippines.*

President and my good people of Linao:[1]

For three months I have been in command of the military
forces of your town, and although promotion severs our official
relations, it cannot alienate the bonds of our affections. The three
months I have been with you, many of you have shown a
disposition to assist me in protecting the cause of my country,
while the soldiers stood on guard and kept all that you held
sacred and dear in sight.

Two hundred and four of you demonstrated your adherence
to the United States of America by accepting the Amnesty
Proclamation; one stating that if he thought that all of the
legislative officials of my country were so human and fair in
their dealings with the Negro races as Col. Hood, military
governor, he would gladly accept the sovereignty of the United
States of America.

My dear people, with the visible Negro blood that flows in the
veins of my body, I would be the last man on earth to try to
deceive you or to sanction the cause of your oppressors. The
United States Government of America is of a true democracy
and the majority of our national legislative representatives are
Christian men, opposed to the oppression of human and religious
rights, and to enforce their protectorate policy to all peoples

---

[1] This circular letter was issued by David J. Gilmer upon leaving his post as
commander of the forces in Linao. A native of Greensboro, N.C., Gilmer had
served in the Third North Carolina Volunteer Infantry and upon being mustered
out joined the Forty-ninth Volunteer Infantry with the rank of lieutenant. His
promotion to Captain was the occasion for assignment elsewhere and his "farewell" letter to the people of Linao.

under the shadow of my country's flag, stands the soldiers of the noble republic, ready and willing to obey the command to march against the iron gateways of infamy in the face of the most destructive fortifications in defense of their country's subjects.

It is true there is a rabble in the United States that runs riot at times but only in the streets of some cities or towns, not in the legislative halls of our national government; yet that mob has some legislative members who are always in a powerless minority, [and whenever it] asserts itself civilization is pained, but is soon consoled by the fact that all nations or countries have a few anarchists. You need not have any fear of that class of Americans, for they cannot reach you; because of that mob I beg of you not to believe all white men of my country are its sympathizers, for there are American white men by the thousands who would die for your rights, with no desire for compensation other than the blessing of heaven.

As I leave you, I turn you over to a kind officer who will share your burdens, and as I do so my last request of you is to dispel the belief that all white men are unfair to the Negro races, and to teach your children to judge men according to the deeds of the individual and not by the color of his skin.

The war of your people against the sovereignty of the United States has been one of misunderstanding, and the loss on both sides can never be compensated; but let us hope that those who encourage its cruel continuation may live to have their hearts renovated by the love of our patron saint, and to see the folly of their great sin, and let us look with love and pity on the mounds over the graves of the Filipinos and the Americans who fell in the recent battle of your town.

David J. Gilmer
Captain, Forty-Ninth Regiment

Frank R. Steward, Forty-ninth Infantry, U.S.V., San Pablo, Philippine Islands, January 22, 1901; from The Bee (*Washington*), *April 6, 1901. Captain Steward, who was provost judge of San Pablo, describes the "hard service" performed by his regiment.*

Lt. Thomas H. R. Clark[1]
Washington, D.C.

My dear Clark:

I received your several letters and have been much enlightened on the situation political and otherwise. You will see by the heading of this letter that we have changed stations. We left Los Pinos and Paranaque early in October, and have been down in this province (Laguna) ever since. I have seen not a little of "scrapping" and service in the last four or five months. In September my command had a considerable scrap with the enemy in and around Los Pinos and Zapote.

The Insurrectos made a desperate attack on Los Pinos and Zapote in the latter part of September. The fight opened up at nearly one a.m., at a time of pitch darkness and continued intermittently until about 7 a.m. We routed the enemy completely, and killed and wounded a number of them. For this bit of service I was commended in fitting terms by battalion [and] regimental commanders, and by the General Commanding the District. The Insurrectos had increased their activity because of the political situation in the United States. They felt pretty sure that [William Jennings] Bryan was to be elected [president] and with his election was to come their "Indepencia"! Peso no!

Since our battalion has been in this province we have seen any amount of hard service. This is a very rich country, full of cocoanuts and fruits of various kinds. It is the chief seat of

[1] Thomas H. R. Clark and the writer of this letter had served together in Eighth Volunteer Infantry (Immunes) in 1898–99.

the cocoanut oil and copra [business]. The people are well-to-do
and the country has been a fat source of revenue to the
Insurgent cause. We haven't had much fighting here because it
is hard to catch the "gugues"[2] together in sufficient bunches. We
are constantly scouting and hiding in the hills; destroying . . .
storehouses, outposts and other sources of supply of the enemy.
I have been in the hills for seven or eight days at a time, packing
our provender on native ponies, and pitching camp where we
happen to light at night.

Last month I got [in] one scrap with the Insurgents. They
had taken a position about four miles south of San Pablo, had
entrenched it, and had planted there also a piece of native
artillery, and sent word for us to "come out and get them." I
was sent out with 100 men; [the] "gugues" had 250 men and
members of the "bolo" people. Their position lay on both sides
of the road, on a hill, which covered the sunken road. If the
troops came down the road, they had to ford a considerable
stream, then come up the sunken road, which also had a sharp
turn in it; the "gugues" would have picked them off almost as
soon as they had shown themselves in the road. Instead of
coming down the road as they expected we took a circuitous
route—flanked them . . . and charged. . . . I don't believe
they've stopped running yet. The "Gugu" is a fleet-footed animal.
I had one musician slightly wounded. I got three Insurgents
killed and I don't know how many were [wounded]. . . .

I am provost judge of San Pablo which gives me jurisdiction
in criminal cases arising between Filipino and Filipino and
between Filipino and American in the neighborhood. So you
see I have been putting my legal training into use. I can
sentence a man to two years in prison and impose a fine of

---

[2] A term of contempt applied by American troops to unfriendly Filipinos. For
obvious reasons, the writer of this letter did not use the other term, "nigger,"
which was commonly applied by white American troops to natives of the Philippines.

1000 pesos. So you see my humble and honorable court has extensive jurisdiction.

Frank R. Stuart [Steward][3]
Captain, 49th U.S. Volunteer Infantry

F. H. Crumbley, Forty-ninth Infantry, U.S.V., Tiason, Philippine Islands, March 7, 1901; from Savannah Tribune, *May 4, 1901. Crumbley urges certain types of black Americans, such as professional men, missionaries, and businessmen, to emigrate to the Philippines.*

Dear Sir:

We are here at this station since Jan. 21st and for a few weeks we been enjoying a rest from active campaigning. The health of the company is very good. Men are well fed and clothed, and stand the climate remarkably well.

As a rule they are well liked by the peaceable natives and many of them will ask for their discharges with a view of staying over here, and will marry native women as soon as they are free of Uncle Sam. We are hoping to leave the Isles for America about May 15th. Some of our officers intend coming back over here after they return to the states.

This is a good place for the active professional Negro, or one who has capital to go into business; but the Negro as a laborer would starve to death here so cheap is native and Chinese labor.

Negroes as missionaries would do well here both for themselves and the natives.

Capt. F. H. Crumbley
49th Infantry

[3] The writer of this letter is obviously Captain Frank R. Steward (not Stuart as printed in the *Washington Bee*) the son of Chaplain T. G. Steward of the Twenty-fifth Infantry and a graduate of Harvard College and of Harvard Law School, who first served as a Second Lieutenant in the Eighth Immunes and later received an appointment as Captain in the Forty-ninth Volunteer Infantry.

Rienzi B. Lemus, Twenty-fifth Infantry, Castillejos, March 17, 1901. from Richmond Planet, *April 17, 1901. Lemus notes that "fights are few and far between" and indicates that the struggle in the Philippines is practically over.*

Sir:

The good work of receiving all the insurgent ordnance and the organization of the civil government continues.

It is reported that Capt. H. A. Leonhauser, commander of the regiment during the Colonel's absence, has surrounded Aguinaldo and his suite in the mountains between Santa Cruz and Dasol with four companies of the 25th Infantry . . . and the Ilocano souts. . . .

Twelve Remington rifles were surrendered here on the 10th inst. in serviceable condition.

The *Manila American* reports that during an engagement in Cuba one officer and thirteen men were killed. Fights are few and far between. The fateful Subig pass and the bloody road from Subig to this station is being rapidly put in passable shape. . . . It now resembles a nice country turnpike.

. . . . .

The latest offered those who surrendered their arms is $20.00 Mexican, a parole, and the release of any friend the surrendering party may pick from the prisoners, not otherwise held than prisoners of war.

The Catholic friars have brought suit against the bolting natives from their faith to recover the church property the latter uses, which they claim is theirs. The suit has not been concluded as yet. . . .

. . . . .

The volunteers are fast returning home. A battalion of the 6th Artillery relieved the 23rd Infantry in Bataan province and the Transport Sheridan arrived on the 15th inst. with new regiments for relief purposes.

. . . .

Rienzi B. Lemus

Rienzi B. Lemus, Twenty-fifth Infantry, Castillejos, April 5, 1901; from Richmond Planet, *June 1, 1901. Lemus reports the capture of the Filipino insurgent leader, Emilio Aguinaldo, by General Frederick Funston.*

[Sir:]

The peace movement is progressing satisfactorily. The much wanted . . . Aguinaldo, who has so long succeeded in eluding the Americans, was captured March 28th by General [Frederick] Funston, and landed safely at Manila, being confined at Malacanan[g].

The first knowledge the public had of the affair was on March 28th in the afternoon when the Manila papers all issued extras. The public was very doubtful owing to the fact that so many stories of like character have been in circulation, but the following morning's issues confirmed their reports which read like a blood and thunder Jessie James and Carl Greene ten cents novel. . . .

. . . .

Indications promise a speedy restoration of complete peace and the good things brought through its medium.

Rienzi B. Lemus

*Rienzi B. Lemus, Twenty-fifth Infantry, Castillejos, April 23, 1901;
from* Richmond Planet, *June 8, 1901. Lemus anticipates a speedy
"winding up of the insurrection" in the wake of Aguinaldo's capture.*

[Sir:]

Right behind the capture of Aguinaldo comes the practical
winding up of the insurrection in this province by the surrender
of the Insurgent General Arsi and his forces to General [A. S.]
Burt, Col., 24th Infantry at this station on April 10th.

General Arsi and his Chief of Staff, Lieutenant Colonel Alva,
with their forces, have harassed this end of the line, especially
Company K, for more than a year, and the fact that they
surrendered to the company they fought so often shows they
appreciated their foes and speaks well of Co. K, 25th Infantry.

. . . .

Aguinaldo has agreed to General [Arthur] MacArthur's terms,
issuing proclamations which will cause the release of 1000
Filipino prisoners of war.

It is said he will leave for the States soon as the guest of the
nation, [but] at present he is at the palace in Malacanan[g].

It is officially announced that civil government will commence
July 1st.

Present conditions are improving wonderfully, but one or
two generals are out and Aggie's proclamation will bring them
in.

. . . .

Rienzi B. Lemus

George W. Prioleau, Ninth Cavalry, Nueva Caceres, Philippine Islands,
ca. June, 1901; from The Colored American *(Washington), July 13,*
1901. Chaplain Prioleau touches upon a variety of subjects in this letter,
including his views on self-government for the Philippine Islands. He
fears that "the Filipino is to be America's 'china' baby while the Negro
will continue to be the 'rag' baby of the republic." Yet, encouraged by
the recent promotion of Benjamin O. Davis—"the first Negro soldier
promoted from the ranks to a commissioned officer . . . through a
competitive examination"—Prioleau maintains that Negro soldiers can
always obtain justice from "officers of the United States army."

Editor
Colored American

There appeared in the Colored American of March 10, 1901, a
clipping from the Daily Record under caption "Questions of
the Hour." Our status in the Philippines was discussed by some
of the leading representatives of the race. Our friend H. Y.
Arnett[1] seemed to have aroused those who followed in the
discussion, Hon. H. P. Cheatham[2] endorsing Mr. Arnett's views
of the subject. Our government is wise in not giving to these
people, "self government;" it is not the purpose of the Congress
and the President to do such. You must understand that the
majority of these people have just taken the oath of allegiance
to the United States of America and a large percent of their
leaders were in a state of insurrection against the rightful
authorities of the island for a number of years and it [has been]
just a few months since they have been captured and the larger
portion of them surrendered. Self government is not to be

[1] H. Y. Arnett, a comparer in the office of the Recorder of Deeds, District of
Columbia, argued against Philippine independence during a debate at the Second
Baptist Church Lyceum in Washington. His was the unpopular side of the debate
with the audience.

[2] Henry Plummer Cheatham, of Vance County, N. C., was a prominent black
Republican, who was a member of Congress from North Carolina from 1889 to
1893. Appointed Recorder of Deeds for the District of Columbia by President
William McKinley in 1897, he served in that office until 1901.

considered for years to come. Comparatively speaking, they know nothing about commercial and agricultural business and a very little about government. There are some intelligent men among them, and they are so conceited that they think that what they do not know is not worth knowing.

The commissioners[3] have been down here in southern Luzon and have established civil government; this city, Nueva Caceres, is the seat of the government; Lt. George Curry, 11th Cavalry, U.S.V., was appointed governor by the commissioners; Major H. B. McCoy, 44th Infantry, U.S.V., inspector of public works; Senor Ramon Eurile, attorney, and Senor Fulgencia Contraras as secretary. Three Americans and two natives. In the wisdom of the commissioners this was the best that could be done for the natives at present. The second term, these officers will be elective, if expedient.

Are they satisfied? Apparently they are, but who knows the character of the Filipino? He is as deep and uncertain as the sea: at present no American is able to definitely state that the Filipinos are contented with the new state of affairs in the island. He differs from the American white man and the American Negro in that he knows how to control his temper; he is calm and deliberate, courteous and polite in debate, and in this, he has it on the Americans. He is not slow, however, in getting out of the way of the muzzle of a carbine. If he were as calm in action against his foe in warfare as he is in debate he would be a hard object to combat against.

With patience and very much labor, schools on the American principle have been established all over the land, and with this potent instrument we will have in a few years a people who will outstrip the American Negro unless he gets up from where [he] is at, and the door of opportunity thrown open a little wider for his entrance. The Filipino is to be America's "china" baby, while

[3] The reference here is to the Civil Commission, headed by William Howard Taft, which superseded the military government of the islands beginning in 1900.

the Negro will continue to be the "rag" baby for the republic. All we ask as ex-Congressman [George H.] White[4] said in his valedictory to the last Congress is "a Man's chance," and thank God friends are arising in every section of our country to champion our cause, "poco tiempo" we will get there. Every year boards are appointed for the examining of soldiers from the ranks for promotions as second lieutenants in the regular establishment. Many soldiers of our race claimed that they have no chance before the board, that they would be turned down if application was made. I have always held that the officers of the United States army are gentlemen, the term "gentlemen" is used in a general sense, and whoever appears before them will be justly dealt with, and in nine cases out of ten this is the case. In every respect the soldier has justice dealt out to him. Courts and boards sometimes make mistakes.

Now see the unreasonableness of the accusation. The 9th United States Cavalry was organized in New Orleans, La., in 1866; from then until May, 1900, there was only one soldier to appear before the board; he failed mentally. That board met at Fort Grant, Ariz. in June 1900. Three soldiers appeared before it, two white and one colored, one white soldier passed but the other two failed. This colored soldier appeared again, so he says, and was turned down at Manila because of physical disability. The second soldier of the 9th Cavalry to appear before the examining board for promotion was Squadron Sergeant Major Benjamin O. Davis, 3rd Squadron, 9th Cavalry.[5] Sergt. Davis appeared before the board at Fort Leavenworth, and . . . Davis passed and stood third on the list. He is the first Negro soldier promoted from the ranks to a commissioned officer in the U.S.

---

[4] George H. White, of Edgecombe County, N.C., was a graduate of Howard University, a successful lawyer, and the last Negro to serve in Congress (1897–1901) until the 1920's. For his famous valedictory speech in the House of Representatives see *Congressional Record*, 56 Congress, 2 Session, pp. 1634–38.

[5] Appointed Brigadier General in 1940, Benjamin O. Davis was the first Negro to hold such rank in the United States.

Army through a competitive examination and the 9th Cavalry has honor of bearing such distinction. I think that he was born and educated in the city of Washington, D.C.

Yes, the soldier, white or black, who appears before an examining board physically and mentally unqualified will be turned down. We have others in the service who will be able to do just what Mr. Davis had done, if they get out of the old rut and get down to study. The door is open; who will be the next to enter?

There were from three to six vacancies in the Naval Academy for every state in the Union up to April 30. Has one Negro youth gone up to take the competitive examination? . . . I have not seen a single item mentioning this fact and urging our youth to make an effort. Our editors and preachers are the educators and advisors of the people. After a while they will begin the hue and cry, "We want a couple of Negro regiments with all Negro officers." . . . I have visited the detachments of my regiment within easy reach of me; was kindly received by officers and enlisted men; it was not necessary at any time to have more than five men as my escort.

The soldiers of the old 9th Cavalry are on very friendly terms with the natives; in fact, I believe it so wherever Negro soldiers are stationed on the island. My second marriage ceremony was that of a corporal of the 9th Cavalry and a native woman, and before this will reach you, I will perform my third, a member of the black 9th Cavalry.

The Congress of the United States has done a handsome thing by providing the chaplain for each regiment of the army [with] an increase [in] pay of $300 per year. They are wise gentlemen, I thank them. In the promotion of Sergt. Major Benjamin O. Davis, 9th Cavalry, the race has scored one more victory. Therefore, all hail to the American Negro! All hail to the Famous 9th! All hail to 2nd Lieut. Benj. O. Davis! All hail to the board of examiners of Fort Leavenworth, Kansas, U.S. Army!

George W. Prioleau

*William R. Fulbright, Twenty-fifth Infantry, Manila, June 10, 1901;
from* The Freeman *(Indianapolis), August 3, 1901. A black infantryman reflecting upon the American struggle in the Philippines pronounces
it "a gigantic scheme of robbery and oppression."*

Editor, Freeman:

Matters are quiet here and ere long the island will be pacified.
"Remingtons" and "Mausers" have been exchanged for plough
shares and where once marked a bloody scene of action can be
seen men who once fought us, but citizens now, plodding along
turning up the soil, sowing rice seed, planting tobacco and
endeavoring to "eat bread by the sweat of their brows." From
Iba, our headquarters, to DaSol on the extreme South, and to
Subig on the North line, two or three soldiers can travel day or
night without arms or any protection whatever. They need not
have any fear for every native is our friend. The insurrection is
almost an incident of the past. Most of the noted leaders have
been captured and many others have surrendered. With them
thousands of soldiers under their supervision, have given up
their arms of war and have taken the oath of allegiance to the
sovereignity of America. Don Emilio Aguinaldo, ex-commander
in chief of the insurgents, has been deceived, surprised and taken;
and by his proclamation, calling upon all armed forces in the
field to come in and submit to the inevitable, 2,000 prisoners
have been set at liberty by Gen. [Arthur] MacArthur. . . .
Everyday hundreds of insurgents, tired and hungry from war,
are surrendering their arms, receiving $13.00 in gold and taking
the oath of allegiance. One thing I don't understand is, if we are
right why should we seek peace by purchase from the treasury
of our government, when American sons have been boloed,
disemboweled, beheaded, and bowed and arrowed to death. War
must be fought with fire and side arms, surrenders should be
voluntary and unconditional, and if peace is to be secured, it
must be gained with bayonets dipped in blood, otherwise it is

temporary and destined to be rekindled and rage with greater destruction than ever. This struggle on the islands has been naught but a gigantic scheme of robbery and oppression. Many soldiers who came here in poverty to battle for the Stars and Stripes have gone home with gold, diamonds, and other valuables, while the natives here who were once good livers are barely able to keep the wolf from the door. Graves have been entered and searches have been made for riches; churches and cathedrals have been entered and robbed of their precious ornaments; homes have been pillaged and moneys and jewelry stolen. The commissary scandal is being thoroughly investigated, and the guilty ones punished. Capt. [James C.] Reed, Capt. [Frederick] Barrows, and Lieut. [Frederick] Boyer[1] of the volunteers have had their insignia torn from their shoulders and have been placed in the penitentiary. . . . The way some of our officers have conducted themselves is enough to cause the worst insurrecto to shudder with fear when he knows the American flag is to wave over his people and that they are to look to the American government for protection. The natives say we have good men for soldiers but drunkards for officers—my lips are closed. The natives unequivocally denounce the attitude of our government and claim its administration is unjust and humiliating. Here are a few reasons: Native policeman receives 24 pesos, or $12 in gold, a month while American policeman gets 120 pesos, or $60 in gold. They are displeased with the rules of the civil authority which allows for same work one price to natives and another to the Americans. The Filipino judges who have been loyal to the American government in times of stress and need claim it is unjust for them to be set aside now that peace has been restored. They are venting their spleen on the American view of justice and have even predicted another insurrection. If we are to unfurl

[1] These three volunteer officers attached to branches of the commissary department in the Philippines were convicted of various crimes including bribery and theft. See *New York Tribune,* April 2, 5, 8, 16, 1901.

our flag on these islands let us make these natives joint heirs
in our citizenship; if we are to institute our government here let it be
a government for the people, of the people and by the people; and
unless we do this we have failed to do our duty. The eyes of the
civilized world are upon us, and now is the time for action.
"Procrastination is the thief of time."

William R. Fulbright,
Private, Co. H, 25th Infantry

*George W. Prioleau, Ninth Cavalry, Guinobatan, Philippine Islands, ca.
December, 1901; from* The Freeman (*Indianapolis*), *January 25, 1902.
For one who formerly made much of the racial affinity between black
Americans and "the dark-skinned people" of the Spanish islands, Chap-
lain Prioleau reveals in the following letter an attitude toward Filipinos
worthy of a white racist.*

[Dear Sir:]

America has been in possession of these islands since 1898.
Great changes have been made in the administration of public
affairs. Government has been established upon American
principles. Wherever the natives have been found competent, they
have been given charge of government in the different provinces.
In many respects this seemed to be satisfactory, and yet from our
observation there seems to be a growing spirit of unrest. There
must be a cause for it, but where lies the cause?

Prosperity is seen on every hand. There is more money in
circulation now than ever in the history of these islands; the
laboring classes are better [off], that is, they have an abundance;
better clothed; they get more for their produce, more for their
labor; the wealthier get better rent and are more promptly paid,
and yet there is a spirit of unrest.

Several months ago, five or six hundred American school

teachers were brought here and put into the schools. These
schools are established upon American principles. A secular
education is to be given each child free of cost; thousands of
books were bought for this purpose: histories, geographies and
arithmetics are printed in Spanish; the primary books in English.
The old Spanish catechism, or book of the doctrine of the
Catholic Church which was taught in the schools was excluded.
A committee of the natives met the commissioners, made a fight
for the continuation of the Book of Doctrine and that Catholic
teachers be given preference; they set forth strong arguments, but
they were of no avail. The catechism had to go. Right here we
will find the cause of this unrest. Someone may smile and say
that is too trivial; if there was any unrest, that is not the cause of
it. The Book of Doctrine has always been taught in the school;
many of them [Filipinos] have no higher education; nearly all
of them can read it; it is required of them. They are a religious
people even though they do not live up to the standard of the
Christian religion. Religion with them is first, that is, the Catholic
religion. Are they guilty of untruthfulness, idolatry, stealing and
every crime in the decalogue? The sin lies at the door of their
religious teachers. I am informed that under Spanish rule the
native priests were secondary in the government of affairs, both
religious and secular. The Spanish priests were blamed for
everything; they wanted them returned to Spain; hundreds of
them returned, and today the native priests are first in the affairs
of religion. They have great influence over the people; they are
capable of doing a great deal of mischief or good; retarding or
accelerating the government as established. The senior priest of
this Pueblo . . . offered one of our American teachers $15 more
in the month than he is getting to teach a parochial school in this
town. This is the first move in the direction to thwart the purposes
of the government. This is the scheme probably in other
places. . . .

They prefer no education if it lacks the teaching and

knowledge of the church. In making the above statement and
that which follows, I have reference in particular to this part of
southern Luzon. . . . The Filipino learns very quickly how to
put a value upon himself and his labor. During the Spanish rule,
they were not asked what will you do this work for or how much
do you want per day? They were ordered to do this or that, [and]
when finished, they would be paid 20¢ or given a little rice. The
Americans fixed a price for them at $1.00 Mexican, or 50¢ per
day. Understand that they can purchase as much for 50¢ as an
American can get for $1.00. They have concluded that their
work is worth more, hence they demand now $1.50 or 75¢ a day
or no work, and it is really hard work to get them to work even at
their own price. The quartermaster at this post has offered $6.00
per cord for wood and he cannot get a stick; they will bring in a
small bundle on their heads and charge you 25¢ for it. It is
fortunate for us that we do not need much wood.

They are tampering with the wrong people. Roads for the
public traffic must be made, bridges repaired and new ones made,
houses built for the accommodation of officers and enlisted men,
transports must be loaded and unloaded; if they will not do the
work, then imported laborers must do it and will do it. The
indolence and laziness of the Filipino must not and will not
retard American progress.

They do not understand or will not understand there are losses
as well as profits in business. They calculate altogether upon the
profit. I am living in a house which is rented for $20.00
Mex[ican]. Our last storm damaged the roof so that it leaked
badly. I requested the landlord to repair it; he replied that he
could not do so when he was getting only $20.00 a month; that
he would lose; that he would do so and raise the rent $5.00. The
roof was repaired and the rent was not raised either.

The Filipino in one respect is like the American Negro. In
business he has no confidence in his fellow Filipino. He will not
patronize him unless he is under obligation. He will deal with the

Chinaman or the Spaniard before he will deal with his own. Senor Mariano Perfecto is a Filipino. He owns the business of four stores under one roof. One of these he conducts himself, assisted by his wife and daughter; the others are conducted by Chinamen. Either of the three does twice as much business as he but they would not if it were known that the business was his.

We have a peculiar people to Americanize. Our knowing men are very sanguine of ultimate success. It may not be in our time, but it will be. The millions of dollars that are being expended in shaping things will return by and by with one hundred per cent profit.

George W. Prioleau
Chaplain, Ninth Cavalry

Rienzi B. Lemus, Twenty-fifth Infantry, Manila, January 15, 1902; from The Freeman (*Indianapolis*), *March 8, 1902. Lemus comments on the nonmilitary contributions of Negro soldiers in the Philippines.*

Editor
The Freeman

Dear Sir:

The conditions in this country have changed beyond comparison since American occupation and the Americans should feel proud of the record of their sons in the Philippines.

The old adage, "The pen is mightier than the sword," was never clearer demonstrated than in the Zambales Province, the home of the 25th U.S. Infantry. The natives have improved fourfold. The regiment, after taking part in the campaigns of central Luzon, marched 12 days across Zambales mountains and took the province in December, '99. "Pay for what you get" was the motto from the start and today the once poor natives are almost as wealthy as their former masters who really kept them in practical involuntary servitude. One poor family of my acquaintance secured a few soldiers' washing in 1900 which increased until now they conduct a laundry and collect an average of $100 at each bi-monthly payday. When we came here they were in debt to one of the supposedly wealthy men of the town, and today they are out of debt and far in advance of their former creditor financially. I pick this family because they are the most prosperous. In many other ways the American colored soldier has taught the Filipino thrift, economy and above all the customs of polite society. But the greatest accomplishments along the educational lines even before the present liberal course was formulated, Chaplain T. G. Steward of the 25th Infantry was in charge of schools taught by soldiers and natives and accomplished excellent results. He got right down to work and, with his knowledge of Spanish, instilled in them ideas which to this day carry them a long way in school. Once while on duty at Headquarters in Iba, Zambales, I was surprised to see two natives going through the service with the Americans. I found they had been early pupils of his and they naturally felt they must attend all meetings he conducted. The 25th Infantry had hard fighting but had the pleasure of receiving the surrenders of their opponents at two different stations and later working side by side making public improvements.

R. B. Lemus
Co. K, 25th Infantry

William F. Blakeny, Twenty-fifth Infantry, Castillejos, January 24, 1902; from The Freeman *(Indianapolis), March 15, 1902. Blakeny encourages black Americans to emigrate to the Philippines and reminds them that "the first to come will be the first served."*

Editor, Freeman

Sir:

Your valuable paper reaches us regularly and we are always pleased at receiving it. To read it is almost like conversing with someone direct from the United States. Sir, you have no doubt seen the Philippines treated by a great many writers as "A God Forsaken Country," but I wish to say, however, that such is not the case. All such ideas concerning this country originated in the minds of men inured to almost incessant fighting Inines[?], that tried men's souls, thereby confirming the famous opinion of a famous general that "war is hell." Nothing but the worry and fatigue caused by sleepless nights and a long and forced march over hills and mountains, through jungles, mud and water will cause such negative opinions to form themselves in the human mind and subsequently find their way into speech. I will say to all colored American[s] . . . that the Philippines are far from being a "God Forsaken Country." The worst that can be said of the Philippines is that they are practically an undeveloped group of islands for which there is in store a brilliant future. I shall say to all industrious and energetic colored Americans, after much reasoning and deliberation, that they cannot do anything more beneficial to themselves than to come over here while the country is still in its infancy and being here to help reap the harvest which we shall soon begin to gather in. In this country will be many fortunes made. Why not come and share with us the glorious good times which are sure to come? Come now. The first to come

will be the first served. Be among the first. A few dollars invested
now will yield big returns. Desirable correspondence a pleasure.

>Respectfully,
>William F. Blakeny
>Co. K, 25th Infantry

Rienzi B. Lemus, Twenty-fifth Infantry, Manila, March 14, 1902; from
Richmond Planet, *April 26, 1902. Lemus describes the return of black
infantrymen to Manila from "hard duty" in Zambales Province and reports various news from the city, including information about a rape
case.*

[Sir:]

The public has plenty of gossip and excitement to enliven the
otherwise dull, monotonous life in Manila. During the past two
weeks a gang of first class road agents and highwaymen have
been developed and seem perfectly contented in confining their
operations to Pasig and the surrounding country thereabouts. At
present there are upwards of three thousand discharged and short
term soldiers . . . at Camp Wallace on the Luneta and their
presence with so much money in their possession seems to be an
inducement for the hold-up business. . . .

Manila had its first threatening of a lynching last Monday
night in the Santa Cruz district when the Americans threatened to
introduce that popular spectacle of "Americanism," but taking
for their model a white policeman of the metropolitan force. It
seems that patrolman George R. Green whose beat was in the
above-named district enticed a young native vagrant into a nearby
house and criminally assaulted her, [then] returned to patroling
as usual. His time being up, he was relieved by another
patrolman, who was accosted by a native woman leading a child
who stated that the latter had been assaulted by a chino. The

good policeman then accompanied them to the scene of the outrage, a chino confectionary stand, where the victim told him she had been assaulted by an American policeman and not by a chino. He hastily reported to the Santa Cruz police station and a municipal physician summoned who pronounced the child in serious condition.

Green walked in attired in civilian clothes exclaiming that he could tell all about the case. His victim immediately recognized him . . . [and] he then admitted his relations with her for a consideration of two pesos. Chief of Police [George] Curry was at once notified. He summarily dismissed Green and ordered him to be confined in the Santa Cruz station for further action. At last accounts the victim of the cowardly policeman was in a precarious position. . . .

.   .   .   .

So strong were the threats of lynching that the prisoner was transferred to Billibid for safe keeping.

When the appeal was made to the city for a company of colored policemen, the Municipal Board, acting thereon, stated that it was impracticable at that time. It is presumed they were afraid they would have too many criminal assault charges against them, which opinion is not well founded, judging by the latest episode among their white brethren, although the metropolitan force cannot be judged by the action of the degenerate Green any more than any other race or body by an individual.

After two years of hard duty in the Province of Zambales, the 25th Infantry has been relieved therefrom and assigned to duty with Headquarters and Co. D at Malabin and Caloocan, the old stamping ground of 1899.

As disinterested as may be our people at home, but a sight worth the eleven thousand mile trip to see was the relief of that black regiment last week.

On February 29, 1902, when companies K, L and B moved

into the towns assigned them, they were greeted by a lot of sneaking natives ready to bolo them at the least favorable opportunity, where two months later they were convinced that we would pay for what we got, it was a case of sneaking natives begging for the opening of the ports to get wares to bolo. "Mr. Soldiers' Pocketbook." Finally came the Redding-Marcelino nuptials which was the keynote of matrimonial unions and when the boys who came away empty-handed in 1900 marched out in 1902 they carried the 25 best looking ladies of Castillejos. . . .

·   ·   ·   ·

The relatives of the Richmond boys who left home three years ago will have the pleasure of seeing them shortly as Camp Wallace is full of Richmonders of the 24th and 25th regiments who will return on the Transport Thomas on the 18th inst. . . .

I was over to Camp Wallace and was surprised to see so many familiar faces.

Rienzi B. Lemus

Rienzi B. Lemus, Twenty-fifth Infantry, Angel Island, Calif., April 17, 1902; from Richmond Planet, *May 3, 1902. Lemus describes the return of his regiment to the United States after almost three years in the Philippines.*

[Sir:]

Once more I have crossed the great western ocean and for the first time in nearly three years set foot on American soil. I am not yet able to realize I am home. It seems like the great hills of Subig Bay or Corregidor. We even find it hard to drop the pigeon Spanish we used to talk to Filipinos and often find ourselves addressing someone to receive a stare for an answer.

With Manila decorated by the sons of Erin in honor of their

patron saint, the Artillery band . . . discoursing patriotic airs, the cheering multitudes, we boarded the lighters in the Pasig and in company with the 3rd U.S. Infantry swung into the bay to embark on the transport "Thomas." When the last of the 3rd Infantry boarded the lighters, fifteen deluded native women, their mistresses, turned away in tears as the Artillery band played, "The Girl I Left Behind," a sentiment under the circumstances very appropriate, and this is a daily example of how the army pacify and civilize the Filipinos, by deluding the females, and returning home to be worshipped as heroes, the officers are no exception to the rule.

At 11:30 a.m., March 18th, General [Adna] Chaffee visited Col. [John H.] Page and as he departed, the hatches were closed and preparations were made to depart by 1:00 p.m. Everything being ready the big 5 ton anchors were drawn up and the transport glided down the bay. . . .

Next day we were well out to sea with nothing but sky and water to look at.

On the 21st we passed the island of Formosa. . . . Toward evening the sea began to get rough and continued so during the voyage. On the evening of the 22nd the high ship began to pitch and in this condition came in sight of the Japanese coast on the morning of the 23rd, arriving at Nagasaki at 11:55 a.m. The Japanese quarantine officers came aboard and were a fine lot by which to judge their hospitable country.

.   .   .   .

After more than three days [at Nagasaki] . . . we weighed anchor and dropped down the channel. . . .

. . . On the morning of the 20th day out of Nagasaki and the 28th day from Manila, we passed in the Golden Gate to the tune of "Home Sweet Home."

After the usual quarantine and customs inspection we landed here.

This is a cool place but more work for soldiers to perform than any other post I ever was in. My service began at Washington, D.C., March 24th, 1899, and expired in Nagasaki, Japan, March 23rd, 1902, but I am still in the service and with my comrades of the same experience, will be for some days yet.

We have served three years, but are still kept here digging sewers, breaking rock, etc., while the clerks are making ready to discharge us. Quite a novel experience.

Rienzi B. Lemus

T. Clay Smith, Twenty-fourth Infantry, Fort Assiniboine, Mont., ca. October, 1902; from Savannah Tribune, *November 1, 1902. A black veteran of the campaign in the Philippines, fully aware of the existence of American race prejudice there, nevertheless believes that Negroes should emigrate to the islands.*

Dear Sir:

Several of our young men are now in business in the Philippines and are doing nicely, indeed, along such lines as express men, hotels and restaurants, numerous clerks in the civil government as well as in the division quartermaster's office, and there are several school teachers, one lawyer and one doctor of medicine.

However, color prejudice has kept close in the wake of the flag and is keenly felt in that far-off land of eternal sunshine and roses.

I think, everything considered, that the Philippines offer our people the best opportunities of the century and would advise emigration.

T. Clay Smith
Sergeant-Major, 24th Infantry

░:░:░:░: SELECTED BIBLIOGRAPHY

AMONG the most important sources of information about Negro soldiers in the era of the Spanish-American War are the collections in the Old Military Division of the National Archives, which contain voluminous records for each Negro unit in both the regular and volunteer armies. The annual reports of the War Department between 1898 and 1902, as well as those of the adjutants general of the various states which mustered in Negro volunteer units, also provide much useful data relating to the organization and activities of Negro troops. A significant supplement to these official records are black newspapers and magazines which, for the most part, are readily available on microfilm or in reprint editions. In addition, numerous military histories of the campaigns in Cuba, Puerto Rico, and the Philippines include commentaries on the role played by Negro soldiers. Unquestionably, the most comprehensive treatment of the Negro regulars and volunteers in the era of the Spanish-American War is Marvin Edward Fletcher's excellent unpublished doctoral dissertation, "The Negro Soldier and the United States Army, 1891–1917" (University of Wisconsin, 1968).

The following bibliography is a selection of published works concerned either wholly or in part with the military history of black Americans between 1898 and 1902.

Bigalow, John. *Reminiscences of the Santiago Campaign.* New York: Harper, 1899.

Bond, Horace Mann. "The Negro in the Armed Forces of the United States prior to World War I," *Journal of Negro Education,* 12 (Summer, 1943): 263–87.

Bonsal, Stephen. "The Negro Soldier in War and Peace," *North American Review,* 186 (June, 1907): 321–27.

Braxton, George H. "Company 'L' in the Spanish-American War," *Colored American Magazine,* 1 (May, 1900): 19–25.

Bullard, R. L. "The Negro Volunteer: Some Characteristics," *Journal of the Military Service Institution,* 29 (July, 1901): 29–39.

Cashin, Herschel V. *Under Fire with the U.S. Tenth Cavalry.* New York: F. T. Neely, ca. 1899.

Chew, Abraham. *A Biography of Colonel Charles Young.* Washington: R. L. Pendleton, 1923.

Coston, W. Hilary. *The Spanish-American War Volunteer.* Middletown, Pa.: Mount Pleasant Printery, 1899.

Curtis, Mary. *The Black Soldier, or the Colored Boys of the United States Army.* Washington: Murray Brothers, 1915.

Edwards, Frank E. *The '98 Campaign of the Sixth Massachusetts, U.S.V.* Boston: Little, Brown, 1899.

Funston, Frederick. *Memories of Two Wars.* New York: Scribners, 1914.

Gatewood, Willard B., Jr. "Negro Troops in Florida, 1898," *Florida Historical Quarterly,* 49 (July, 1970): 1–15.

Glass, E. N. *History of the Tenth Cavalry.* Tucson: Acme Printing Co., 1921.

Goode, W. T. *The "Eighth Illinois."* Chicago: Blakely Printing Co., 1899.

Hall, Charles W. "The Eighth Illinois, U.S.V.," *Colored American Magazine,* 1 (June, 1900): 94–103.

Johnson, Edward A. *History of Negro Soldiers in the Spanish-American War.* Raleigh: Capital Publishing Co., 1899.

Johnson, William H. *History of the Colored Volunteer Infantry of Virginia, 1871–99.* Richmond: n.p., 1923.

Lee, Irvin. *Negro Medal of Honor Men.* New York: Dodd, Mead, 1967.

Lemus, Rienzi B. "The Enlisted Man in Action, or the Colored American Soldier in the Philippines," *Colored American Magazine,* 5 (May, 1902): 46–54.

Lynk, Miles V. *The Black Troopers, or the Daring Heroism of the Negro Soldiers in the Spanish-American War.* Jackson, Tenn.: Lynk Publishing Co., 1899.

Marks, George P. "Opposition of Negro Newspapers to American Philippine Policy, 1899–1900," *Midwest Journal,* 4 (Winter, 1951–52): 1–25.

Muller, William G. *The Twenty-fourth Infantry, Past and Present.* n.p., 1923.

Nankivell, John H., *History of the Twenty-fifth Regiment of the United States Infantry, 1869–1926.* Denver: Smith-Brooks Printing Co., 1927.

"Race Discrimination in the Philippines," *The Independent,* 54 (February 13, 1902): 416–17.

Reddick, L. D. "The Negro Policy of the United States Army, 1775–1945," *Journal of Negro History,* 35 (January, 1949): 9–29.

Sexton, William T. *Soldiers in the Sun: An Adventure in Imperialism.* Harrisburg, Pa.: Military Service Publishing Co., 1939.

Steward, Theophilus G. *Colored Regulars in the United States Army*. Philadelphia: A. M. E. Book Concern, 1904.

———. "Two Years in Luzon," *Colored American Magazine*, 4 (November, 1901): 4–10.

"Virginia's Colored Volunteers," *Southern Workman*, 27 (July, 1898): 132.

Washington, Booker T. *A New Negro for a New Century*. Chicago: American Publishing House, 1900.

African Methodist Episcopal Church, 13, 271

Aguinaldo, Emilio, 12, 13, 241, 245, 258, 259, 286, 298, 299, 304

Alabama: Negro volunteers in, 10, 101, 102. *See also* Third Alabama Infantry, U.S.V.

Alexander, C. R.: letter from, 128–29

Alexander, James, 36, 62

Alger, Russell, 125, 147, 216

Ames, Adelbert, 121

Anderson, Charles J., 136

Anderson, E. D., 78

Anderson, J. H., 282

Anderson, R.: letter to, 50–52

Anderson, W. H.: letter from, 128–29

Anderson, W. T., 82

Angeles, P.I., 261

Anti-imperialism: among Negroes, 5

Arnett, H. Y., 300

Arringi, P.I., 283

Arzat, P.I., 289

Assiniboine, Mont., 31, 316

Associated Press: on Negro soldiers, 224

Atlanta Constitution: on Negro soldiers, 176

Atlanta, Ga., 65, 176

Attucks, Crispus, 45, 108

Augusta, Ga., 139, 178, 207

Bailey, W. H., 165

Baker, Edward L., 37, 263

Baker, W. A.: letter from, 177–78

Balanga, P.I., 275

Baldwin, James: quoted, 3

Baldwin, T. A., 73

Bamban, P.I., 258, 264

Barrows, Frederick, 305

Bass, Emmanuel, 263

Batchelor, Joseph B., 241

Bates, John C., 158

Beard, George J.: letters from, 202–3, 209–12, 229–31

Beck, James, 183

Beck, William J., 77, 80

Belden, Ga.: election in, 164–65

Bell, J. Franklin, 258

Bentley, George A., 132

Berry, George, 78

Bigalow, John, 23

Binn, T. F., 139

Bivins, H. B.: letter from, 49–50; mentioned, 80

Black, Frank S.: and Negro volunteers, 9

Black, James C., 207

Blakeny, William F.: letter from, 311–12

Bonsal, Stephen, 15, 44–45

Booker, James: letter from, 284–85

Botolan, P.I.: battle of, 13, 241, 265, 266, 285

Boyer, Frederick, 304

Breckinridge, J. C., 125, 136, 147

Brice, A. C., 194

Brooks, John R., 88–89

Brown, Arthur, 82

Brown, Bart, 201

Brown, Belton, 206

Brown, D. T., 65
Brown, Edward: letter from, 276–77
Brown, J. M., 165
Brown, Simon: letter from, 193–94
Bruce, N. C.: letter from, 106–8
Bryan, William Jennings, 294
Buckner, John C., 181–82, 228
Burns, Frank: letter from, 205–6
Burt, A. S., 265, 299
Bushnell, Asa, 101, 147

Cabanatuan, P.I., 241
Caloocan, P.I., 249, 289, 313
Camp Alger, Va., 111–12
Camp Corbin, Va., 122–25, 147
Camp Haskell, Ga.: Negro soldiers at, 12, 104–5, 138–77 passim
Camp Marion, S.C., 121
Camp Poland, Tenn.: Negro soldiers at, 125–37 passim; mentioned, 147
Camp Shipp, Ala., 177
Camp Tanner, Ill., 229
Camp Wallace, P.I., 312, 314
Camp Wikoff, N.Y., 82. See also Montauk Point, N.Y.
Carl, Charles, 201
Castillejos, P.I., 275
Certificate of Merit: to Negro soldiers, 43
Chaffee, Adna, 315
Charleston, S.C., 74–75, 121
Chase, Calvin, 17
Chattanooga, Tenn., 31
Chavis, Jordan, 210
Cheatham, H. P., 300
Chickamauga Park, Ga., 22, 25, 31, 233
Christian Endeavor Society, 209, 264
Clark, H. C., 266
Clark, Thomas H. R.: letter to, 294–96
Cole, James F., 77
Collin, James M.: letter from, 128–29
Collins, Joab: shooting of, 32, 35–36
Comfort, C. D., 164, 169, 171, 172
Conly, Pasco, 37, 58
Conn, John R.: letter from, 65–71; mentioned, 46
Consunji, Tomas, 254

Contraras, Fulgencia, 301
Cordin, C. W.: letters from, 157–73, 249–51, 255–56, 259–62; mentioned, 16, 105
Cox, W. H.: letters from, 272–73, 282–84
Croxton, R. C., 103, 132, 146, 147, 148, 149. See also Sixth Virginia Infantry, U.S.V.
Crumbley, F. H.: letters from, 269–71, 296
Cuba: Negro soldiers in, 8–9, 41–96 passim, 181–235 passim; description of, 207–9; opportunities in, 53–54, 184–85, 187, 191, 231–32, 234–35; conditions in, 186, 188, 189, 191, 194–95; mentioned, 4, 5, 6, 11, 14, 25, 29, 33, 146, 153, 158, 161, 169, 270, 291
Cullom, Shelby, 223
Curry, George, 313

Daiquiri, Cuba, 50
Dasol, P.I., 297, 304
Davis, Benjamin O., 302, 303
Davis, Jefferson, 161
Davis, Richard Harding, 43
Dewey, George, 239
Dewey, Taliaferro Miles: letters from, 115–16, 119–20; mentioned, 117
Dickens, Harry, 211
Dixie, 54
Douglass, Charles, 111
Douglass, Frederick, 108
Duvall, W. P., 272

Early, C. C., 230
Eighth Illinois Infantry, U.S.V.: origins of, 181–82, 216; letters concerning, 186, 188–89, 197–98, 202–6, 209–30; morale in, 182, 209–30 passim; mentioned, 10, 11
Eighth Infantry, U.S.V., 11, 104
El Caney: battle of, 42, 43, 45, 55–56, 68, 97, 207, 241, 247
El Deposito, P.I., 252
El Hebro, Cuba, 42
Elliot, James, 80

Eleventh Cavalry, U.S.A., 301
Emancipation Day: celebration of, 164
Engiles, P.I., 255
Eurile, Ramon, 301
Evans, S. T.: letter from, 273–74
Ewers, Ezra P., 189, 192, 200

Fagan, David, 15
Falls Church, Va., 113–14
Farmer, William, 210
Fifty-fourth Massachusetts Infantry, U.S.V., 248
First Cavalry, U.S.V., 41, 66
First Delaware Infantry, U.S.V., 114
First Georgia Infantry, U.S.V., 125–26
First Illinois Infantry, U.S.V., 229
First Infantry, U.S.A., 60
Fleming, R. J., 94
Fleming, William H., 207
Ford, Frank, 211
Ford, William: arrest of, 172
Foreman, George W.: letter from, 128–29
Formosa, 315
Fort Camansi, P.I., 265, 268
Fort Grant, Ariz., 84
Fort Leavenworth, Kans., 303
Fort Macon, N.C., 110
Fort Myers, Va., 7–8
Fortune, T. Thomas, 7
Forty-fourth Infantry, U.S.V., 301
Forty-eighth Infantry, U.S.V.: in the Philippines, 14, 240; letters concerning, 272–73, 277–79, 281–82, 282–84
Forty-ninth Infantry, U.S.V.: in the Philippines, 14, 240; letters concerning, 269–71, 292–93, 294–96
Forty-sixth Infantry, U.S.V., 261
Forty-third Infantry, U.S.V., 263
Fourteenth Pennsylvania Infantry, U.S.V., 121
Fourth Kentucky Infantry, U.S.V., 177
Fourth Wisconsin Infantry, U.S.V., 178
Fulbright, William R.: letter from, 304–6
Fulton, John C., 116
Funston, Frederick, 298

Galloway, John W.: letter from, 251–55
Gardner, Cornelius, 243
Garrett, Daniel, 88–89
Gazette (Cleveland, Ohio), 16, 120
Georgia: Negro militia of, 9; Negro soldiers stationed in, 138–77 passim. See also Camp Haskell, Ga.; Macon, Ga.
Giddings, Joshua, 165
Gillipse, James R., 36–37
Gilmer, David J.: letter from, 292–93
Gilpin, James S.: letter from, 128–29
Givens, William, 58
Gleaves, William, 35
Godwin, E. A., 164n
Gomez, Maximo, 42, 81
Gould, Edward W.: letter from, 134–37
Graham, W. M.: and Negro soldiers, 113–14, 118, 120
Grant, U. S., 197
Graves, Benjamin A.: letter from, 128–29; mentioned, 122, 134, 141, 142
Green, George R., 312
Griffith, Thomas, 78

Hall, Charles E.: letter to, 202–3
Hammons, Henry, 161
Hampton Institute, 49
Hankins, William A., 122
Hanna, Marcus A., 101
Harrisburg, Pa., 114
Haskell, James T., 138
Hatcher, Charles C., 206
Hawkins, William H., 199
Healy, John W., 132
Henry, Guy V., 36, 62, 73
Hill, Ebenezer J., 207
Hill, James E.: letter from, 134–37
Hill, John H.: letter from, 128–29
Hill, Richard: letter from, 128–29
Hill, William H., 221
Hobson, Richmond, 201, 226
Hobson, Winslow: letter from, 117–19
Holliday, Presley: letter from, 92–97
Hopkinsville, Ky., 31
Howard, O. O., 111

Hughes, Robert P.: quoted, 14
Humphrey, Brad, 226
Hunt, C. L., 218
Hunt, Levi P., 36
Huston, Adam, 78

Iba, P.I., 13, 241, 265, 266, 285, 304, 310
Igorrotes: description of, 278
Illinois: Negro volunteers in, 10. *See also* Eighth Illinois Infantry, U.S.V.
Illinois Record, 17, 36, 37, 59, 203, 213
Immunes, 11, 104, 107, 138, 148, 151, 157, 167, 168, 181, 183, 187, 206, 207–9
Imperialism: Negroes on, 4–5
Indiana: Negro volunteers in, 103

Jackson, Robert R., 182, 189
Jefferson, Eddie, 127
Jefferson, William T., 218
Jenkins, Albert, 127
Johnson, Carter P., 81
Johnson, J. B.: letter from, 128–29; mentioned, 142. *See also* Sixth Virginia Infantry, U.S.V.
Johnson, J. E., 201
Johnson, James H., 186
Johnson, Smith, 77
Johnson, William H.: letter from, 134–37
Jucaro, Cuba, 42

Kansas: Negro volunteers in, 10, 182–83. *See also* Twenty-third Kansas Infantry, U.S.V.
Kent, Jacob F., 57
Key West, Fla.: Negro soldiers at, 22, 25
Kirby, C. D.: letter from, 47–49
Kirby, Mrs. Charles, 47
Knoxville, Tenn.: press of, 103. *See also* Camp Poland, Tenn.

La Luma, P.I., 249
Lakeland, Fla.: Negro soldiers at, 24, 31–32, 50, 60, 63–64, 72
Lamar, William, 160

Las Guasimas: battle of, 41–42, 45, 50, 59, 96
Lawton, Henry W., 57, 186
Leedy, John W., 103, 182–83, 193
Lemus, Rienzi B.: letters from, 246–47, 297, 299, 309–10, 312–16
Leonhauser, H. A., 258, 259, 260, 297
Lewis, John E.: letters from, 30–33, 58–60, 233–35; mentioned, 46, 62, 72, 76, 85
Lincoln, Abraham, 4, 108, 197
Logan, John A., 197
Logan, William H.: letter from, 290–91
Los Pinos, P.I., 294
L'Ouverture Rifles, 121
Low, A. S., 33
Lynch, John R., 250
Lynching, 74, 84, 89, 105, 106, 139, 162, 247, 312
Lyons, Judson W., 111
Lytle, Ga., 31

Mabalacat, P.I., 258
MacArthur, Arthur, 246, 286, 299, 304
McCoy, H. B., 201
Maceo, Antonio, 187, 195–96
McKee, William J., 141, 164, 169
McKinley, William, 9, 108, 158, 188, 207, 212
Macon, Ga.: racial climate in, 12, 104–5, 139, 157–77 passim; Negro business in, 161, 165; mentioned, 127, 138. *See also* Camp Haskell, Ga.
Malabin, P.I., 280, 313
Mangrum, Frederick E.: letter from, 128–29
Maine, 21, 83, 197
Manila, P.I., 242, 248, 250, 255, 263, 264, 265, 269, 273, 275, 277, 284, 288, 298
Manila Times, 242, 243
Marshall, John R.: letters from, 186, 188–89; accusations against, 203–5, 212–39 passim; mentioned, 181, 182, 185, 209, 210. *See also* Eighth Illinois Infantry, U.S.V.
Marshall, Lewis, 94
Martin, Carl A., 260, 260*n*

Martin, William L., 220
Masinloc, P.I., 284, 288
Mason, Patrick: letter from, 257
Mason, William, 223
Massachusetts: Negro militia of, 10, 101, 102. *See also* Sixth Massachusetts Infantry, U.S.V.
Masurier, R. L., 132–33
Matthews, George, 283
Medal of Honor: to Negro soldiers, 42
Merchant, Walter E.: letter from, 281–82
Meredith, Amos, 211
Mexico, P.I., 252
Middletown, Pa., 114
Miles, Nelson A., 29, 48, 118
Miller, James: letter from, 60–61
Mississippi: Negro volunteers in, 9
Mitchell, John, 103
Mitchell, Joseph G., 77
Montauk Point, N.Y., 60, 65, 74, 75, 82
Moore, Preston: letter from, 288–90
Morgan, A. L., 211
Motalokie, P.I., 261
Mount, James A.: and Negro volunteers, 103

Nagasaki, Japan: Negro soldiers in, 215–16, 273
New Orleans, La.: riot in, 286, 286n; mentioned, 302
New York: Negro volunteers in, 9. *See also* Black, Frank S.
New York Journal, 73
New York Loan Company, 160
Newells, Gustavus A., 227
Nicholas, C. B.: letter from, 134–37
Negritos: description of, 241, 276–77
Ninth Cavalry, U.S.A.: poem about, 45; letters concerning, 27–29, 47–49, 74–76, 82–84, 290–91, 300–303, 306–9; mentioned, 6–7, 21, 22, 33, 43, 45, 57, 63, 116, 187, 201, 240, 247
Ninth Infantry, U.S.V.: letters concerning, 207–9, 231–32; mentioned, 11, 104, 183, 200, 206. *See also* Immunes

Ninth Ohio Battalion, U.S.V.: letters concerning, 111–21; discontent within, 115–20; mentioned, 102, 105. *See also* Young, Charles
North Carolina: Negro volunteers in, 10, 103. *See also* Third North Carolina Infantry, U.S.V.
Norvell, S. T., 50

O'Donnell, P.I., 13, 241, 258, 265
Ohio: Negro volunteers in, 10, 101, 102. *See also* Ninth Ohio Battalion, U.S.V.
O'Neil, Joseph P., 267, 267n
Otis, Elwell, 247, 270

Page, John H., 315
Page, William, 127
Palma Soriana, Cuba, 182, 189, 218
Palmer, Frederick, 243
Paranaque, P.I., 294
Parham, John: letter from, 128–29
Patterson, George L., 218–19
Payne, W. C.: letter from, 53–54
Peal, Allen S.: letter from, 174–77
Peking, China, 291
Pendergrass, J. C.: letter from, 50–53
Perfecto, Mariano, 309
Peterson, Arthur E.: letter from, 277–79
Philippine Islands: Negro soldiers in, 13–15, 239–316 passim; Filipino-Negro relations in, 15–16, 243, 251–55, 271, 310; natives of, 250, 251, 256, 262–63, 276–77, 278, 289–90, 300–301; Chinese in, 249, 251, 268, 308; opportunities for Negroes in, 254–55, 296, 311, 316; depredations of soldiers in, 280, 287, 305; Catholic church in, 289, 297, 307–8; mentioned, 4, 6, 12–13, 18
Pierce, J. Madison: letters from, 111–15
Pogue, P. C.: letter from, 258–59
Populists, 182, 183
Prayal Cabial, P.I., 252
Press: and Negro soldiers, 16–18, 32–33, 175–76

Prioleau, George W.: letters from, 27–29, 74–76, 82–84, 300–303, 306–9; mentioned, 26
Puerto Rico: conquest of, 43–44, 53–54, 102; conditions in, 60–61; mentioned, 4, 6, 10, 18, 112, 116, 207, 270

Rabi, Jesus, 234, 234n
Racial prejudice: evidence of, 9, 11–12, 121, 139; against Negro soldiers, 17–18, 26, 28, 31, 63–65, 83–91 passim, 152, 153–54, 157–77 passim, 199–200, 243–44, 257
Randolph, S. B.: letter from, 134–37
Ray, Alfred M., 176
Red Cross Society, 82, 189, 227
Reed, James C., 305
Republican party, 4, 9, 183
Rice, J. K.: letter from, 128–29
Richardson, Frank, 214
Richardson, John, 127
Richmond Planet, 103, 123
Risinger, Paul, 36
Roberts, W. B.: letters from, 190–92, 194–96, 199–201
Robinson, Charles H.: letter from, 128–29
Robinson, Michael H.: letter from, 264–69
Rollins, Will, 206
Roosevelt, Theodore: in Spanish-American War, 42, 43, 44, 73, 76, 118; controversial article by, 92–97. See also Rough Riders
Ross, Charles, 211
Ross, Harry H.: letter from, 197–98
Rough Riders, 41, 42, 59, 66, 67, 76, 77, 93–97 passim, 187, 291. See also First Cavalry, U.S.V.
Russell, Daniel L., 103

Saddler, M. W.: letters from, 55–57, 247–49
St. Augustine, Fla., 25
St. Louis, Mo., 168
Salem, Peter, 45
San Fernando, P.I., 252, 255, 256

San Francisco, Calif., 288
San Isidro, P.I., 252
San Jose, P.I., 277
San Juan Hill: battle of, 42, 43, 44, 45, 48, 51–52, 69–71, 73, 83, 93–97, 182, 201, 208, 241, 247. See also Roosevelt, Theodore; Rough Riders
San Luis, Cuba: Negro soldiers at, 183–282 passim
San Pablo, P.I., 294, 295
San Pedro, P.I., 269
Santa Anna, P.I., 252
Santa Cruz, P.I., 276, 285, 297
Santa Rita, P.I., 14
Santiago, Cuba, 41, 50, 51, 55, 67, 191, 219, 226, 231, 232, 247
Santos, Tordorica, 253
Sattoliav, P.I., 255
Schenck, William T., 260, 260n
Scott, Reefus, 275
Second Arkansas Infantry, U.S.V., 178
Second Infantry, U.S.A., 178
Second Ohio Infantry, U.S.V., 139, 157, 168, 170, 173
Seventh Cavalry, U.S.A., 151
Seventh Infantry, U.S.V.: letters concerning, 157–77; mentioned, 11, 16, 104, 105, 138. See also Immunes
Seventy-first New York Infantry, U.S.V., 71
Shafter, William T., 22
Shepard, William: murder of, 268
Siboney, Cuba, 41, 66, 207
Singleton, Will: lynching of, 162
Sixth Massachusetts Infantry, U.S.V., 44, 102
Sixth Virginia Infantry, U.S.V.: "mutiny" in, 104, 131–32, 140; letters concerning, 122–56; Negro officers resign from, 126–31 passim; arrest of, 139–47 passim; muster out of, 155–56; mentioned, 103, 104, 105
Smith, Carter, 77
Smith, Harry C.: letters to, 27–29, 157–58; mentioned, 16
Smith, James C.: letter from, 128–29
Smith, James W., 282
Smith, John, 210

Smith, Luschious, 80
Smith, Saul, 228
Smith, T. Clay: letter from, 316
Smith, William, 283
Spaniards, 5, 47, 48, 49–50, 51–52, 56, 61, 66, 67, 68, 78, 187, 192, 279
Springer, Ruter W., 29
Sterp, Jo Lane, 136
Stevens, J. A. C.: letter from, 134–37
Steward, Frank D.: letter from, 294–96; mentioned, 263
Steward, Theophilus G.: letters from, 25–26, 252–64; mentioned, 82, 310
Subig, P.I., 264, 266, 275, 285, 304
Summerville, S.C., 121
Sumner, Charles, 165
Sunday, Charles S., 215

Taft, William H., 243
Taliaferro, S. W., 57
Tampa, Fla.: Negro soldiers at, 8, 22–24, 28–29, 62; racial incidents in, 8, 24; mentioned, 41
Tanner, John R.: letters to, 186, 188–89; mentioned, 103, 181–82, 197, 216, 223, 224
Tayabocoa, Cuba: rescue operation at, 42
Taylor, George, 77, 282
Teller Amendment, 181
Temple, Bonus: letter to, 273–74
Tenth Cavalry, U.S.A.: letters concerning, 30–37, 49–50, 50–53, 58–60, 62–65, 72–73, 76–79, 79–81, 85–97, 233–35; mentioned, 6, 7, 8, 21, 22, 41, 42, 45, 57, 66, 116, 184, 187, 201, 240, 247, 291
Tenth Infantry, U.S.V., 104, 138, 157, 164, 167, 168, 170, 171. See also Immunes
Tenth Pennsylvania Infantry, U.S.V., 272
Texarkana, Ark.: racial incident at, 90–91
Third Alabama Infantry, U.S.V.: letter concerning, 177–78; mentioned, 102, 105

Third Connecticut Infantry, U.S.V., 121
Third Missouri Infantry, U.S.V., 114
Third North Carolina Infantry, U.S.V.: letters concerning, 106–10; mentioned, 10, 103, 105, 125, 138, 148, 153, 154, 157, 161, 164, 167, 173
Third Virginia Infantry, U.S.V., 143
Thirteenth Minnesota Infantry, U.S.V., 288
Thirty-second Infantry, U.S.V., 275
Thirty-fourth Infantry, U.S.V., 258
Thonge, P.I., 259
Tillman, Benjamin R., 75, 84
Tuguegarao, P.I., 241
Turner, Elijah: death of, 153–54
Turner, Henry M.: anti-imperialism of, 13; mentioned, 234
Turner, J. D., 226
Tuskegee Institute, 74
Twentieth Kansas Infantry, U.S.V., 272
Twenty-fifth Infantry, U.S.A.: letters concerning, 25–26, 55–57, 246–47, 247–49, 249–51, 255–56, 258–59, 259–62, 262–64, 264–69, 275–76, 284–88, 297–99, 304–6, 309–16; mentioned, 6–8, 21, 22, 27, 29, 42–43, 187, 201, 240, 247, 276, 279
Twenty-fourth Infantry, U.S.A.: letters concerning, 65–71, 251–55, 257, 273–74, 276–77, 288–90, 316; mentioned, 6–8, 21, 22, 27, 29, 43, 46, 57, 60, 187, 201, 240, 242, 247, 249, 258, 279
Twenty-third Kansas Infantry, U.S.V.: origins of, 182–83; letters concerning, 187, 190–96, 199–201; mentioned, 10, 11
Tyler, J. Hoge, 103

Vernon, Frank, 211
Virginia: Negro volunteers in, 10, 103–4. See also Sixth Virginia Infantry, U.S.V.

Walker, C. T.: letter from, 207–9
Walker, Edwin T.: letter from, 128–29

Waller, John L.: letter from, 187–88; mentioned, 210, 221–22
War Department, 8, 9, 13, 101, 130, 183
Warmsley, W. C.: letter from, 231–32
Washington, Booker T., 13, 252
Washington, George, 260
Wasp, 54
Watson, James W., 80, 93
Webb, Pleasant: letter from, 128–29
Wesley, Allen A., 214, 215, 227
Westberry, R. W., 210
Weyler, V., 239
Wheeler, Joseph, 41, 57
White, Charles, 80
White, George H., 302
Wilberforce University, 102, 262
Wilder, Harvey, 124
Williams, John H., 77
Williams, Noah, 211
Williams, Reuben, 211
Wilson, J. M., 151, 152
Wint, Theodore, 73, 78

Wiseman, T. H.: letter from, 275–76
Wood, Leonard, 181, 207
Worrell, David: letter from, 134–37
Wren, William G., 115
Wyche, Lee J.: letter from, 128–29; mentioned, 122

Xenia, Ohio, 282

Yale, 182
Yokohama, Japan: Negro soldiers in, 272, 273
Young, Charles, 101–2, 105, 112, 113, 115, 116, 118, 119, 120. *See also* Ninth Ohio Battalion, U.S.V.
Young, James: letter to, 205–6
Young, James H., 103. *See also* Third North Carolina Infantry, U.S.V.
Young, S. B. M., 288

Zapote, P.I., 294
Ziegenheim, Henry, 169, 169*n*

WILLARD B. GATEWOOD, JR., born on February 23, 1931, grew up on a farm near Pelham, North Carolina. After graduating from George Washington High School in Danville, Virginia, he attended Duke University, where he received the A.B., M.A., and Ph.D. degrees. He taught history at East Tennessee State University, East Carolina University, North Carolina Wesleyan College, and the University of Georgia prior to his appointment in 1970 as Alumni Distinguished Professor of History at the University of Arkansas in Fayetteville. His previous publications include four books, Eugene Clyde Brooks: Educator and Public Servant (*1960*), Preachers, Pedagogues and Politicians: The Evolution Controversy in North Carolina, 1920–1927 (*1966*), Controversy in the Twenties: Modernism, Fundamentalism and Evolution (*1969*), *and* Theodore Roosevelt and the Art of Controversy (*1970*) *as well as thirty articles which have appeared in journals such as* Journal of Negro History, Journal of Southern History, American Quarterly, Phylon, South Atlantic Quarterly, Ohio History *and* Florida Historical Quarterly.

A member of Phi Beta Kappa and several historical associations, Gatewood received the M. G. Michael Research Award in 1966 and the J. H. Parks Teaching Award in 1969, both at the University of Georgia.